Modules 7 – 12 FOUNDATIO

# MODUL
# SCIENCE
## for Edexcel



Graham Booth
Bob McDuell

Heinemann

Heinemann Educational Publishers
Halley Court, Jordan Hill, Oxford, OX2 8EJ
a division of Reed Educational & Professional Publishing Ltd
Heinemann is a registered trademark of Reed Educational & Professional Publishing Ltd

OXFORD MELBOURNE AUCKLAND
JOHANNESBURG BLANTYRE GABORONE
IBADAN PORTSMOUTH NH (USA) CHICAGO



First published 2002

ISBN 0 435 58467 7

06 05 04 03 02
10 9 8 7 6 5 4 3 2 1

Edited by Helen Juden, Allan Masson and Sarah Ware

Designed and typeset by Hardlines, Charlbury

Illustrated by Hardlines, Charlbury

Printed and bound in Spain by Edelvives

**Acknowledgements**
The authors and publishers would like to thank the following for permission to use photographs:

Cover photos: Macrophotography of maple leaf - SPL/Rod Planck; Crash test dummy on motorcycle - SPL/TRL Ltd; Sodium reacting with water - SPL/Charles D. Winters.

***T* = *top*  *B* = *bottom*  *R* = *right*  *L* = *left*  *M* = *middle***

**1** NHPA/G.I. Bernard; **2** ***T*** Rex Features, ***B*** FLPA/J Van Arkel; **3** SPL; **4** Photodisc; **8** Photodisc; **10** and **12** Holt Studios/Nigel Cattlin; **13** Roger Scruton; **16** Holt Studios/Nigel Cattlin; **18** Bruce Coleman/Hans Reinhard; **20** Bruce Coleman; **22** Photodisc; **23** Still Pictures/Mark Edwards; **24** and **25** Photodisc; **26** ***T*** SPL/Bill Barksdale, ***B*** Photodisc; **27** SPL/Claude Nuridsany and Marie Perennou; **28** Holt Studios/Nigel Cattlin; **29** Roger Scruton; **30** Photodisc; **31** ***T*** Photodisc, ***M*** SPL/Vaughn Fleming, ***B*** Photodisc; **35** Photodisc; **44** SPL/Saturn Stills; **48** John Birdsall Photography; **50** Photodisc; **52** Science Photo Library/Hattie Young; **61** Photodisc; **62** NHPA/Alan Williams; **63** ***L*** SPL/Pat and Tom Leeson, ***M*** and ***R*** Photodisc; **65** Art Directors and TRIP/Andrew Lambert; **66** ***T*** Roger Scruton, **B** Peter Gould; **68** SPL; **74** Oxford Scientific Films/Angus Palmer; **75** ***T*** Corbis; ***B*** Johnson Matthey; **76** and **77** Peter Gould; **78** ***TL*** and ***TM*** Geoscience Photo Library, ***TR*** Oxford Scientific Films/Norbert Rosing, ***BL*** and ***BR*** Geoscience Photo Library; **80** ***T*** Oxford Scientific Films/E R Degginger, ***B*** SPL/Alfred Pasieka; **81** SPL/Alfred Pasieka; **84** Oxford Scientific Films; **85** Corbis; **86** ***T*** Peter Gould, ***B*** SPL; **89** SPL/David Campione; **90** Corbis/Bettmann; **93** Peter Gould; **94** and **95** Photodisc; **97** ***T*** Roger Scruton, ***B*** SPL/John Reader; **100** Geoscience Features, **105** and **106** Peter Gould; **107** Roger Scruton; **108** ***T*** Trevor Clifford, ***B*** Peter Gould; **111** Mary Evans Picture Library; **112** SPL/Colin Cuthbert; **113** SPL; **119** Photodisc; **123** Alvey and Towers; **124** ***T*** Getty Images/FPG International, ***B*** Trevor Clifford; **126** Rex Features; **127** SPL/Jim Varney; **129** Alvey and Towers; **130** ***L*** Frank Spooner Pictures/John Pool, ***R*** Rex Features; **132** Genesis Space Photo Library; **133** Getty Images/FPG International; **136** ***T*** Alvey and Towers, ***B*** Corbis; **139** ***L*** SPL/Rosenthal Images Plc, ***R*** Corbis Vince Steano; **142** Trevor Clifford; **144** ***T*** Corbis/James L Amos, ***B*** SPL/Peter Menzel; **145** ***L*** Camera Press, ***R*** Mary Evans Picture Library; **149** Photodisc; **150** SPL; **152** ***T*** Mark Wagner, ***B*** Photodisc; **154** SPL; **156** ***L*** and ***M*** Morphy Richards; ***R*** Rupert Horrox; **157** SPL; **162** ***T*** Photodisc; ***B*** Holt Studios; **163** Getty Images/Peter Sterling/FPG; **164** SPL/Deep Light Production; **165** SPL; **166** John Birdsall; **167** SPL; **168** Aerofilms; **172** Photodisc.

SPL = Science Photo Library

The publishers have made every effort to trace the copyright holders, but if they have inadvertently overlooked any, they will be pleased to make the necessary arrangements at the first opportunity.

Picture research by Thelma Gilbert

# About this book

This is the second book in the Edexcel Modular Science series and is designed to guide you through modules 7–12 of GCSE study. It has been written to help you find everything you need to prepare for your exams.

We have named each module in the book with the title of the module test that you will be set. This is so that you can be sure of what you need to study.

The introductory page to each module will help you get a feel of the module. It explains the topics covered and gets you thinking about the science that you already know.

To help you study we have included some useful features in the book. Here are a few:

**Double-page spreads**
Everything you need to know for each module is covered in double-page spreads. These pages will cover all the topics you need to understand for your exams. To help you find all of the important points we have included questions to test yourself as you learn.

**End of module questions**
At the end of each module you will find three pages of test questions. Answering lots of questions will help you check what you have learnt and prepare for exams.

**Did you know?**
These boxes contain extra information about the topic that you are studying. The information in these boxes will not be tested in module tests or exams.

**Key ideas**
The information in these boxes summarises the most important points on the page. In your exams you will be tested on your knowledge of the points in the Key ideas boxes. These boxes will also help you make notes and answer questions.

**Key words**
Important words are listed at the back of this book to aid revision. These are ordered according to spread, so that you can check what you need to learn and easily find the page in which it is covered. Writing these out and filling in your own definitions will help you to prepare for your exams.

# Contents


**Module 7 – Food and the environment** **1**

| | | |
|---|---|---|
| 7:1 | Plant cells | 2 |
| 7:2 | Photosynthesis | 4 |
| 7:3 | Using glucose | 6 |
| 7:4 | Growing crops | 8 |
| 7:5 | Why do plants need water? | 10 |
| 7:6 | Plants and minerals | 12 |
| 7:7 | Movement through plants | 14 |
| 7:8 | Plant hormones | 16 |
| 7:9 | Energy in ecosystems | 18 |
| 7:10 | The carbon cycle | 20 |
| 7:11 | Trees and the atmosphere | 22 |
| 7:12 | Maintaining a balance | 24 |
| 7:13 | Controlling pests | 26 |
| 7:14 | Environmental control | 28 |
| 7:15 | Biodiversity | 30 |
| End of module questions | | 32 |

**Module 8 – Health and exercise** **35**

| | | |
|---|---|---|
| 8:1 | Take a deep breath | 36 |
| 8:2 | Exchanging gases | 38 |
| 8:3 | Heart beat | 40 |
| 8:4 | Blood transport | 42 |
| 8:5 | Controlling blood sugar | 44 |
| 8:6 | Releasing and using energy | 46 |
| 8:7 | Making the body work hard | 48 |
| 8:8 | Misuse of steroids | 50 |
| 8:9 | Inherited disorders | 52 |
| 8:10 | Sickle cell disease | 54 |
| 8:11 | Gene therapy | 56 |
| End of module questions | | 58 |

**Module 9 – Chemicals and the Earth** **61**

| | | |
|---|---|---|
| 9:1 | Metals and their uses | 62 |
| 9:2 | Metals from the Earth | 64 |
| 9:3 | Displacement reactions | 66 |
| 9:4 | Making iron | 68 |
| 9:5 | Electrolysis | 70 |
| 9:6 | Industrial electrolysis | 72 |
| 9:7 | Transition metals | 74 |
| 9:8 | The alkali metals | 76 |
| 9:9 | Making and changing rocks | 78 |
| 9:10 | Igneous rocks | 80 |
| 9:11 | The atmosphere | 82 |
| 9:12 | Keep it in balance | 84 |
| 9:13 | The Haber process | 86 |
| 9:14 | The importance of fertilisers | 88 |
| 9:15 | The noble gases | 90 |
| End of module questions | | 92 |

**Module 10 – Understanding chemical reactions** **95**

| | | |
|---|---|---|
| 10:1 | Atoms and isotopes | 96 |
| 10:2 | Joining atoms together | 98 |
| 10:3 | More about ionic compounds | 100 |
| 10:4 | Covalent bonding | 102 |
| 10:5 | More covalent bonding | 104 |
| 10:6 | Energy given out | 106 |
| 10:7 | Energy taken in | 108 |
| 10:8 | Chemical formulae | 110 |
| 10:9 | Chemical equations | 112 |
| 10:10 | Using chemical formulae | 114 |
| End of module questions | | 116 |

**Module 11 – Movement and change** 119

| | | |
|---|---|---|
| 11:1 | Distance–time graphs | 120 |
| 11:2 | Speeding up | 122 |
| 11:3 | Acceleration | 124 |
| 11:4 | Stopping in time | 126 |
| 11:5 | Balanced forces | 128 |
| 11:6 | Unbalanced forces | 130 |
| 11:7 | Moving through the air | 132 |
| 11:8 | Forces doing work | 134 |
| 11:9 | Kinetic energy and power | 136 |
| 11:10 | Inside the Earth | 138 |
| 11:11 | Moving plates | 140 |
| 11:12 | Radioactive decay | 142 |
| 11:13 | Dating using radioactivity | 144 |
| End of module questions | | 146 |

**Module 12 – Energy, force and communication** 149

| | | |
|---|---|---|
| 12:1 | Static electicity | 150 |
| 12:2 | Some dangers and uses of static electricity | 152 |
| 12:3 | Charge in motion | 154 |
| 12:4 | Electrical power | 156 |
| 12:5 | Electric motors | 158 |
| 12:6 | Transformers | 160 |
| 12:7 | The wave equation | 162 |
| 12:8 | Total internal reflection | 164 |
| 12:9 | Analogue and digital | 166 |
| 12:10 | Wave diffraction | 168 |
| 12:11 | Changing shape | 170 |
| 12:12 | Gas pressure | 172 |
| End of module questions | | 174 |

**Periodic table** 177

**Key words** 178

**Index** 181

# Module 7 – Food and the environment

Plants are important to all aspects of life on the Earth. They provide food for animals and help keep the levels of oxygen and carbon dioxide in the atmosphere the same.

This module starts with a study of the processes that go on inside plants. Including:

- photosynthesis;
- what happens in the roots of a plant;
- how the activity of a plant is controlled.

It is important that we understand ecosystems so that we can exploit them without destroying them. Your study of ecosystems includes:

- the interdependence of living things;
- the role of forests and decay organisms in maintaining life on our planet.

The module ends by considering the impact of farming on the environment and by looking at the range of organisms that exist in the world.

Try these questions first.

1 Which cells have cell walls, plant cells or animal cells?

2 Which part of a plant takes in water from the ground?

3 Which parts of a plant cell contain chlorophyll?

4 What is the purpose of immunisation?

5 What type of organism is the producer in most food chains?

# 7:1 Plant cells

Plans have already been made to construct manned spacecraft that can visit other planets in the Solar System. The voyages in these craft will take years. A major problem is how to provide enough food and oxygen for such a long voyage. The answer is not finding extra storage space but using tiny plants to recycle human waste products into both food and oxygen.

**a What waste product do humans breathe out?**

The tiny plants that the voyagers plan to use are aquatic plants. Each of these plants consists of only one cell. They will be grown in tanks on the spacecraft.

Animal cells cannot produce food and oxygen, so we rely on plant cells.

**Plant cells seen through a microscope.**

## Structure of a plant cell

These are plant cells as seen through a light microscope. Apart from having a regular shape and a green colour you cannot see much further detail.

The diagram shows the differences between plant and animal cells.

**b List the differences between the plant cell and the animal cell.**

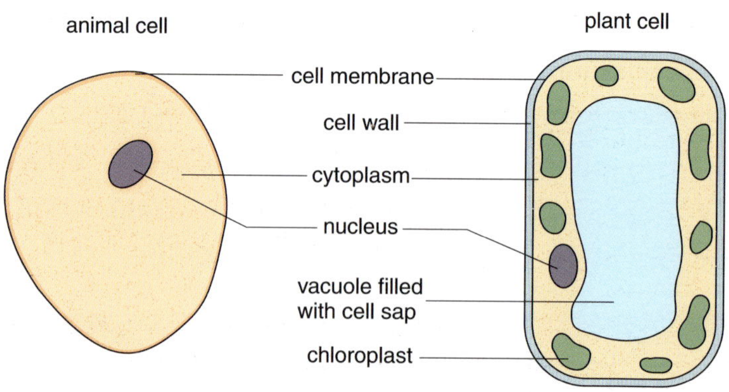

It is one of these differences that enables plant cells to produce food and oxygen. Plant cells have **chloroplasts**. These are able to use energy from light to make food and oxygen.

In plant cells the **nucleus**, **cytoplasm** and **cell membrane** have the same job as in animal cells. The jobs of the parts of a plant cell are shown in the table.

| Part of plant cell | Job |
|---|---|
| nucleus | controls the activities of the cell |
| cytoplasm | where many of the chemical reactions occur |
| cell membrane | controls the passage of substances into and out of the cell |
| cell wall | strengthens the cell |
| chloroplasts | absorb energy from light to make food |
| permanent vacuole filled with cell sap | helps to support the cell |

**c Explain how the cell membrane controls the passage of substances into and out of the cell.**

Chloroplasts are green because they contain the green pigment **chlorophyll**. It is this pigment that absorbs energy from light. Cells can only produce chlorophyll in the light. Plants grown in the dark are yellow.

**d Would you expect root cells to have chlorophyll? Give the reason for your answer.**

**Did you know?**

The photograph shows the chemical factory of the future. This particular crop is oilseed rape. As the name suggests the plant produces oil. Scientists are now genetically engineering crop plants to produce many chemicals that are usually produced in factories.

## Questions

1 Copy and complete these sentences. Use words from this list.

**cell membrane** **nucleus** **chemical reactions** **food** **cell wall** **supports**

The passage of substances into and out of a cell is controlled by its ____________. The ____________ controls the activities of a cell. The cytoplasm is where many ____________ take place. Chloroplasts make ____________. A plant cell is strengthened by its ____________. The vacuole ____________ the cell.

2 Can you think of the advantages of producing chemicals by growing crops rather than using factories? Are there any disadvantages?

## Key ideas

- *Plant and animal cells have nuclei, cytoplasm and cell membranes.*
- *Plant cells also have cell walls, chloroplasts and vacuoles.*

# 7:2 Photosynthesis

The photograph shows the traditional way of harvesting rice in Thailand. Rice is the staple diet of over half of the world's population.

Rice is the fruit of grass plants. The fruit is packed with the food needed for young grass plants to grow. The food is made by **photosynthesis**, the most important chemical process on Earth.

## The photosynthesis equation

Photosynthesis consists of many chemical reactions, but these can be summarised by the word equation:

carbon dioxide + water + [energy from light] → glucose + oxygen

## Investigating photosynthesis

Plants use photosynthesis to make carbohydrates. If we want to find whether a plant has photosynthesised we need to test it for carbohydrate. The carbohydrates made by plants include glucose and starch.

It is not very easy to test leaves for glucose, so we test the leaves for starch.

We use iodine solution to test for starch. If the leaf turns blue/black in the test, the leaf has made starch.

### Is light needed for photosynthesis?

We can check this by doing an experiment. To do this we allow some parts of the leaf to receive light but not others. A foil stencil should be attached to the leaf as shown in the diagram. The plant is left in the light for a few hours then the leaf is tested for starch.

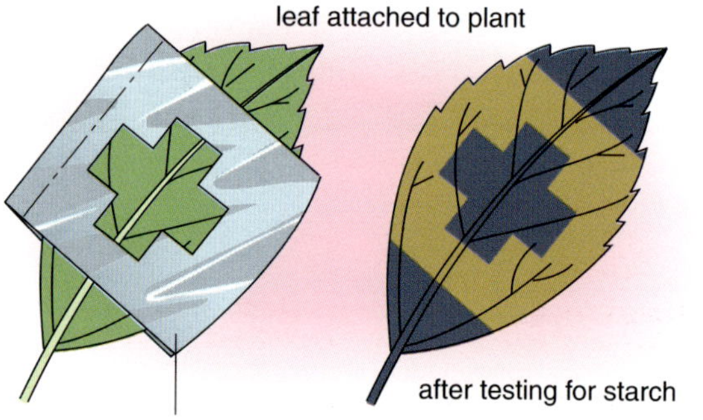


The diagram shows the set up and the results of this experiment.

Only the parts of the leaves that were not covered turned blue in the iodine test.

**a Explain the appearance of the leaf after the starch test.**

### Is carbon dioxide needed for photosynthesis?

To test for this we must stop one leaf of a plant getting carbon dioxide. The diagram shows how this is done.

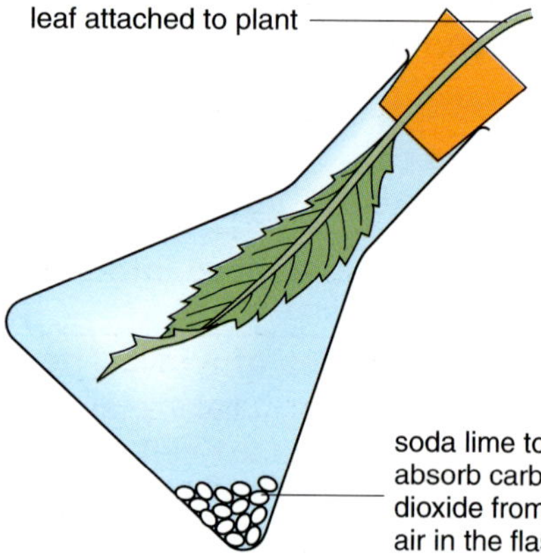


After a few hours in the light, the leaf may be tested for starch.

The leaf in the flask did not turn blue in the starch test, but a leaf that had not been in the flask turned blue.

**b What is the control in this experiment? Explain the results of the starch test.**

**Showing that chlorophyll is needed for photosynthesis**
We can't take chlorophyll out of a leaf without killing it. Some leaves have patches without chlorophyll. These leaves are called **variegated** leaves.

**c What colour would you expect the parts of the leaf without chlorophyll to be?**

A plant with variegated leaves is left in the light for a few hours. One of its leaves is then tested for starch. The results of the starch test are shown in the diagram.

**d Explain the results of the starch test.**

These three experiments confirm that green plants need carbon dioxide, light and chlorophyll to make starch.

## Oxygen

**What gases do plants give out?**
We can collect the gas given out by aquatic plants using the equipment shown in the diagram. Aquatic plants are ones that grow naturally underwater. They can obtain dissolved oxygen and dissolved carbon dioxide from the water.

When the gas in the tube is tested we find that it is mainly oxygen when the plant is in the light.

**e How would you show that the gas in the tube was oxygen?**

**Did you know?**
Green plants look green because they reflect green light. The other colours are absorbed.

## Questions

**1** Copy and complete these sentences. Use words from this list.

**carbon dioxide   water   chlorophyll   glucose   starch   oxygen**

To photosynthesise plants need to take in _______________.

In photosynthesis, energy is absorbed by _______________. The first carbohydrate produced in photosynthesis is _______________. Some of this carbohydrate is converted into _______________. The gas given off in photosynthesis is _______________.

**2** Over two hundred years ago, a scientist called Joseph Priestley put a potted plant, a mouse and some mouse food in an a large, airtight jar. He left them for several weeks. Both the plant and the mouse survived. Explain why.

## Key ideas

- *Chlorophyll absorbs energy from light.*
- *In photosynthesis this energy is used to drive the reactions between carbon dioxide and water that produce glucose.*
- *Oxygen is released as a by-product of photosynthesis.*
- *Some of the glucose is converted into starch.*

# 7:3 Using glucose

## Storing carbohydrate

Chips seem to be the staple diet of most teenagers. Chips are made from potatoes. Potato plants store lots of starch in their tubers; the part that we call potatoes.

Potato plants store starch to survive over winter, and to produce more potato plants the following spring.

The diagram summarises the processes involved.

**Did you know?**
Potatoes orginally came from Peru. They were introduced into Europe in the sixteenth century by Spanish explorers.

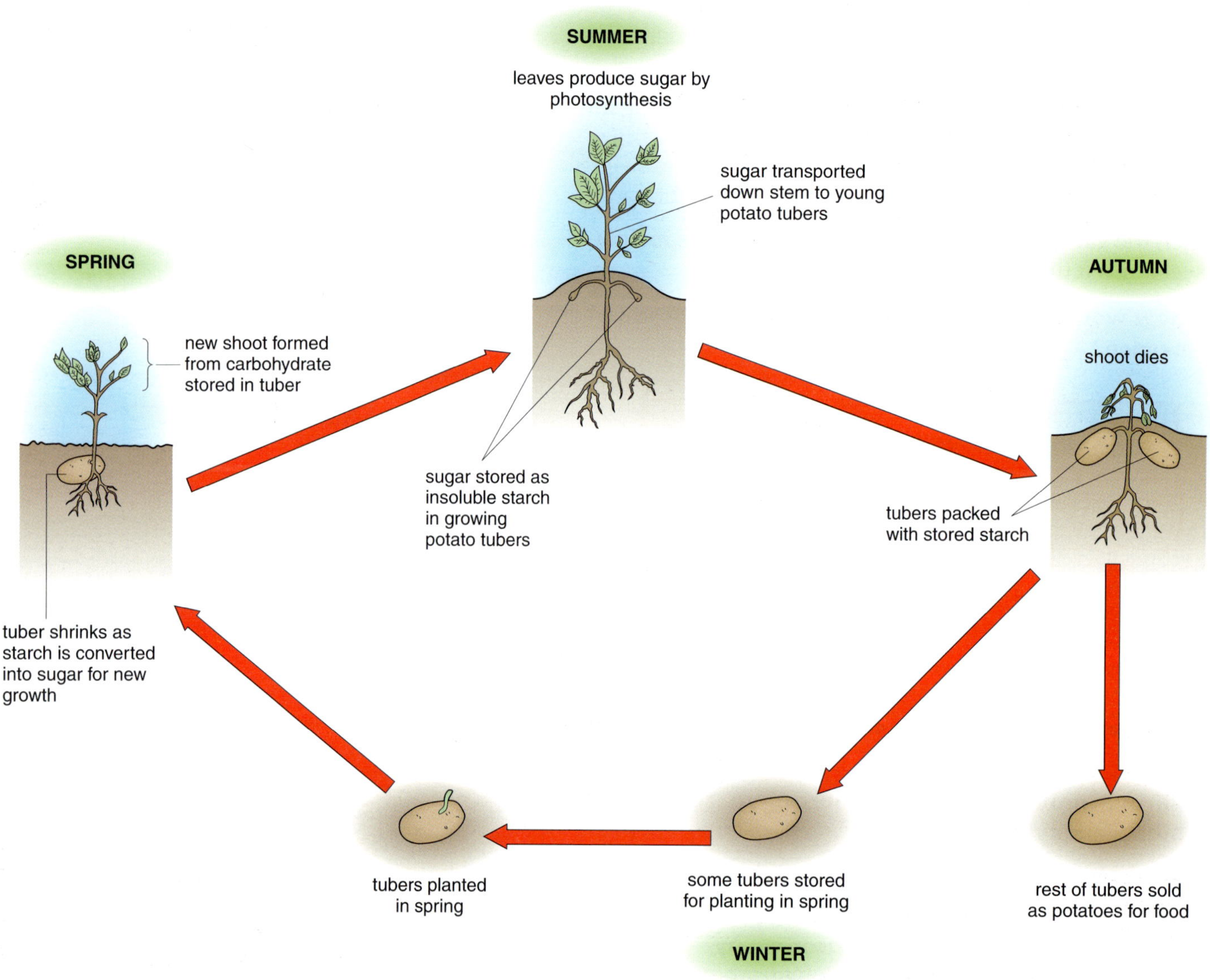


**a Why do potato plants store starch?**

## Plant respiration

All living things need energy for their life processes. Animals get their energy from the food they eat.

Plants make their own food during photosynthesis, but they still need to break it down to use the energy.

Respiration in plants is very similar to respiration in animals. The big difference is that plants make their own sugar for respiration while animals get theirs by eating food.

Respiration is breaking down glucose to release energy.

glucose + oxygen → carbon dioxide + water + [energy]

We can check if plants are carrying out respiration by detecting carbon dioxide.

Plants respire 24 hours per day but we can only detect carbon dioxide being given off during the night.

The diagram explains why this is.

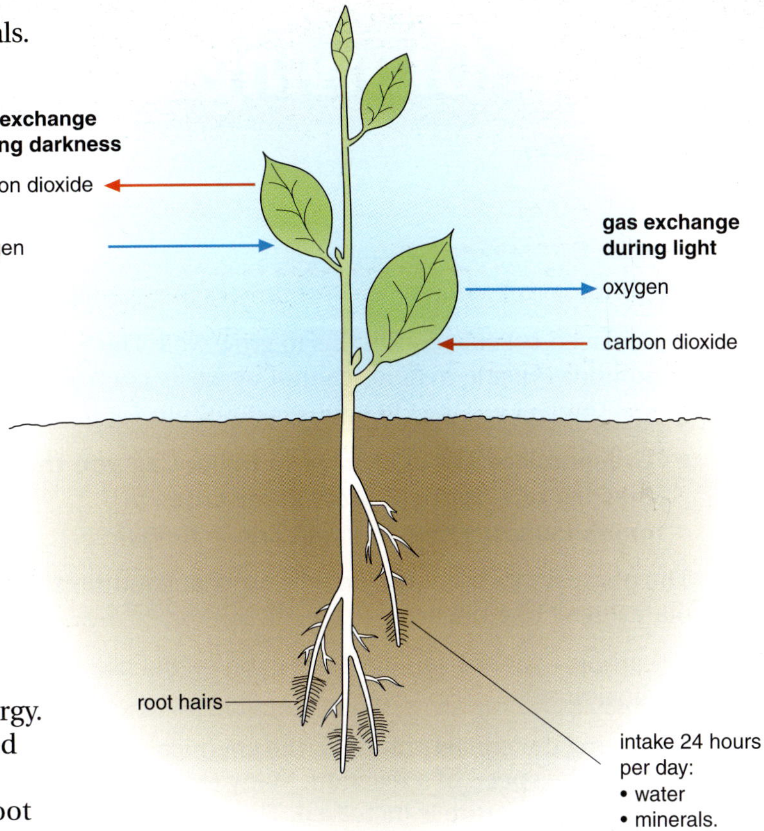


**b Why is it not possible to detect the carbon dioxide given off during the day?**

### What do plants use energy from respiration for?

The sugars produced by the potato in photosynthesis are not all stored. Some are used in respiration to release energy. Most of this energy is used to make the substances needed to make new cells. New cells are needed for the tuber to grow in autumn. They are also needed to produce the shoot in spring.

Materials needed for making new cells include:

- cellulose – to make the cell walls;
- proteins – to make proteins the plant needs **nitrates** from the soil in addition to carbohydrates;
- fats.

**c Give *two* reasons why a potato plant needs to make new cells.**

## Questions

**1** Copy and complete these sentences. Use words from this list.

**starch cellulose nitrates twenty-four energy**

Plants store carbohydrates mainly as __________. Glucose can also be converted to __________ to make cell walls. To make proteins plants need both glucose and __________.

Plants respire __________ hours per day. They respire in order to release __________ from carbohydrates.

**2 a** In potato plants, how does sugar made in photosynthesis reach the tubers?

**b** Givc *onc* important differencc between sugar and starch.

**c** Suggest *one* advantage of storing carbohydrate in the tubers as starch rather than as sugar.

**d** Plants have similar enzymes to humans. What type of enzymes do you think plants use to convert starch to sugar in Spring?

## Key ideas

- *Plant cells respire using some of the glucose produced during photosynthesis.*
- *The glucose is also used for growth and to make cellulose.*
- *Glucose that is not needed can be stored as starch.*

# 7:4 Growing crops

## Limiting factors

The photograph shows a crop of flowers in a greenhouse.

Plants need specific conditions to grow well. The conditions outside in fields cannot be easily controlled. In greenhouses it is easier to control conditions for the plants.

**a Greenhouses are expensive to build. Can you think of reasons why farmers grow some crops in greenhouses rather than outside in fields?**

The photosynthesis equation tells us what conditions plants need to grow.

carbon dioxide + water + [energy from light] → glucose + oxygen

Increasing the concentration of the chemicals can usually increase the speed of a reaction. Many reactions also go faster if temperature is increased. This also makes the plants grow more quickly.

Changes that can increase the speed of a reaction are called limiting factors. A plant's growth is slowed (limited) if any of these **limiting factors** are in short supply.

The factors that may limit the rate of photosynthesis are:

- low temperature;
- shortage of carbon dioxide;
- shortage of light.

### Carbon dioxide as a limiting factor

The atmosphere has a very low concentration of carbon dioxide. This limits the rate of photosynthesis.

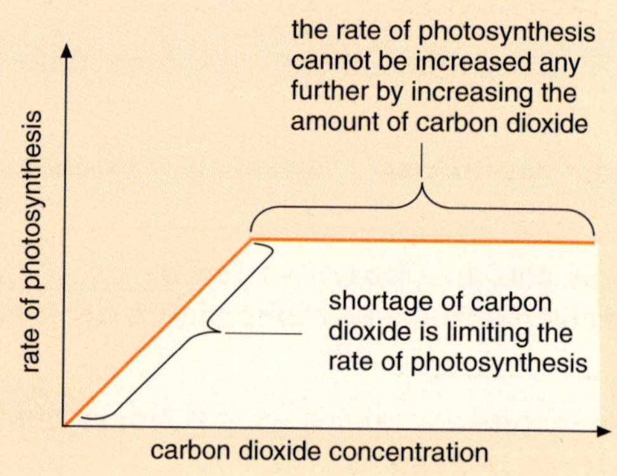


We cannot improve the carbon dioxide supply to crops growing in fields but we can give plants growing in greenhouses more carbon dioxide.

Growers can increase the amount of carbon dioxide in a greenhouse by burning fossil fuels such as propane. They find that they can only increase the rate of photosynthesis up to a certain level.

**b Why is it easier to control the amount of carbon dioxide in a greenhouse when this level is reached?**

### Light as a limiting factor

Photosynthesis needs light. Plants do not photosynthesise in the dark, and they only photosynthesise slowly in dim light.

We can give plants growing in greenhouses more light. This is not needed in summer, but it is often done in winter for valuable crops.

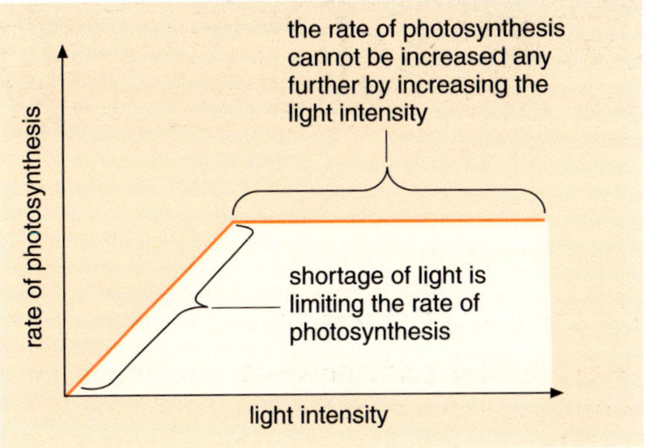


### Temperature as a limiting factor

Temperature speeds up the rate of photosynthesis in *two* ways:

- it speeds up the molecules that react inside the chloroplasts;
- it speeds up the rate at which carbon dioxide from the atmosphere gets into the leaves.

We cannot increase the temperature for crops growing in fields but we can for plants growing in greenhouses. This is not needed in summer, but it is often done in winter for valuable crops. The heat is usually supplied by burning propane.

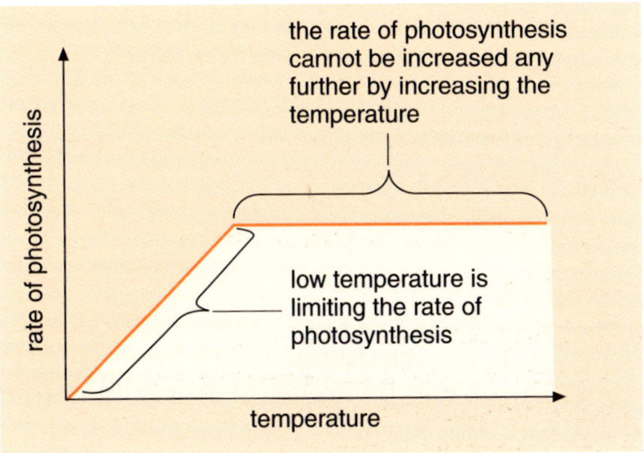


**c Apart from cost, what is the advantage of heating a greenhouse by burning propane rather than using electric heating?**

**Did you know?**

Computers are used to control the conditions in commercial greenhouses. They open vents and switch lights and heaters on and off when necessary.

## Questions

**1** List *three* factors that may limit the rate of photosynthesis.

**2** Copy and complete these sentences. Use words from this list.

**propane carbon dioxide low temperature**

Growers can increase the amount of carbon dioxide in a greenhouse by burning ______________.

At noon on a hot, sunny summer-day, the rate of photosynthesis is most likely to be limited by low ______________ levels.

At noon on sunny winter day the rate of photosynthesis is most likely to be limited by ______________.

**3** Sketch a graph to show how the rate of photosynthesis of a crop plant changes through 24 hours of a day. Start the horizontal axis at midnight on one day and finish it at midnight on the next day.

**4** Gardeners at stately homes in Victorian times were asked to provide fresh fruit and vegetables in the winter. They did this by having beds of manure in small greenhouses. The manure gave off both heat and carbon dioxide. Can you explain why the gardeners did this?

## Key ideas

- *The rate of photosynthesis can be limited by temperature and the availability of carbon dioxide and light.*

# 7:5 Why do plants need water?

Water is an important substance! All plant and animal life needs a constant supply of it. The photograph shows what happens to a plant that does not have enough water.

**a Which of the two plants in the picture is short of water?**

People take in water by drinking and they get rid of water by excretion from the lungs and the bladder. Like people, plants take in and excrete water. However, the way they do it is different.

**b Which organ excretes water as you breathe?**

## Osmosis

If you squirt a perfume spray in one corner of a room, within a few minutes the perfume can be detected everywhere in the room. This is an example of **diffusion**. The particles that form the perfume spread out as they mix with air particles. Cooking smells travel in a similar way. The diffusion, or spreading out, of particles in a gas is a rapid process. It is much slower in liquids.

**c Use your knowledge of the structure of liquids and gases to explain why diffusion is slower in liquids than in gases.**

**Osmosis** is a similar to diffusion. In osmosis:

- some particles of water move from where there is a lot of it (a high concentration) to where there is less of it (a low concentration);
- the movement is through a **selectively permeable membrane** – it allows small particles (like water particles) to pass through it but blocks the movement of large particles (like salt particles).

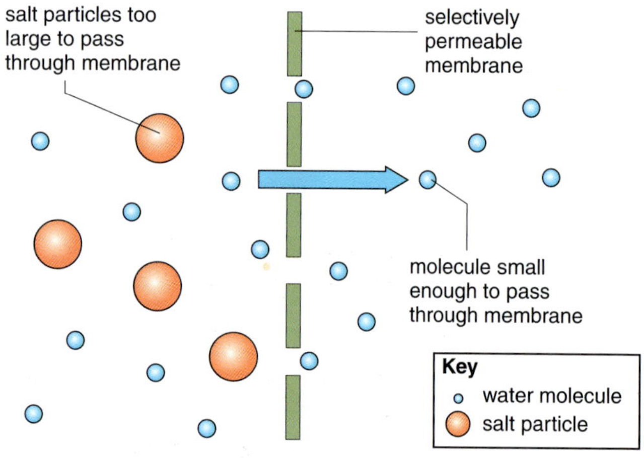


**Cell membrane is selectively permeable.**

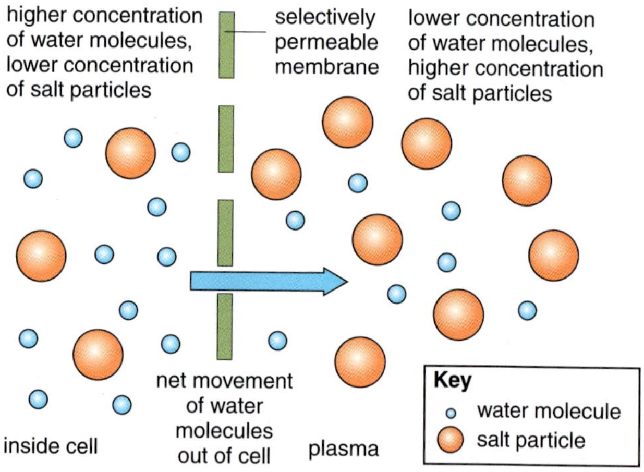


**Water molecules move from high to low concentration through a selectively permeable membrane.**

In plants osmosis occurs when water moves from dilute solutions of salts (high water concentration) to more concentrated solutions of salts (low water concentration).

**An osmosis experiment**

The effects of osmosis can be seen by using slices of potato.

1 Place one slice of potato in water, and another in sugar solution.

2 Inspect them one day later.

3 The slice of potato placed in water has swollen, due to water moving into the potato.

4 The slice of potato placed in sugar solution has shrunk, due to water moving out of the potato.

**d How do the results of this experiment show that particles move from where there is a lot of them to a region where there are less of them?**

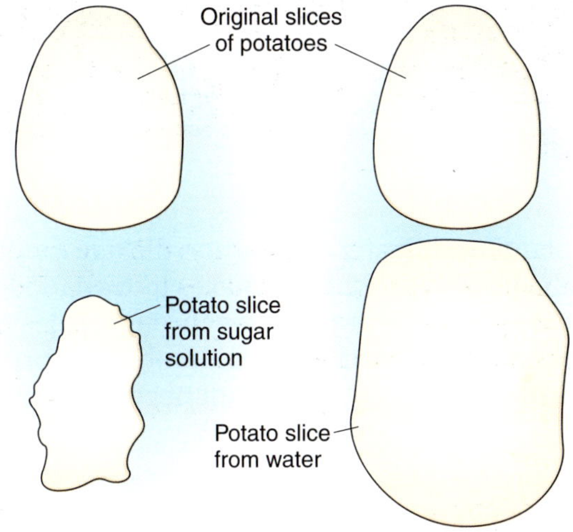


## Wilting

Water travels from the ground into the roots of a plant by osmosis. However, if the ground is dry the plant may not be able to take in enough water. Just as we sweat in hot weather, plants lose water by evaporation from their leaves. If more water is lost from the leaves than it can draw in through its roots, the plant is in trouble!

Without a good supply of water, a plant cannot photosynthesise. More importantly, it cannot keep its shape.

When plant cells are full of water, they are **turgid**. The pressure of the water inside the cells pushes out on the cell walls. This makes them difficult to squash, like a balloon that is fully inflated. With less water, the cells lose their shape and cannot support the plant. The plant **wilts** and becomes floppy.

A layer of wax covering the surface of leaves reduces the amount of water lost from leaves. This layer of wax is called the **cuticle**.

**e A gardener grows tomato plants in a greenhouse. Explain why they need to be watered frequently in sunny weather.**

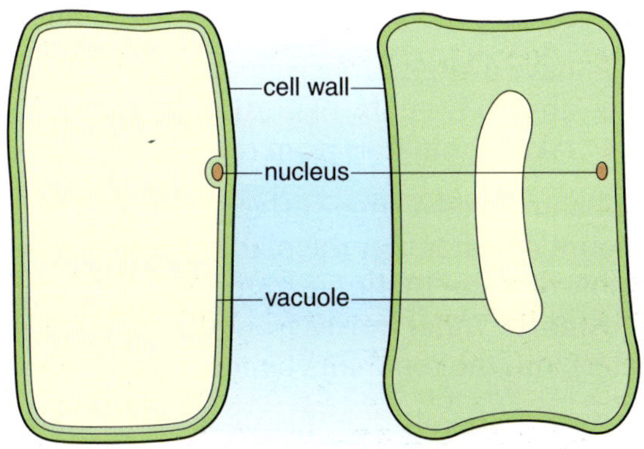


A turgid plant cell A flacid plant cell

**Did you know?**

Plants do not need a skeleton. They remain upright due to:

- the strength of their cell walls;
- the turgidity of their water-filled cells.

## Questions

**1 Copy and complete these sentences. Use words from this list.**

**small membrane low high**

**Osmosis is the movement of particles from where their concentration is ______________ to where it is ______________. Osmosis takes place through a selectively permeable ______________ that only allows ______________ particles to pass through it.**

**2 Explain why pieces of potato:**

**a shrink when they are placed in sugar solution;**

**b expand when they are placed in water.**

**3 Cacti are plants that grow in hot deserts. Explain why they have a very thick cuticle.**

## Key ideas

- *Osmosis involves the movement of water across a membrane.*
- *Water moves from a dilute solution of salt (high water concentration) to a concentrated solution of salt (low water concentration).*
- *Water is needed in plants for photosynthesis and to keep cells turgid.*

# 7:6 Plants and minerals

A plant needs water and carbon dioxide for photosynthesis. This is the process by which it makes its own food. It takes in carbon dioxide from the atmosphere through its leaves. Water is taken in through the roots along with other important substances, called **minerals**, that the plant needs for healthy growth.

## Taking in water

The roots of a plant have lots of tiny growths branching off them. These are called **root hairs**. Root hairs:

- have a large surface area;
- absorb water by osmosis;
- take in minerals from the surrounding soil.

Root hairs need a large surface area to be able to take in the amount of water that the plant needs. When there is a plentiful supply of water in the surrounding soil, it enters the root hairs by osmosis. Water moves from the soil (where there is a lot of water) into the root hairs (where there is less water).

Essential minerals that the plant needs for growth also pass from the soil into the root hairs.

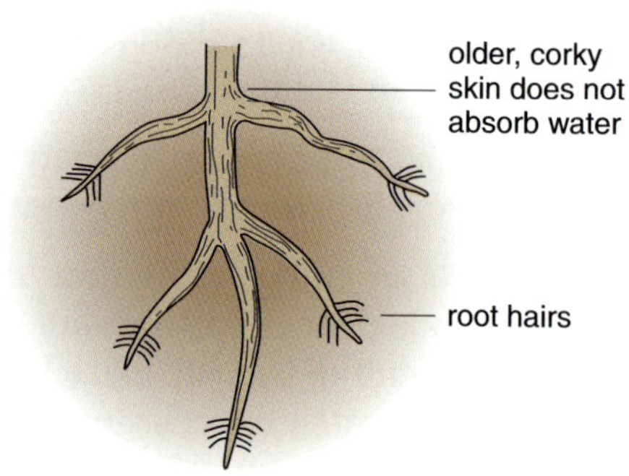


**a i Where on a root are the root hairs?**

**ii The root grows at the tip. Explain why root hairs do not grow from the tip of the root.**

## What minerals does a plant need?

When a farmer puts artificial fertiliser on a field, the fertiliser is often labelled NPK.

- N stands for nitrogen, used by plants to make proteins for growth.
- P stands for phosphorus, essential for respiration.
- K stands for potassium, needed to form cell membranes.

Two other important minerals that all plants need are:

- sulphur, for making protein;
- magnesium for making chlorophyll.

If a plant does not have enough magnesium it cannot absorb enough light to make food, so it does not grow properly. With crop plants, the result is a low yield.

**b Which *two* minerals named above are needed for making protein?**

## Organic or inorganic?

If you go along to a supermarket, you may have a choice of whether to buy food grown organically or inorganically. People are increasingly concerned about where their food has come from.

**Did you know?**
Less than 1% of the vegetables sold in the UK are grown organically.

Most farmers in this country use artificial fertilisers to make sure that their crops have the correct balance of minerals. These crops are grown inorganically.

Some farmers use organic farming methods. Only fertilisers that are produced from plants or animals are used. Organic fertilisers release their nutrients more slowly than inorganic fertilisers, so they need applying less often.

Unlike artificial fertilisers, the contents of organic fertilisers, such as manure, cannot be precisely controlled.

**c How can waste vegetable material be turned into fertiliser?**

### Questions

**1** The diagram shows the structure of a root hair. A root hair consists of just one cell.

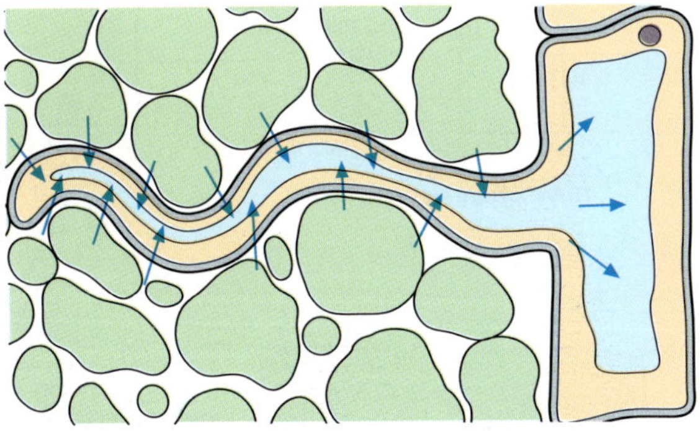

**a** What feature of the root hair cell makes it suitable for the job it has to do?

**b** How does water enter the root hair cell?

**c** What other substances enter the plant through the root hairs?

**2** Horse manure contains the eggs of worms that are parasites. They live in the horse's intestine where they feed on the food that the horse has digested.

Explain why horse manure should not be used for fertiliser on fields where horses graze.

**3** If a plant does not have enough magnesium, it may turn yellow. Explain why this happens.

### Key ideas

- *Plants obtain water by osmosis from the soil into their root hairs.*
- *Plants need minerals such as nitrogen (for growth) and magnesium (to make chlorophyll).*

# 7:7 Movement through plants

Plants have tubes for transporting materials.

- The tubes that carry water and minerals in a plant are called **xylem**.
- The tubes that transport sugars are called **phloem**.

The diagram shows where these tissues are found in a root and a stem.

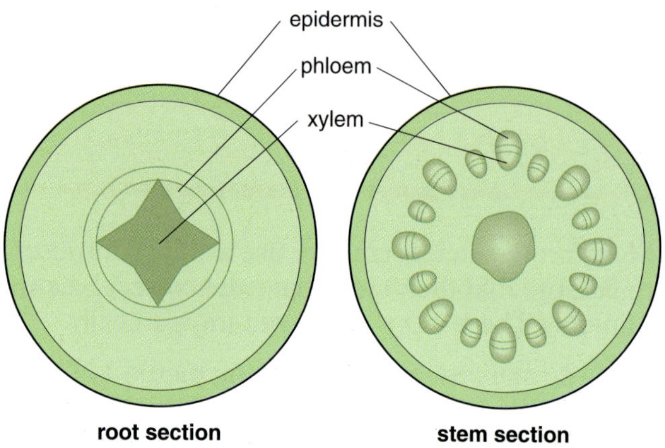


## Xylem

There are different kinds of cells in xylem, but the ones that transport most water and minerals to the leaves are called **xylem vessels**.

Xylem vessels are formed from dead xylem cells whose end walls have broken down. These form continuous tubes. The xylem vessels act like pipes, transporting water up the plant.

Wood is made of xylem cells. Most xylem cells have substances in their walls that strengthen the cells. This is why wood is so strong. The diagram shows how xylem vessels form.

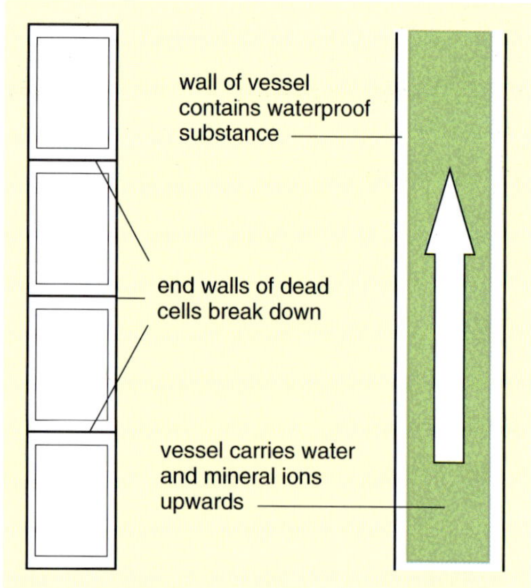


How xylem vessels form.

**a Celery is stringy. Suggest what the stringy tissue is.**

## Phloem

Sugar made in photosynthesis needs to be moved around the plant. The sugar is made in the leaves. All the plant cells need sugar for respiration. Some parts of a plant, for example the tubers in a potato plant, store food as starch.

Phloem cells form a system of tubes that move the sugar to all parts of the plant.

## Water loss

Leaves contain a lot of water. Water evaporates from a leaf surface, this is known as **transpiration**.

Leaves have cells called **stomata** (singular: stoma) that allow carbon dioxide to enter the leaf for photosynthesis. **Guard cells** open and close the stomata. When the stomata are open, they allow water to leave the leaf by diffusion. The diagram shows the path taken by water vapour out of the leaf.

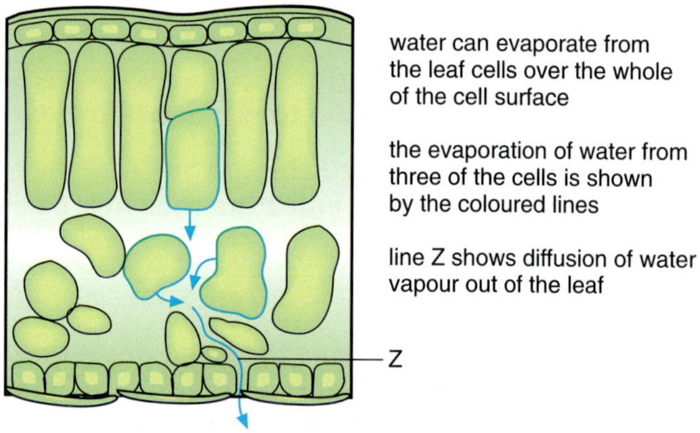


**b Why do the guard cells not need to be open at night?**

Stomata are not open all the time. The diagram below shows when stomata are open and closed during a 24-hour period.

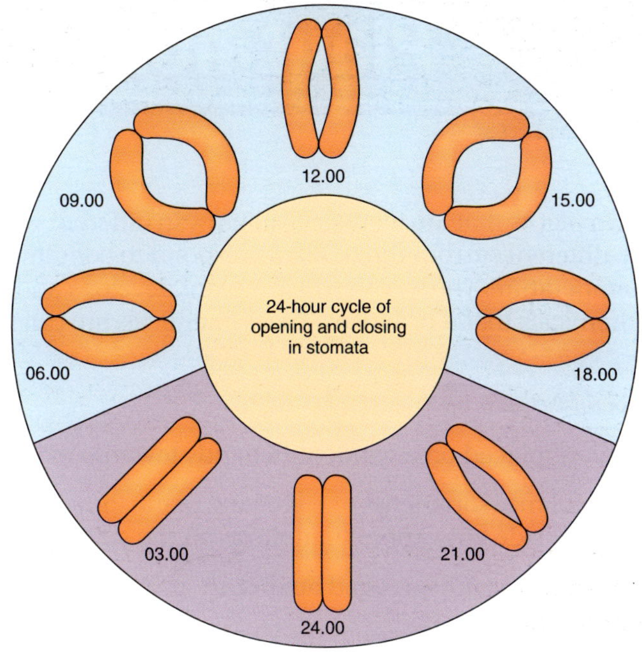


**Did you know?**
There are thousands of stomata on each square centimetre of the lower leaf of a plant.

At night-time, when the stomata are closed, less water is lost.

The other factors that affect water loss through the stomata are temperature, air movement and humidity.

- The higher the temperature, the greater the amount of water lost through evaporation.
- Wind increases the rate of water loss by removing the water vapour particles that have evaporated and diffused out of the leaf. This allows more water to diffuse out of the leaf.
- In a similar way dry conditions increase the rate of water loss because there is a lower concentration of water vapour particles in the air so diffusion occurs more rapidly. If the air is damp there is less diffusion of water vapour out of the leaf.

**c Why are plants more likely to wilt on a sunny day in summer than on a rainy day in summer?**

## Questions

1 Copy and complete these sentences. Use words from this list.

**transpiration diffusion xylem minerals**

Water and ______________ flow up a plant stem in ______________ vessels.

The loss of water from a leaf is known as ______________. When the stomata are open water passes into the air by ______________.

2 Explain why less water moves up a plant stem at night than during the day.

3 Stomata are normally open at midday. This is when the plant is photosynthesising most rapidly. If water is in short supply the stomata may close.

a Why do the stomata close?

b How does the closing of the stomata affect the rate of photosynthesis?

## Key ideas

- *Xylem vessels consist of dead, hollow cells. They transport water and minerals from the roots to other parts of the plant.*
- *Sugars are transported in tubes called phloem.*
- *During transpiration, water diffuses out of the plant through the stomata.*
- *The rate of water loss through the stomata depends on the temperature, light level, humidity and air movement.*

# 7:8 Plant hormones

Two plants that are identical can grow in different ways if they are placed in different surroundings. Plants respond to conditions such as light and temperature. The way in which a plant develops and grows is controlled by chemicals that it produces. These chemicals are called **plant hormones**.

## Responses of plants to light

A plant placed on a windowsill bends towards the light as it grows.

Careful measurements of a growing plant show that the cells on the shaded side grow more than those on the side that has light shining on it.

1 Plant hormones called **auxins** are produced in the tip.

2 More auxin diffuses to the shaded side than to the side with light shining on it.

3 This makes the cells on the shaded side grow faster.

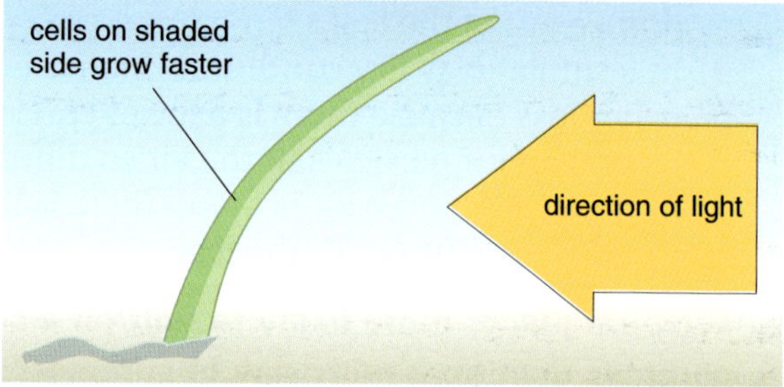


Light is the stimulus and the bending of the shoot is the response.

**a Why should plants that grow on windowsills be turned round every few days?**

## Responding to the Earth's pull

Shoots grow up towards the light and away from the Earth's pull. Roots respond to two factors – the Earth's pull and the presence of water. Unless there is more water near the surface, roots grow down.

If a plant is placed on its side the roots grow down towards the Earth. The effect of the auxins produced in the root makes one side grow faster than the other so that the root grows round a corner.

The Earth's pull is the stimulus and the bending of the root is the response.

**b Plants grown in pots are sometimes watered from the bottom, rather than from the surface of the compost. What is the advantage of this?**

## Tissue culture

Some plants are difficult to grow from seed or by taking cuttings. In these cases plants can be raised in their thousands by a process known as **tissue culture**. Small pieces of plant tissue are placed in a liquid culture. The culture contains:

- the nutrients that the plant needs for growth;
- hormones to promote growth.

After a few weeks, when there is enough root growth, the new plant can be transferred to normal compost.

These plants growing in culture are about four weeks old.

## Taking cuttings

Gardeners often reproduce plants by **cutting** a piece of shoot from an existing plant. This is then planted in compost.

Some plants develop roots easily and others do not. The cutting needs to grow roots quickly if it is to survive. To make the roots grow quickly, the cut end of the shoot is dipped into **rooting powder** before being planted. The rooting powder contains plant hormones that stimulate the roots to grow from cells at the base of the shoot.

**c Why do the roots of a cutting need to develop quickly?**

**Did you know?**
Plants grown from cuttings are identical to their parent as they are grown by asexual reproduction.

## Selective weed killer

Some weed killers kill all the plants that they come into contact with. If a gardener wants to kill the weeds growing in his lawn, he does not want to kill the grass as well. A **selective weed killer** contains hormones that only affect plants with broad leaves.

The hormones make the shoots grow much faster than the roots. As the roots cannot provide enough water and nutrients for the plant, it wilts and dies.

Cereal crops are narrow leafed grasses, so selective weed killers are useful to farmers as well as to gardeners.

## Fruit

In fruit production, hormones are used produce seedless grapes and to control the ripening of fruit such as apples.

To produce seedless grapes:

1 the flowers are sprayed with auxins normally provided by pollen;

2 the auxins prevent the flowers from dropping off the plant and cause the fruit to set;

3 since there has been no pollination or fertilisation the grapes do not have any seeds.

**d Why do fruit growers want to produce seedless grapes?**

## Questions

**1** Copy and complete these sentences. Use words from this list.

**down    light    auxins**

Plant stems grow towards ______________. This response is caused by chemicals called ______________ moving to the shaded side of the stem. Plant roots grow ______________ if the soil at the surface is dry.

**2** A commercial plant grower needs to produce one million African violet plants.

**a** What are the advantages of growing them by tissue culture rather than by taking cuttings?

**b** Suggest why all the equipment used needs to be thoroughly sterilised.

**3** Explain why weeds wilt after they have been sprayed with selective weed killer.

### Key ideas

- *The growth of roots and shoots in a plant is affected by plant hormones.*
- *Plant hormones are used in tissue culture, rooting compounds, weed killers and in fruit growing.*

# 7:9 Energy in ecosystems

Plants produce food. Animals feed on plants and in turn become food for other animals. A community of plants and animals that depend on each other is an ecosystem. The ecosystem on a seashore is very different from that in woodland.

A moorland food chain.

## Food chains

When animals eat plants, they obtain **biomass** from the plants. When one animal eats another animal it obtains biomass from that animal.

In the **food chain** shown in the diagram, the mouse obtains energy from the plants and the kestrel obtains energy from the mouse. The arrows in a food chain or food web show the energy flow.

**a What is the source of energy for the plants?**

## Pyramids of biomass

In an area of moorland there are many plants, a smaller number of mice, and very few kestrels.

The diagram shows how this information is represented in a **pyramid of numbers**.

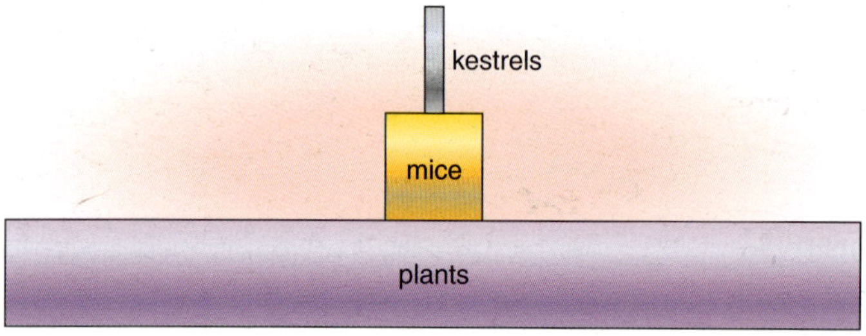


A pyramid of numbers.

**b Draw a pyramid of numbers for a single oak tree that supports thousands of insects and a few birds.**

The table shows the amount of biomass in each square metre of moorland.

| Organism | Biomass ($g/m^2$) |
|---|---|
| plants | 500 |
| mice | 1 |
| kestrels | 0.1 |

Another way of showing this information is in a **pyramid of biomass**. In a pyramid of biomass:

- a rectangle is drawn for each level of the food chain;
- the length of the rectangle represents the amount of mass at that level.

For this particular food chain, the pyramids of numbers and biomass have the same shape. That is not always true. However, in a pyramid of biomass the next level is always smaller than the one beneath it.

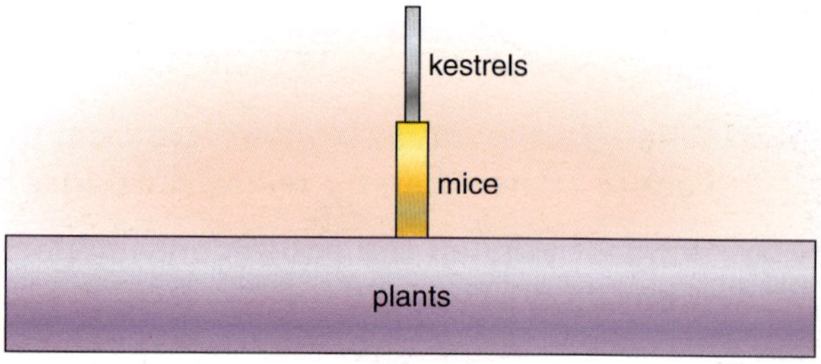


A pyramid of biomass.

## Losing energy

Energy enters a food chain via the producer, in this case the plants. This is where energy from the Sun is used to make food. The producer uses most of this energy for respiration and only a small amount for growth.

As the plants grow they are eaten by the mice. The mice use the energy from their food in a number of ways:

- most is used in respiration of body cells;
- some is lost in excretion of waste products;
- a small amount is used for growth and reproduction.

The result of this is that very little of the biomass that the mice obtain from the plants ends up as biomass in the form of mouse tissue. So the kestrels have less biomass to feed on.

**c Why do the mice use most of their energy in respiration?**

**Did you know?**
Eighty-five per cent of all the eggs eaten in the UK are produced by battery farming, where hens are kept in cages with little room to move.

## Efficient feeding

Which is your favourite meal, breakfast or dinner? For many people, breakfast consists mainly of carbohydrate. Breakfast cereals and toast are good foods for starting the day. They are mainly carbohydrate, so they provide lots of energy that is readily available.

For dinner, many people eat meat along with vegetables. Meat is a good source of protein. One disadvantage of eating meat is that a lot of energy is wasted in producing it.

The diagram shows how much of the energy a battery-reared chicken takes in is available to the consumer.

Chickens are usually fed on cereals.

If you buy a chicken from your local butcher or supermarket, you may have a choice between free-range and battery-reared. The free-range chicken is the more expensive because more food and energy are needed to produce it. A free-range chicken is allowed to walk about, using energy for movement rather than for growth.

Vegetable and cereal crops do not walk about and they do not need to generate heat to keep their bodies warm. Because they are not constantly emitting heat to their surroundings, less energy is wasted and more is passed on to the next level.

**d Explain why more people can be supported by growing crops than by raising cattle.**

### Key ideas

- *The amount of biomass present in each level of a food chain is shown by a pyramid of biomass.*
- *In an ecosystem, energy is transferred from producers to organisms higher in the food chain.*
- *Energy is lost at each level of a food chain by respiration and excretion.*
- *Mammals lose a lot of energy because they need to respire to produce body heat.*

## Questions

**1 a** State *two* ways in which energy is lost from a food chain.

**b** What happens to the energy that is lost from a food chain?

**2** What are the advantages of people eating cereals and vegetables rather than meat?

# 7:10 The carbon cycle

## Compost heaps

**Microorganisms** break down dead organisms and waste materials. In autumn, in a garden, many plants lose their leaves. These leaves contain nutrients that can be recycled by soil microorganisms. Many gardeners collect all the dead leaves and use them to make **compost**. Compost contains nutrients such as nitrates, so it acts as a natural fertiliser when it is spread on the garden. The diagram shows one way of making compost.

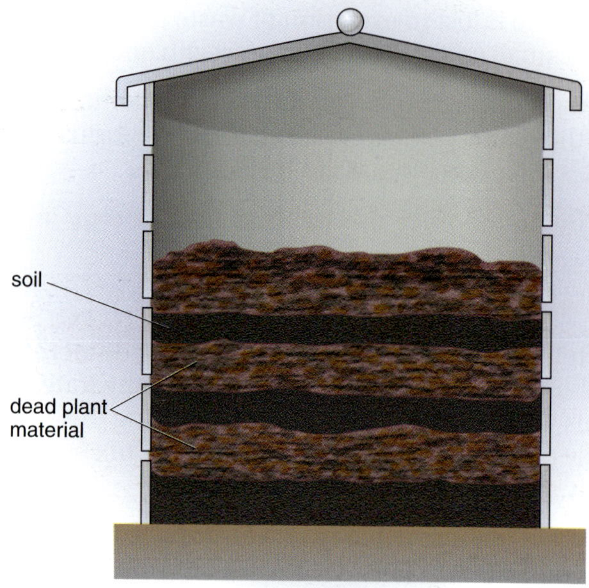


**The formation of compost is an example of decay.**

### Decay conditions

**Decay** is rapid if the conditions are moist, warm and there is a good supply of oxygen.

- Moisture is needed for the microorganisms to digest the waste outside their bodies.
- An increase in temperature increases the activity of the digestive enzymes.
- Oxygen is needed by the microorganisms for respiration.

**a Explain why waste material decays more rapidly in a large compost heap than in a small one.**

## Recycling carbon

When organisms die, small animals and microorganisms feed on their bodies. The **carbon compounds** in the dead organisms become carbon compounds in the bodies of these small organisms. When the small organisms respire, some of the carbon compounds in their food are converted into carbon dioxide.

**This is the Amazon rainforest in South America.**

### How plants recycle carbon

The photograph shows a tropical rainforest. It exchanges thousands of tonnes of carbon dioxide with the atmosphere every year. There are two processes involved in this exchange – **photosynthesis** and **respiration**. These are summarised in the diagram.

Forest fires can wipe out many square miles of trees and the other organisms that depend on them. When wood burns the gas exchange with the atmosphere is the reverse of that in photosynthesis. Oxygen is taken out of the atmosphere and replaced with carbon dioxide.

**b Why is photosynthesis important to all organisms?**

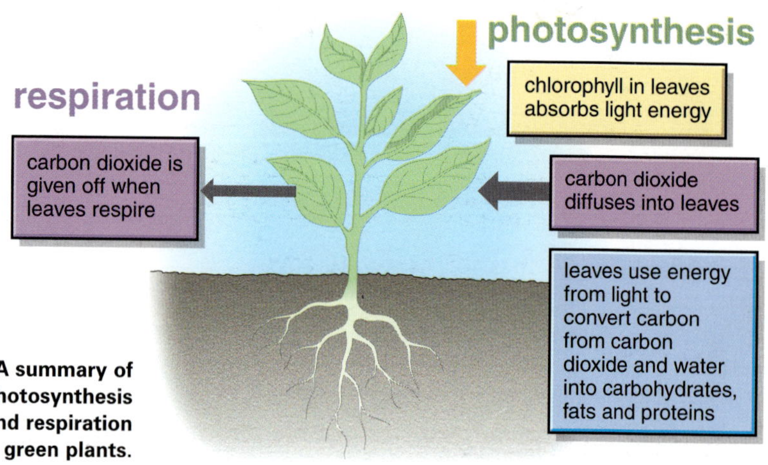


**A summary of photosynthesis and respiration in green plants.**

### A question of balance

Without plants, animals could not live. They are the source of all our food and they also keep the atmosphere fit to breathe. All plants and animals respire, taking oxygen from the atmosphere and replacing it with carbon dioxide. Other human activities such as burning fuel have the same effect as respiration.

Plants also photosynthesise, taking in carbon dioxide and replacing it with oxygen. These processes need to be in balance to keep oxygen and carbon dioxide at their current levels.

**c Explain why some people are concerned that large areas of the world's forests are being destroyed to create land for agriculture.**

**Did you know?**
An increase in the level of carbon dioxide in the atmosphere will result in more wind and rain in the UK.

**Putting it all together**

Carbon in the form of carbon dioxide is continually being taken out of the atmosphere and put back in. Plants, animals and microorganisms all play an important part in recycling carbon. This process is known as the carbon cycle. It is shown in the diagram.

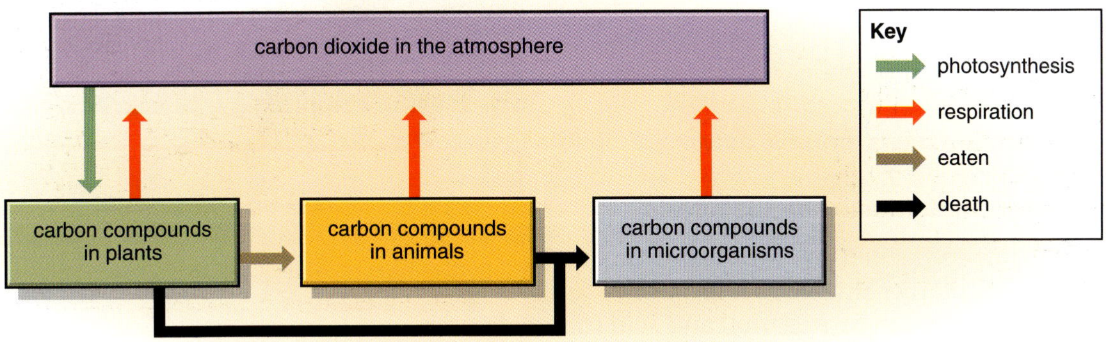


## Questions

1 Copy and complete these sentences. Use words from this list.

**carbon dioxide oxygen photosynthesise respire**

All living organisms __________. They take __________ from the atmosphere and replace it with __________.

Plants also __________. This removes __________ from the atmosphere and replaces it with __________.

2 The diagram shows the result of an experiment on soil organisms.

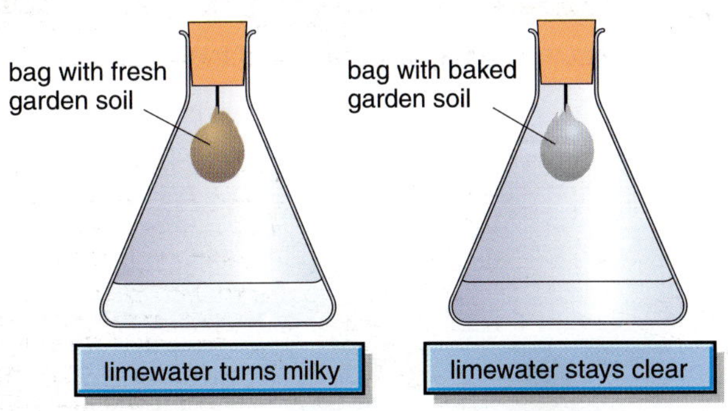


Explain the results of the experiment.

3 You eat some potato crisps. The crisps contain carbon compounds.

a How do plants make carbon compounds?

b What happens to the carbon compounds in the crisps in your body?

## Key ideas

- *When organisms decay, microorganisms recycle nutrients.*
- *The carbon cycle describes the ways in which carbon dioxide enters and leaves the atmosphere.*
- *Plant and animals depend on each other to keep the balance of oxygen and carbon dioxide in the atmosphere.*

# 7:11 Trees and the atmosphere

When trees are removed from an area it is known as deforestation. Forests cover six per cent of the Earth's land, but they are home to half of all the species that live on Earth. Since 1945 nearly half of the world's rainforests have disappeared and up to a hundred species of plants and animals are being lost each day.

**a Why does deforestation result in the loss of plant and animal species?**

## Why are forests being destroyed?

There are a number of reasons for deforestation:

- wood is a useful building material;
- land is needed for farming;
- land is needed for building roads, houses, power stations and factories;
- valuable minerals are found underneath the forests.

Trees have been felled for burning as fuel and for making fences. Wood from rainforests is particularly valuable as it is mainly hardwood such as mahogany. This can be exported and sold to companies that make furniture.

**Did you know?**
Furniture manufacturers do not need to use mahogany. They could use cherry wood instead.

What was once forest is now being used for agriculture to grow crops such as bananas and coffee. It is also used for grazing cattle. The land does not make good agricultural land and so after a few years it is abandoned and more forest is cleared.

Countries need to develop. This can involve destroying forest to build roads so that people can travel. Factories need to be built near to the resources that they use. These factories need power stations and the factory workers need somewhere to live.

Forests are destroyed to mine metals such as manganese and tin. These are exported, earning foreign currency that can be used to buy consumer goods such as televisions and video recorders.

Building roads causes large areas of forest to be destroyed.

**b Give *three* reasons why forests are being destroyed.**

## How can forests be kept?

It is possible to use the timber that grows in forests without having a large impact on the environment. This is known as **sustainable forestry**. It involves planting new trees to replace those that are cut down.

The forests in the UK are expanding. Each year the area that is planted and replanted is greater than that cleared by felling trees. This also helps to conserve species such as deer, pine marten and the great crested newt.

**c What is the meaning of sustainable forestry?**

The forest provides a habitat for this deer.

## Changing carbon dioxide levels

Plants remove carbon dioxide from the atmosphere during photosynthesis. Most living organisms pass carbon dioxide back to the atmosphere when they respire. These two processes have been in balance for thousands of years.

In the last few centuries humans have interfered with this balance in two major ways.

- There has been a big increase in the combustion of fossil fuels. This has increased the amount of carbon dioxide in the atmosphere.
- Large areas of forest have been cleared in deforestation.

When trees are cut down, only the trunk is used. The branches are burned. This combustion releases carbon dioxide into the atmosphere. The roots of the trees die. They decompose and release carbon dioxide.

Cutting down trees also means that the amount of photosynthesis in the world is reduced. Trees take in millions of tonnes of carbon dioxide every year. Most of this is converted into the cells that form new wood. The carbon dioxide is trapped in the wood.

The graph shows how the carbon dioxide levels in the atmosphere have changed in the past 250 years.

**The carbon locked away in the biomass of the forest is released suddenly into the atmosphere when trees are felled and burned.**

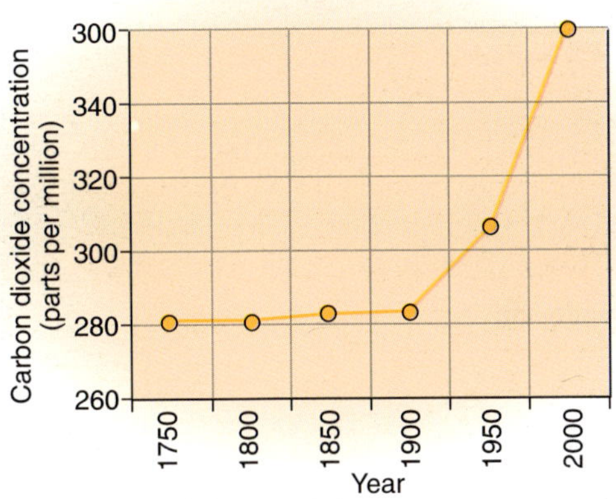


**Concentration of carbon dioxide in the atmosphere since 1750.**

**d** **Describe how the amount of carbon dioxide in the atmosphere has changed in the last 250 years and whether this has been a constant rate of change.**

### Questions

**1** **State *three* causes of deforestation.**

**2** **State *three* ways in which deforestation increases the amount of carbon dioxide in the atmosphere.**

**3** **Some countries rely on exports of timber for their economy. What should they do to make sure that there will be more timber to export in future years?**

### Key ideas

- *When trees are cut down it is called deforestation.*
- *Deforestation puts more carbon dioxide into the atmosphere and takes away the plants that remove carbon dioxide from the atmosphere.*
- *Sustainable forestry is the planting of new trees to replace those that have been cut down.*

# 7:12 Maintaining a balance

## Plants and animals

All living organisms need proteins to grow. Plants can make their own proteins if they are supplied with nitrates. Proteins contain nitrogen. Plants cannot absorb nitrogen from the air, they have to obtain nitrates from the soil.

When herbivores eat plants, or carnivores eat other animals, some of the nitrogen compounds in the food are used to make new proteins in the animals.

In uncultivated land such as a rainforest nitrates are released when faeces or dead organisms decay. On farms, harvesting crops removes nitrogen compounds. These have to be replaced before more crops can be grown.

Harvesting this crop removes nitrogen compounds from the land.

## The rainforest

**Rainforests** are wet places. Their rainfall is in excess of 2.5 m each year, about eight times the average rainfall in the UK. They are also warm, with an average temperature of around 25 °C and no extremes of hot or cold.

Most of the world's rainforests are on and around the Equator. The largest is the Amazonian rainforest. These forests are home to many species of plants and animals. The table shows the large number of species found in a relatively small area.

Part of the Amazonian rainforest.

| Type of organism | Number of species per $km^2$ |
|---|---|
| flowering plant | 1500 |
| tree | 750 |
| mammal | 125 |
| bird | 400 |
| butterfly | 150 |
| reptile | 100 |
| amphibian | 60 |

**a Present this information as a bar chart.**

**Did you know?**

Because they have not been affected by glaciers, the world's rainforests have been in existence for many millions of years.

## Deforestation

There are six million square kilometres of rainforest remaining in the world. This is much less than there was 200 years ago. Rainforest is disappearing at the rate of five hundred square kilometres each day. At this rate, they will be destroyed within a hundred years resulting in:

- changes in the concentration of carbon dioxide in the atmosphere;
- fertile rainforest being converted into poor quality grassland;
- many species of animals and plants being lost forever;
- the soil being eroded by the high rainfall and being washed into rivers and lakes;
- small human societies who have a detailed knowledge of the rainforest being lost;
- rainfall patterns changing as water is not being recycled by the trees.

**b What is causing the loss of the rainforest?**

The clouds above the rainforest are due to evaporation of water from the trees.

## Why the rainforest should be preserved

Scientists suspect that the majority of the world's species of plants and animals are in rainforests. Most of these have not been identified. Some could be useful sources of food or drugs for use in medicines. We could be losing sources of life-saving drugs that we do not yet know anything about.

Rainforests are not only not only sources of timber, they also provide rubber, resins and vegetable oils.

Rainforests can continue to provide these resources without being destroyed if they are managed properly. Preserving the rainforest also enables countries to generate income from tourism.

**c Suggest why there may be many unidentified species in rainforests.**

Rainforest plants are the source of the drugs used in many medicines.

### Key ideas

- *Rainforests are found on and around the Equator.*
- *The habitats of the most the world's species of plants and animals are found in rainforests.*
- *The destruction of rainforests is causing problems. These could be avoided by conservation.*

### Questions

**1 a** Where are the world's rainforests?

**b** Describe how the climate in a rainforest differs from that in the UK.

**2** Name *three* valuable resources that rainforests provide.

**3** Explain why it is important to preserve rainforests.

# 7:13 Controlling pests

Farmers face a continual battle against organisms that reduce their harvest of crops. Weeds compete with crops for nutrients, light and water. Insects feed on crops and destroy them. Fungi such as mould also feed on crops. The farmer needs to destroy these pests, but their destruction can harm our environment.

## Pesticides

Farms are essential to produce the food that we eat. Unfortunately they destroy the habitats of many kinds of animals and plants, and they use chemicals that have undesirable effects on the environment.

Farmers use different kinds of chemicals, called **pesticides**. There are *three* types of pesticide:

- **insecticides** – used to kill insects that eat crops;
- **herbicides** – used to kill weeds;
- **fungicides** – used to kill moulds.

Insecticides also kill harmless insects that provide food for birds. The populations of many kinds of birds have decreased over the last 50 years as farmers have increased their use of pesticides. If pesticides are washed by rain into streams and ponds they kill the plants growing there.

This aircraft is spraying the crop with insecticide.

**a Explain how the use of pesticides has affected bird populations.**

Herbicides kill weeds growing in fields but they also kill wild plants that are not a nuisance to the farmer. Many of these wild plants provide food for animals such as butterflies. If the wild plants are killed the butterflies have nothing to feed on so they die too. The numbers of most kinds of butterflies in this country have declined over that last 50 years due to the use of more herbicides. Rainfall washes herbicides into streams and ponds where they kill the plants growing there, just as insecticides do.

Careless use of herbicides can destroy the habitats of insects such as butterflies.

Fungicides are sprayed onto crops to prevent the growth of moulds and mildew that feed off the plants and reduce the crop yield.

**b What is a herbicide used for?**

## The dangers of using pesticides

A chemical called DDT was first made on a large scale in 1939. DDT kills all insects so it is a very effective insecticide. DDT has been used to kill the insects that carry malaria and those that damage crops. Unfortunately DDT kills useful insects such as:

- insects that pollinate flowers;
- insects such as wasps that are predators of insect pests.

**Did you know?**

DDT is short for dichlorodiphenyltrichloroethane. Try saying that!

Another problem with DDT is that it is not broken down into simpler, harmless chemicals. It passes along the food chain, becoming more concentrated at each level. This results in the poisoning and death of animals at the top of the food chain. The use of DDT is now banned in most countries.

**c State *one* advantage and *one* disadvantage of using the chemical DDT.**

## Biological pest control

New organisms can be added to a habitat to control pests in **biological pest control**. Two ways of doing this are:

- using predators of the pest;
- using sterile males of the pest species.

Beetles, spiders and wasps prey on many insects and mites. They kill or eat many individuals and keep the population under control.

Some wasps and flies are **parasites**. The female lays its eggs in, or on, the pest. As the young develop they feed on the host's body fluids and organs, eventually killing it.

Pests attacked by parasites die more slowly than those that are simply killed or eaten by their predators.

In the sterile insect method of pest control, large numbers of the pests are bred in a factory. The males are selected and sterilised with low doses of radiation. The sterile males are then released to mate with wild females. When a female mates with a sterile male, there are no offspring. For this technique to be successful, the sterile males need to greatly outnumber the fertile wild males.

An advantage of biological pest control is that it is usually cheaper than using chemicals. A danger is that an organism introduced into a habitat can itself become a pest.

**d Why might a gardener introduce ladybirds into a greenhouse?**

These ladybirds feed on whitefly and other aphids.

## Questions

**1** Copy and complete these sentences. Use words from this list.

**mould chemicals insects herbicides pests**

Pesticides are ______________ that are used to control ______________. Insecticides kill ______________. Pesticides used to kill weeds are called ______________ and fungicides are used to kill ______________.

**2** Explain how a parasitic predator kills its prey.

**3** When sterile males are used to control pests, why is important that the sterile males greatly outnumber the fertile wild males?

## Key ideas

- *Farmers use pesticides to control pest such as insects, weeds and moulds.*
- *The overuse of pesticides can damage the environment.*
- *Biological control of pests can be an effective alternative to chemical control.*

# 7:14 Environmental control

There are several ways in which humans affect the environment. It is not possible to control the global climate, but human activity has affected it. A greenhouse is an example of a habitat where humans are able to control the climate and produce foods that would otherwise only be available by importing them.

Pesticides are used both in the greenhouse and world-wide. These pesticides affect the environment and the organisms that live in different habitats.

## DDT and malaria

**DDT** is a chemical that was first made in 1873. Its usefulness as an insecticide was not discovered until 1939. In World War II, it was used by the US army in Naples to stop an epidemic of typhus that was being caused by lice. DDT is cheap and not very poisonous to mammals. Its use has probably saved about twenty-five million lives.

**Malaria** is an illness that causes bouts of fever. It is spread by mosquitoes and affects about a hundred million people each year. When it was discovered that DDT can kill the mosquitoes, it was sprayed in the parts of the world where these insects live. The effect was dramatic. In India the number of deaths from malaria fell from five hundred thousand a year to only one thousand.

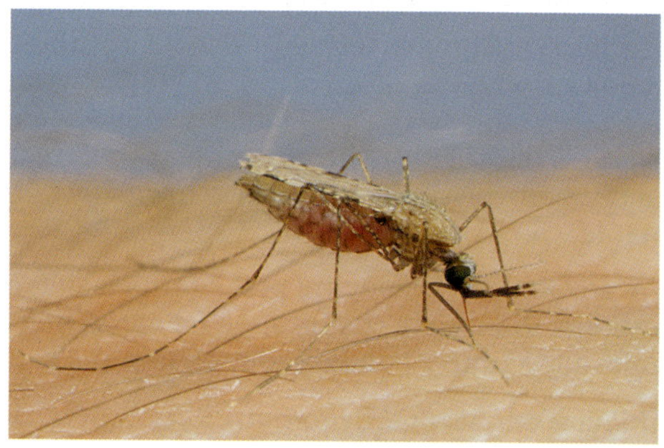

Some insect pests developed new strains that were resistant to DDT. They survived the spraying but their natural predators, such as wasps, were being killed.

**a State *one* advantage and *one* disadvantage of using DDT for pest control**

## DDT in the food chain

It was noticed that in areas where DDT had been used birds were laying eggs with very thin shells that broke. This resulted in a decrease in the number of sparrow hawks and falcons.

DDT enters the **food chain** when it is washed into rivers and streams. It is present in low concentrations in fish. At every step up the food chain, its concentration increases. In the falcon shown in the diagram the concentration of DDT is so high it poisons the bird.

**b Explain how the use of DDT affected bird populations.**

| Organism | DDT concentration (parts per million) |
| --- | --- |
| trout  | 6 |
| herring gull  | 99 |
| peregrine falcon  | 5000 |

**Did you know?**
DDT is very effective because it attacks the nervous systems of insects.

## DDT and humans

The long-term effects of DDT on humans are not known. Scientists in the United States think there may be a link between DDT and premature births.

Scientists in Belgium studied children who had emigrated from countries such as India where DDT is still used. They found that:

- girls had a much greater chance of starting puberty at a very young age;
- most of the girls who started puberty early had high levels of a chemical that comes from DDT in their blood – the chemical has a similar effect to the sex hormone oestrogen;
- some girls developed breasts before they were eight and started their periods before they were ten.

Scientists are also concerned that there may be a link between DDT and cancer, but this has not been proved.

**c Explain why DDT caused early puberty in girls but not in boys.**

## A world-wide ban

DDT is still used in twenty-five countries in the world. It is banned in Europe and in the United States of America. Some environmentalists would like every country in the world to stop using it.

Some health experts are opposed to a ban. They state that:

- DDT is cheap and developing countries in Africa and Asia do not have the money to buy alternatives;
- a ban will result in millions more deaths from malaria;
- DDT may be harmful to the environment, but its benefits in fighting malaria far outweigh this.

Even though DDT has not been used in the UK for thirty years, we still take it into our bodies through the food that we eat. We import food from countries that still use DDT, and the chemical is present in this food. In the body it concentrates in fatty tissue such as the breasts and is passed on to children in breast milk.

The story of DDT shows how important it is to find out the effects of new pesticides before they are used on a large scale.

This food is imported from India, a country that still uses DDT.

### Key ideas

- *DDT has been beneficial, eliminating malaria from some parts of the world.*
- *DDT has known harmful effects on the environment and may have harmful effects on people.*

### Questions

1 **What beneficial effects has DDT had for people?**

2 **What harmful effects has DDT had on the environment?**

3 **Write *two* leaflets, one in favour of the continued use of DDT and one that supports a ban on its use.**

# 7:15 Biodiversity

There is a vast range and variety of living things. Scientists estimate that the world contains about five million different **species** of plants and animals. However, less than two million of these have been identified and classified. The range and number of species that exist in a **habitat** or **ecosystem** is known as the ecosystem's **biological diversity** or **biodiversity**.

## Maintaining diversity

If we are to keep the diversity of habitats then we do not want any species to die out. As agriculture develops and wild uncultivated land is built on, the habitats of some rare plants and animals disappear. The numbers of some plants and animals are so low that they are classified as **endangered species**. Endangered species can be protected by:

- laws that prohibit the picking of some wild flowers and the collection of the eggs of some birds;
- keeping their location secret;
- re-introducing organisms into habitats where they have died out.

The osprey is a hawk that feeds on fish. Ospreys build nests in the shape of baskets in tall trees. Ospreys breed in Scotland and NW England but there are very few breeding pairs left. The sites where ospreys nest are kept under constant watch to guard them from human predators. Stealing an egg from an osprey's nest is an offence that can carry a prison sentence.

The lady's slipper orchid is a plant that is rare in the wild. There are only a few sites where it occurs in the UK. Like the osprey, it is legally protected. It is an offence to pick a flower or dig up a plant.

**a Explain how human activity can cause species to die out.**

**Did you know?**
International law requires governments to protect the diversity of habitats in their countries.

## A playing field

A school playing field or a football pitch provides a habitat that is not very diverse. Few plants can grow there and there is too much human activity for many animals to be able to live there. For a plant to be able to survive it needs to have leaves that grow close to the ground so that they can survive mowing and trampling. Apart from grass, plants that are commonly found on playing fields and football pitches include:

- daisies, their leaves and many of their flowers are so low that they escape the grass cutter;
- dandelions, although their flowers are cut off by the grass cutter, they can produce new ones and distribute the seed between mowing;
- plantains, their leaves grow flat along the ground and they produce long spiked flowers;
- chickweed or stitchwort, this is a low-growing plant with small leaves.

**b How are daisies adapted to survive in grass that is cut frequently?**

The daisies growing in this meadow can survive the effects of a lawn mower.

## A more diverse habitat

A wood can support hundreds of different species. Several habitats exist in a wood.

Birds and large mammals such as deer, badgers and squirrels use the whole of the wood as their habitat. They roam freely to find their food.

Many species of insect can live on a single oak tree. Here they find food and shelter and they provide food for birds.

At ground level, spring-flowering plants such as bluebells and anemones are found in clearings where light can penetrate. They are dormant in summer when direct sunlight does not get through the canopy of leaves.

**A wood provides a habitat for the grey squirrel. There are very few red squirrels left in the UK.**

Small animals such as mice and voles nest in hedges and bushes.

A rotting log provides a habitat for wood lice.

Below ground there are many different species of insect that feed on the fallen leaves and recycle the nutrients.

**c Why are decomposers important to the woodland habitat?**

**An oak tree provides food for decomposers as well as for squirrels.**

## Questions

1. Explain the meaning of the term **biodiversity**.
2. Suggest why less than half of the estimated species of plants and animals in the world have been classified.
3. Many small towns and villages have a lot of heavy traffic flowing through them. This is seen as a problem by many people living these towns and villages. An answer to their problem may be to build a by-pass around the town or village.
   - **a** Why can this cause conflict with environmental groups?
   - **b** Write a letter to a local newspaper, giving a reasoned argument either in favour or against a proposed by-pass.

### Key ideas

- *Biodiversity describes the different types of organism in an ecosystem.*
- *The more organisms that a habitat supports, the greater its biodiversity.*

# End of module questions

## Low demand

1. Plant and animal cells both have
   **A** cell walls
   **B** chlorophyll
   **C** chloroplasts
   **D** nuclei

2. Plants produce their own food in a process called
   **A** excretion
   **B** ingestion
   **C** photosynthesis
   **D** respiration

3. In a plant cell, chlorophyll is found in the
   **A** cell membrane
   **B** cell wall
   **C** chloroplasts
   **D** vacuole

4. Sugars are moved to all parts of a plant through the
   **A** leaves
   **B** roots
   **C** phloem
   **D** xylem

5. In a plant, photosynthesis occurs
   **A** only in the light
   **B** only in the dark
   **C** both in the light and in the dark
   **D** in neither the light nor the dark

6. A plant absorbs water from the soil through its
   **A** fruit
   **B** leaves
   **C** roots
   **D** stem

7. Vegetable material in a compost heap decays best in which conditions?
   **A** cold and dry
   **B** cold and wet
   **C** warm and dry
   **D** warm and wet

8. Some pyramids are shown in the diagram.

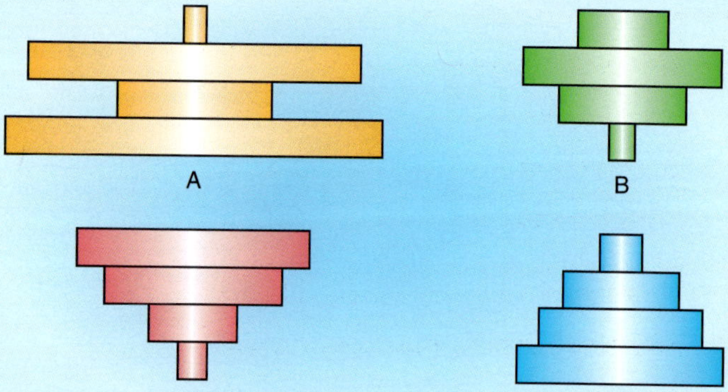


   Which diagram could represent the pyramid of biomass for a food chain that begins with an oak tree?

9. In a sustainable forest
   **A** trees are cut down and replanted
   **B** trees are cut down and left to rot
   **C** trees are cut down and the land is used to grow crops
   **D** trees are cut down and burned

10. The biodiversity of an ecosystem is a measure of the number of different
    **A** animals
    **B** flowers
    **C** plants
    **D** organisms

**11** A weedkiller is

**A** an antibiotic

**B** a fungicide

**C** a herbicide

**D** an insecticide

**12** Pests on food crops can be controlled biologically by using

**A** fungicides

**B** herbicides

**C** insectides

**D** predators

## Standard demand

**13** Photosynthesis requires energy from

**A** diffusion

**B** excretion

**C** respiration

**D** the Sun

**14** In the process of photosynthesis

**A** carbon dioxide and glucose react to form water and oxygen

**B** carbon dioxide and water react to form glucose and oxygen

**C** glucose and oxygen react to form water and carbon dioxide

**D** glucose and water react to form carbon dioxide and oxygen

**15** Plants need nitrates to make

**A** carbohydrates

**B** carbon dioxide

**C** oxygen

**D** protein

**16** Osmosis is an example of

**A** absorption

**B** diffusion

**C** excretion

**D** respiration

**17** Plant cells need water to maintain

**A** floppiness

**B** frigidity

**C** turgidity

**D** wilting

**18** Mammals lose more energy than plants because they

**A** have a greater body mass

**B** take in more minerals

**C** take in more water

**D** are warmer than plants

**19** In root hair cells water enters the roots because

**A** water moves from a region of high salt concentration a region of low salt concentration

**B** water moves from a region of low salt concentration a region of high salt concentration

**C** salt moves from a region of high salt concentration a region of low salt concentration

**D** salt moves from a region of high salt concentration a region of low salt concentration

**Questions 20–22**

The diagram shows the carbon cycle.

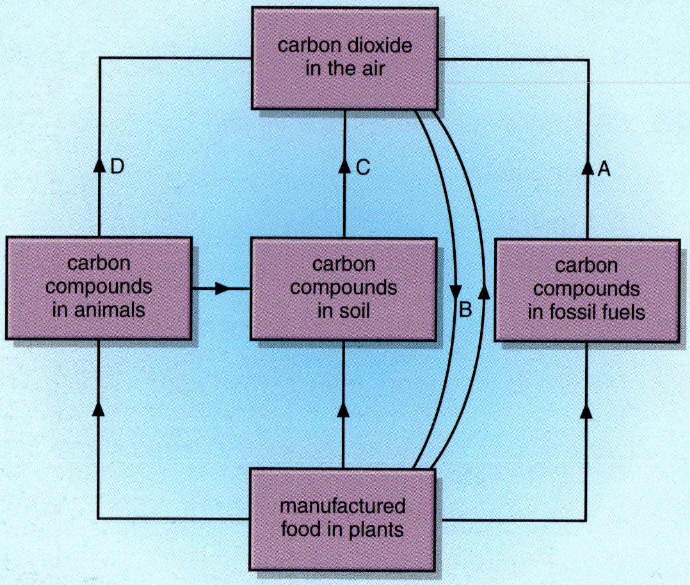


**20** Which letter shows combustion?

**21** Which letter is caused by microorganisms?

**22** Which letter shows photosynthesis?

**Questions 23–24**

The diagram shows the food web of a seashore habitat.

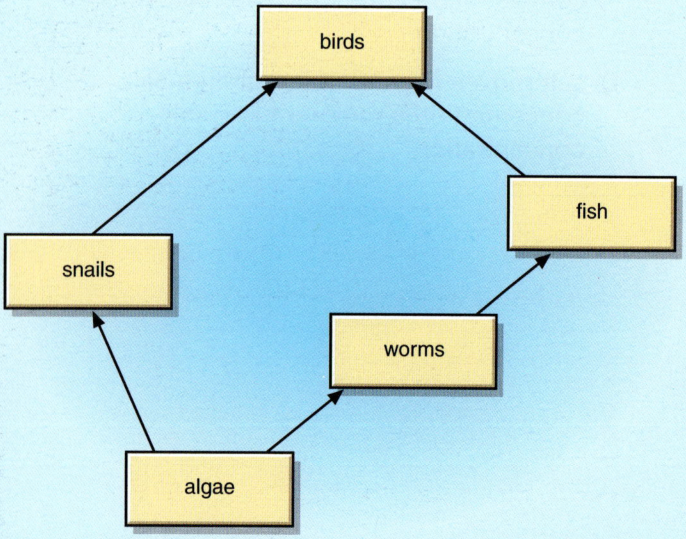


**23** Poisonous chemical waste is absorbed by the algae.

The concentration of chemical waste is likely to be highest in the bodies of the

**A** birds

**B** fish

**C** snails

**D** worms

**24** Energy is lost from the food web by respiration and by excretion.

Which statement is correct?

**A** more energy is lost by the algae than by the worms

**B** more energy is lost by the worms than by the fish

**C** more energy is lost by the fish than by the birds

**D** more energy is lost by the birds than by the fish

# Module 8 – Health and exercise

This module is divided into five parts.

1 An exchange of gases takes place in the lungs. Oxygen from the air is transferred to the blood. Carbon dioxide from the bloodstream is taken into the lungs and breathed out. The structure of the lungs makes them good at exchanging gases. Smoking, however, can seriously affect this process.

2 Blood circulates around the body through arteries, capillaries and veins. The heart pumps the blood through *two* separate systems. The efficiency of the circulatory system can depend on life style and diet.

3 At the cells respiration takes place. There are *two* types of respiration – aerobic and anaerobic.

4 Misuse of steroid drugs by athletes and young people.

5 Inherited diseases such as cystic fibrosis and sickle cell disease.

Try these questions first.

**1** **Which gas in the air is needed for respiration?**

**2** **Finish the equation for respiration.**

**Glucose + oxygen → ______________ + ______________**

**3** **Which gas is at a higher concentration in the air we breathe out when compared to the air we breathe in?**

**4** **Write down *four* components of blood.**

**5** **Which part of blood carries oxygen around the body?**

**6** **What is the job of the heart in the body?**

**7** **What measurements does a doctor make to judge how well your circulatory system is working?**

# 8:1 Take a deep breath

## Climb to the top

We all need oxygen to keep us alive. In a healthy body your breathing system is working all the time to provide a continuous supply of oxygen.

The air around very high mountains contains less oxygen. This is why mountaineers have to take a supply of oxygen with them.

Fortunately, the air you breathe contains enough oxygen to keep you fit and healthy.

### Air passages

The job of your breathing system is to get air into and out of your body.

This brings in a fresh supply of oxygen and removes carbon dioxide. This is called **ventilation**.

The diagram shows your breathing system.

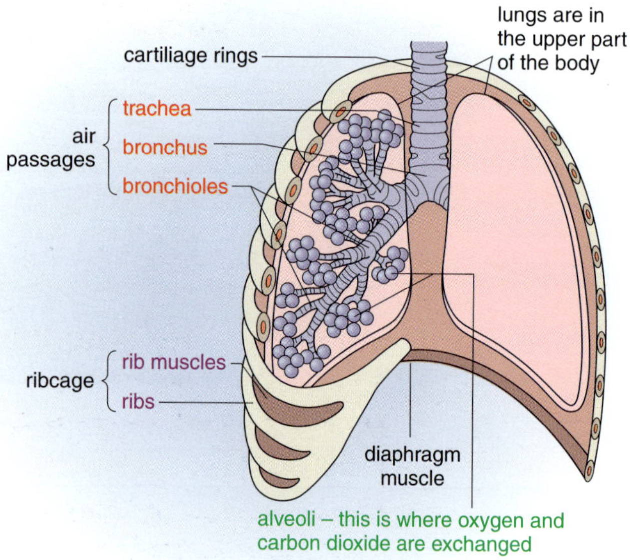


There are *three* main parts:

- a series of **air passages** that connect your lungs with the outside;
- gas exchange tissues made from millions of tiny air sacs called **alveoli**;
- the ribcage made from bone and muscle that protects your lungs and is used to pump air in and out of your lungs.

### What happens when we breathe in and out?

The series of diagrams show how your breathing system works.

In the first diagram you are breathing in. The space inside your chest (called the **thorax**) is made bigger. The pressure of the air inside the lungs is reduced. Air enters to make the pressure the same as it is outside your body.

**a Look at the diagram. What *two* things make the thorax bigger?**

In the second diagram you are breathing out. The space inside the thorax is made smaller. The pressure of the air inside the lung gets greater. Air is pushed out to reduce the pressure.

**b Look at the diagram. What *two* things make the thorax smaller?**

**Breathing in**

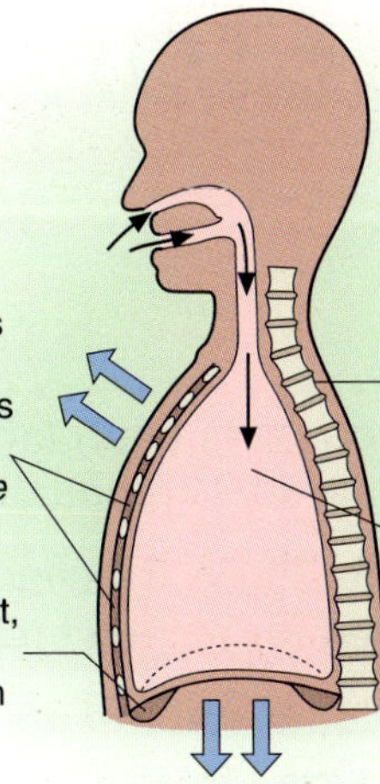


**Breathing out**

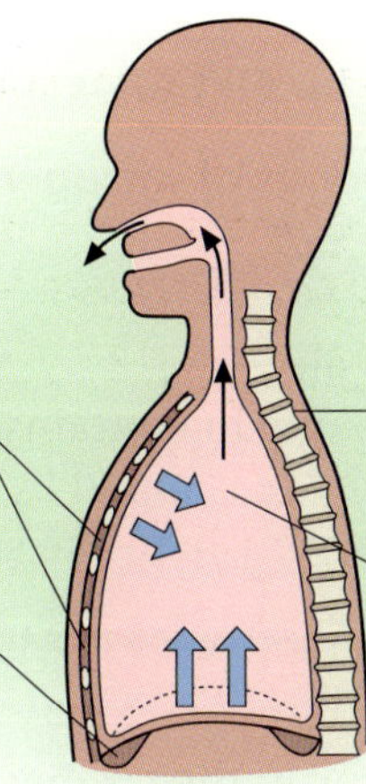


### Investigating breathing

As you become more active your cells need more energy. To provide more energy you need to break down more glucose during respiration. This means that you need to get more oxygen into your body. The table below shows the results of an investigation carried to find out how breathing changes during exercise.

| Activity | Volume of each breath ($cm^3$) | Number of breaths taken per minute |
|---|---|---|
| rest | 500 | 18 |
| 20 step-ups per minute | 500 | 25 |
| 50 step-ups per minute | 1200 | 34 |

**c How does breathing change as activity becomes more demanding?**

## Key ideas

- *The thorax is made up of three parts:*
  - *air passages that connect the lungs with the outside air;*
  - *the tiny sacs where gas exchange takes place;*
  - *the ribcage made of bone and muscle to protect the lungs and pump air in and out.*
- *Air is breathed in (inhaled) when the pressure of air inside the lung is reduced.*
- *Air is breathed out (exhaled) when the pressure of the air inside the lung is increased.*

## Questions

**1 Look at the diagram of the breathing system. Use it to answer these questions.**

**a What strengthens the trachea and stops it collapsing?**

**b What raises and lowers the ribs?**

**c Where does gaseous exchange take place?**

**2 Copy and complete this sentence. Use words from this list.**

**body contract diaphragm ribs ventilation**

**When a person breathes in the _______________ move out and the _______________ becomes flatter.**

**3 Use the results from the breathing investigation to answer the following questions.**

**a How many breaths did the person take per minute at rest?**

**b How many more breaths were taken when the person was doing 20 step-ups?**

# 8:2 Exchanging gases

## A fair swap

As you breathe you are not only taking in the oxygen you need you are also getting rid of waste carbon dioxide. In your alveoli you exchange what you need for your waste.

The table opposite shows the concentration of gases in the air you breathe in and the air you breathe out.

| Gas | Inhaled air (%) | Exhaled air (%) |
|---|---|---|
| oxygen | 20 | 16 |
| carbon dioxide | 0.04 | 4 |
| nitrogen | 78 | 78 |

**a Sam makes some statements about differences between the air we breathe in and the air we breathe out. Which are true and which are false?**

**A We breathe in more oxygen than we breathe out.**

**B We use up all the oxygen we breathe in.**

**C The amount of nitrogen we breathe in is the same as the amount we breathe out.**

### Filtering the air

The air we breathe in contains dust particles and other microorganisms including bacteria. These are trapped by **mucus** in our throat. This is then moved to the back of the throat by tiny hair-like structures called **cilia**.

The mucus and particles are usually swallowed so that the acid in the stomach can kill any bacteria.

Cilia and mucus in the trachea continue the process of cleaning up the air.

The aim of all this is to stop harmful microorganisms reaching the lungs.

### Exchanging gases

Once the air you breath in reaches the alveoli, oxygen and carbon dioxide are exchanged by **diffusion**. The diagram below shows how the oxygen you need diffuses into the bloodstream and how waste carbon dioxide diffuses out of the blood.

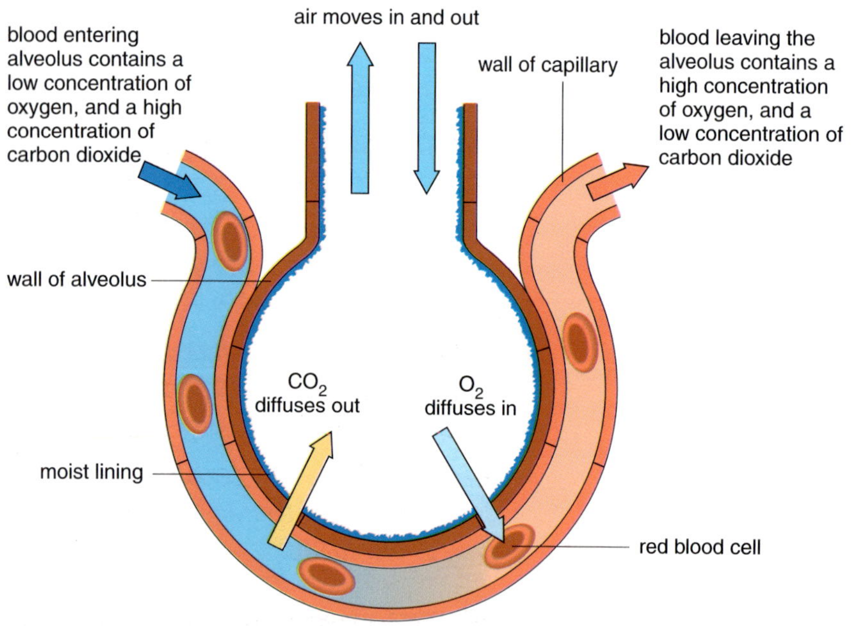


**Thin walls allow diffusion of gases in and out of alveoli in the lungs.**

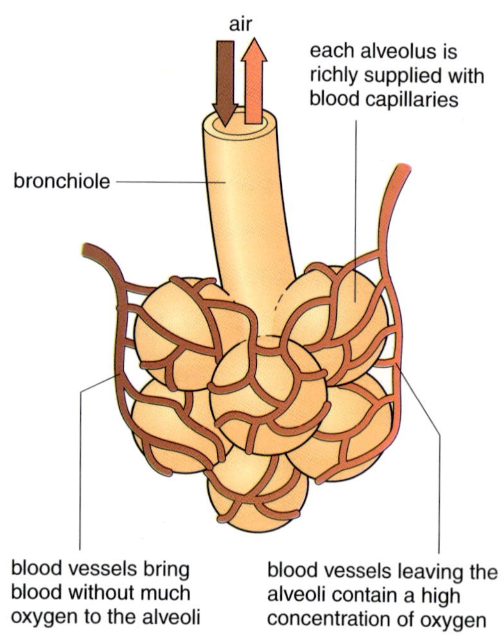


**Alveoli are richly supplied with blood vessels.**

In all organisms gas exchange surfaces:

- have a large surface area for diffusion;
- have a rich supply of blood vessels;
- have very thin walls so gases have only a short distance to move.

**Smoke gets in your lungs**

Tars in cigarette smoke stop the cilia from working.

This means that they cannot remove the mucus and bacteria from the system. This leads to problems such as **bronchitis**.

Tars also damage the walls of the alveoli making them break down and reducing the surface area for gas exchange. This causes **emphysema**. The diagram shows the change that takes place.

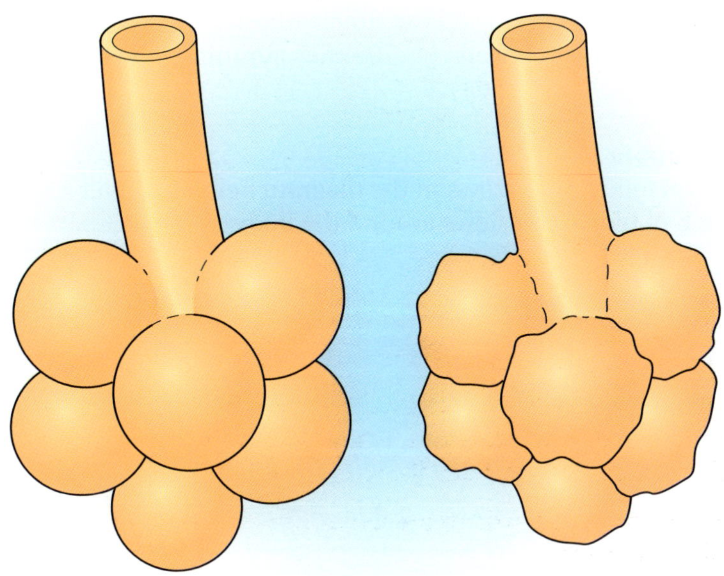

**Healthy alveolus.** **Alveolus from a person with emphysema.**

**b What warning is given to smokers when they buy a packet of cigarettes?**

***Lung cancer***

Cancer occurs when cells divide in the wrong way. This is caused by mutations and can lead to the formation of a **tumour**. There is evidence that chemicals, called **carcinogens**, in cigarette smoke cause mutations that lead to cancerous tumours.

***Giving up smoking***

Smoking is **addictive**. Once you start smoking it gets harder and harder to stop. Smokers can use nicotine patches, gum, etc. to help them break the habit. By using these they gradually reduce the amount of nicotine their body wants.

**Did you know?**

Nicotine in cigarettes used to be used by gardeners to control pests. They can't now because it is too dangerous.

## Questions

1 Copy and complete these sentences. Use words from this list.

breathing carbon dioxide diffuses digestion oxygen respiration

The air entering the alveoli contains a high concentration of ______________. This gas ______________ into the bloodstream and is transported to all body cells and used in ______________.

2 An exchange of gases takes place in the lungs. Write down *three* things that make this efficient.

3 Write down ways that smokers can try to give up smoking.

## Key ideas

- *The lining of the nose and lungs traps particles and bacteria and with the help of the cilia destroy these.*
- *Cigarette smoke can lead to emphysema.*
- *Cigarette smoke contains carcinogens that cause lung cells to mutate to form lung cancer.*
- *Smokers use different methods to give up smoking.*

# 8:3 Heart beat

## Pumping the system

Blood flows around your body through a network of blood vessels that make up your **circulatory system**. Blood is kept flowing around the system by the pumping action of your heart. Your heart is the circulatory system's pump.

Your heart is working all the time without pausing to rest. It pumps (beats) between 60–70 times per minute, which is about 100 000 beats every day

### A double pump

If you follow the arrows in the diagram below you will trace the path of blood as it flows around the body.

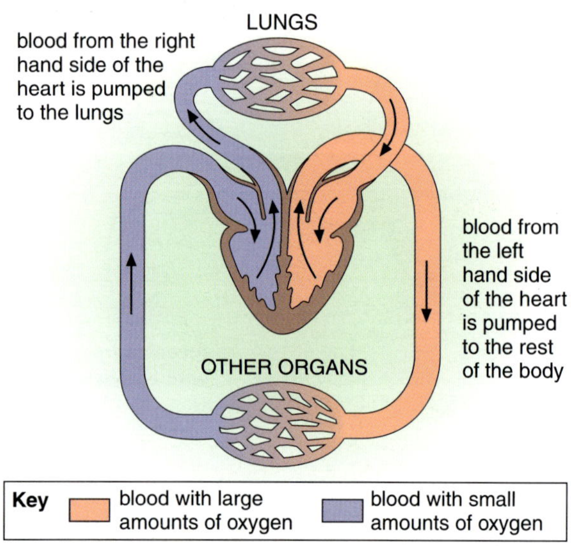


Blood from the right hand side of the heart is pumped to your lungs where it picks up oxygen before returning to the heart.

Blood from the left hand side of the heart is pumped all around the rest of your body before returning to the heart.

This is called a **double circulatory system** because blood travels through the heart twice as it flows once around the body.

The big advantage of double circulation is that the blood is returned to the heart to gain a high enough pressure to get it through the capillaries of the body.

### A pump with four chambers

The diagram shows what the inside of your heart looks like. You can see that it is divided into four chambers – two **atria** and two **ventricles**.

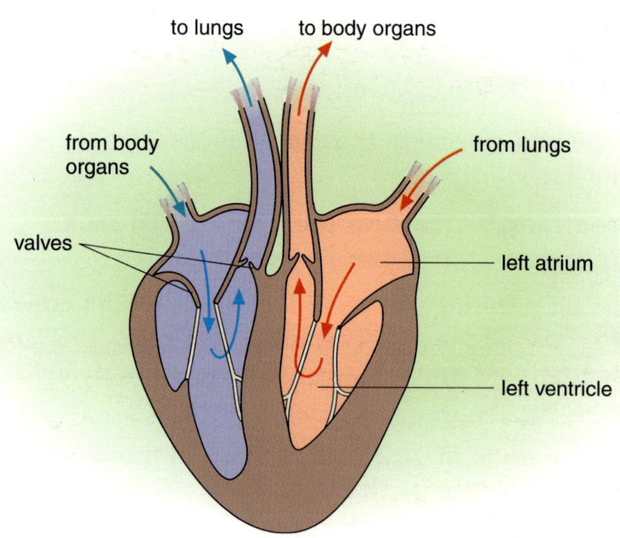


**The right side of the heart is on the left as you look at it.**

Blood flows to and from the heart through the blood vessels connected to it.

Blood flows *from* the heart through **arteries**.

Blood flows *back to* the heart through **veins**.

There are valves inside the heart and in blood vessels to ensure that blood flows in the right direction.

**Heart action**

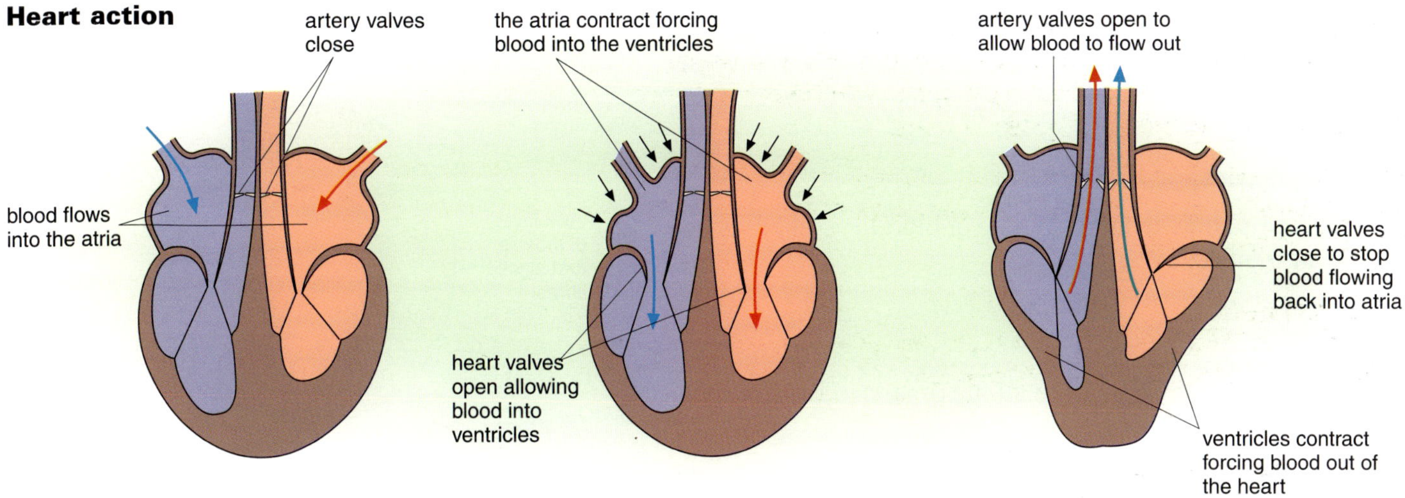


**Your heart muscles and valves ensure blood flows in the right direction.**

Its thick muscular walls produce the pumping action of your heart.

When the muscles around the chambers *contract* blood is squeezed out.

When the muscles *relax* blood enters the chambers.

The heart muscles receive the glucose and oxygen they need through coronary blood vessels.

**Did you know?**
William Harvey was the first person to realise that blood circulated around the body. This was in 1628.

**Measuring heart action**
Each time your heart beats blood is forced into arteries. When this happens the arteries expand as blood flows through them. Once the blood has passed through the arteries contract. This is your **pulse**. A pulse in an artery happens once every heartbeat.

**a Why does your pulse rate increase when you exercise?**

**b What happens when you rest after exercise?**

## Questions

**1** Write the list below in the correct order of circulation starting from blood flowing from body organs.

**blood flowing from body organs** **left atrium**
**right atrium** **right ventricle** **left ventricle**
**blood flowing to body organs**
**blood flowing to the lungs**

**2** Why is it important to have valves in the heart?

## Key ideas

- *The heart pumps blood around the body through a double circulatory system.*
- *The heart consists of four chambers – two ventricles and two atria.*
- *There are valves in the heart and veins to make sure the blood flows in one direction.*
- *The coronary blood vessels supply the heart muscle with the glucose and oxygen it needs.*
- *The pulse is caused by blood pumping along an artery from the heart.*

# 8:4 Blood transport

## Supply lines

Blood is pumped around your body through a highly complex system of blood vessels. There are *three* types of blood vessel:

- **arteries;**
- **veins;**
- **capillaries.**

The diagrams show what each type of blood vessel looks like and what they do.

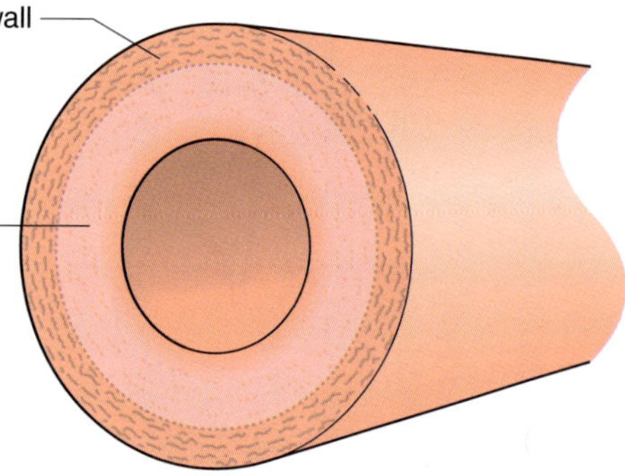


**An artery.**

## Arteries

Blood flows from your heart to all the organs in your body through arteries.

The blood in arteries is under high pressure because blood is pumped into arteries by the heart.

Arteries have thick walls containing muscle and elastic fibres to withstand the pressure.

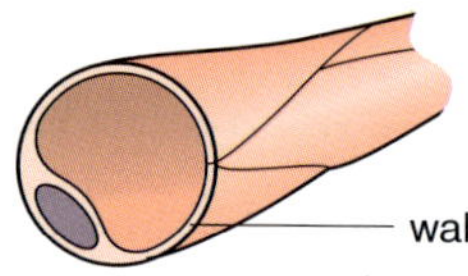


**A capillary.**

### Capillaries

Arteries branch to form smaller and smaller blood vessels and eventually form capillaries.

Capillaries are found inside organs. They are very narrow and have thin walls that are only one cell thick.

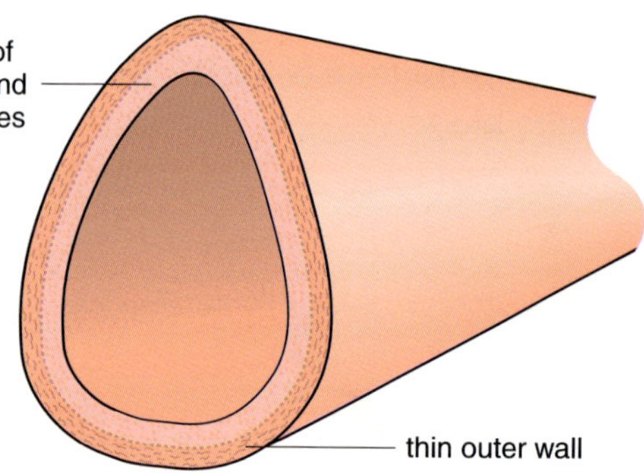


**A vein.**

### Veins

Capillaries gradually join up again to form veins.

The pressure in veins is very low so blood flows much more slowly than in arteries.

Veins have thin walls as they do not have to withstand high pressure. They also have valves to stop any blood flowing backwards.

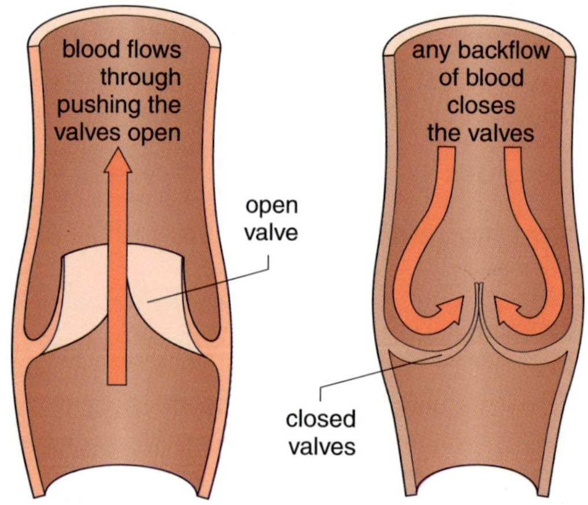


**Valves in a vein.**

**a Blood flows away from the heart pump in arteries. Explain:**

**i why the blood pressure in arteries is high;**

**ii why arteries have thick walls;**

**iii why arteries do not have valves.**

> **Did you know?**
> When William Harvey proposed the circulation of the blood in 1628 he did not know about capillaries. He predicted they existed and is was Malpighi who first found capillaries in 1661.

**Exchanging substances**

The thin walls of capillaries allow substances needed by cells to pass *from* the blood.

The thin walls also allow waste substances produced by cells to pass *into* the blood.

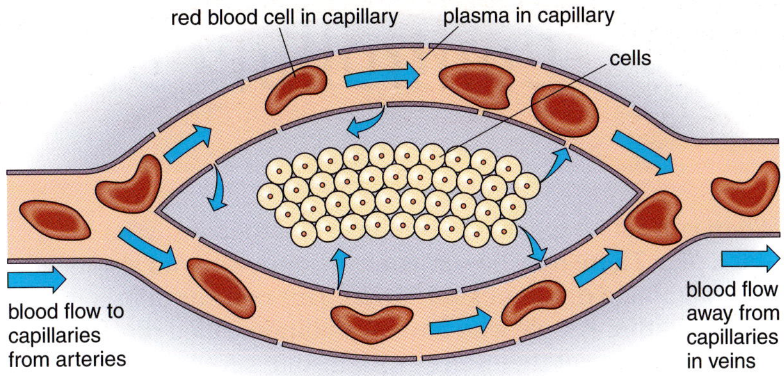


**Moving in and out**

Capillaries are the part of your circulatory system where substances enter and leave the blood. Here are three examples of organs where substances move in and out of blood through capillaries.

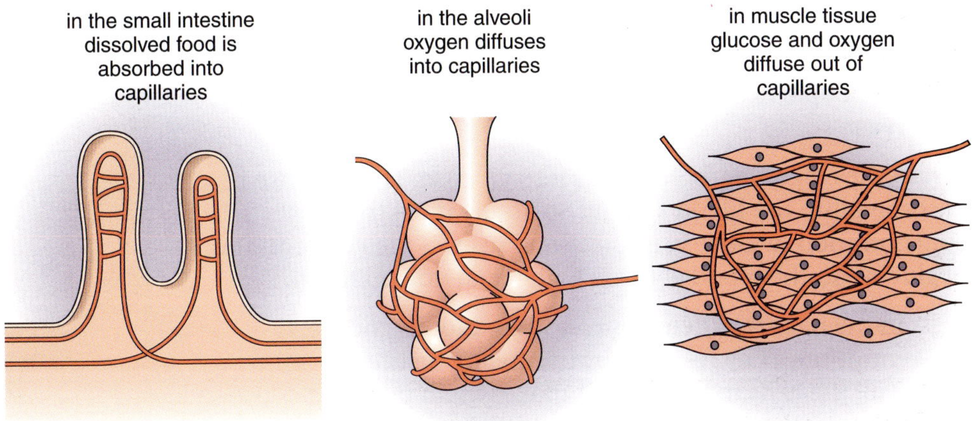


**Substances move into and out of capillaries.**

**Problems with the circulatory system**

Exercise will make your heart more efficient so that it can beat less often but still pump the same amount of blood.

On the other hand, blocking the coronary artery starves the heart muscle of glucose and oxygen. This leads to coronary heart disease and possibly death.

The *three* factors associated with heart disease are:

- diet;
- raised blood pressure;
- smoking.

With age the arteries become less flexible. This is called hardening of the arteries.

## Questions

**1** Copy and complete these sentences. Use words from this list.

**capillaries muscle pressure veins**

Blood is carried back to the heart in _______________ at low _______________. Arteries have thick walls made from _______________ and elastic fibres. The smallest blood vessels are called _______________ and have walls that are one cell thick.

**2** Copy and complete this table.

| | Veins | Arteries | Capillaries |
|---|---|---|---|
| wall thickness (thick or thin) | | | |
| valves (present or absent) | | | |
| blood pressure (high or low) | | | |

## Key ideas

- *Arteries, capillaries and veins carry blood around the body. They have different structures for the different uses they have.*
- *Substances are transferred between cells and capillaries by diffusion.*
- *The circulatory system can be affected by diet, age and lack of exercise.*

# 8:5 Controlling blood sugar

When you set off for school you have to remember your books and a pen. There may be someone in your year who also needs to remember a different kind of pen. This pen contains a drug called **insulin**. People who have a condition called **diabetes** may have to inject themselves with insulin several times per day. The pen is used to inject the insulin.

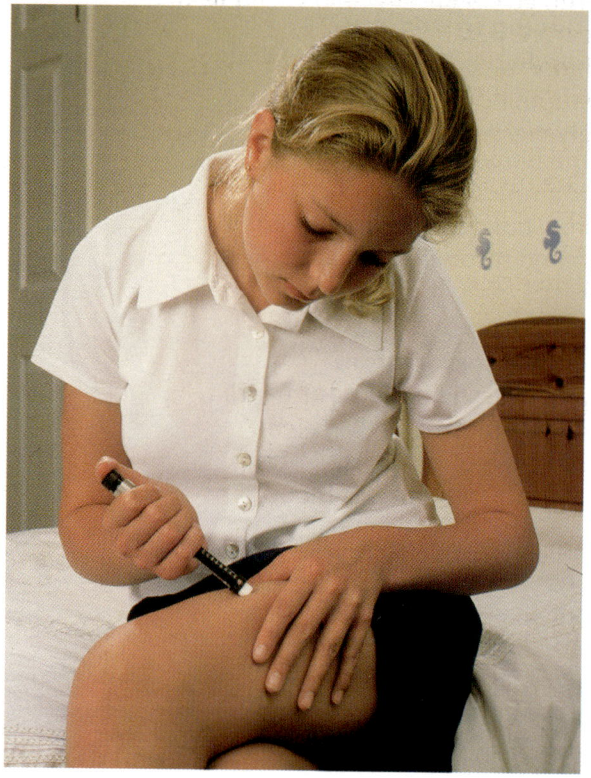

## Insulin

Healthy people make their own insulin. It is produced by the **pancreas**.

Our bodies digest carbohydrates into glucose. This glucose is absorbed into the blood stream. So after a meal the concentration of glucose in the blood rises. If the concentration of glucose in the blood gets too high it can do you harm.

Cells in the pancreas detect increases in blood glucose concentration. They respond by producing insulin. Insulin affects all the cells in the body. It makes them take in glucose so the concentration of glucose in the blood comes down.

The amount of insulin produced is controlled by cells in the pancreas, not by the brain.

**a The pancreas also secretes enzymes for digestion. Where do these enzymes go as they leave the pancreas?**

### Diabetes

In some people, cells in the pancreas do not secrete enough insulin. This condition is called diabetes. The majority of people who have diabetes can control the condition by watching their diet. They have to careful about the amounts of sugar-containing foods that they eat.

**b Explain why people with diabetes must not eat too much sugar-containing food.**

In some people suffering from diabetes many of the insulin-producing cells deteriorate. These diabetics have to make up for the loss of insulin by injecting themselves with insulin several times a day.

**c Suggest why these diabetics inject small amounts of insulin several times a day rather than just injecting one large dose of insulin.**

## Getting the balance right

The pancreas secretes another hormone called **glucagon**. Glucagon has the opposite effect to insulin. If the blood glucose concentration drops too low, the pancreas secretes glucagon. Glucagon causes the blood glucose concentration to rise to normal levels.

**d i Give *two* reasons why the blood glucose concentration might fall.**

**ii Explain why it is important that blood glucose concentration should not be allowed to fall too low.**

## Glycogen

The liver plays an important part in blood glucose regulation. When blood glucose concentration is high, insulin stimulates enzymes in the liver to convert excess glucose into glycogen. Glycogen is an insoluble carbohydrate that is stored in the liver. When blood glucose concentration is low, glucagon stimulates enzymes in the liver to convert glycogen back into glucose.

Chemical firms are able to make insulin by extracting it from the pancreas of pigs, sheep and cattle. Now it can be made from genetically engineered bacteria.

**Did you know?**

Insulin was not discovered until 1921. In 1922 a 14 year-old Canadian boy with diabetes was treated with extract from the pancreas of a dog. After treatment, the teenager was able to eat a normal diet and began to put on weight and lead an active life. Without this treatment he would have died.

## Questions

**1** Copy and complete these sentences.
Use words from this list.

**diabetes glucagon glucose glycogen hormones insulin liver pancreas**

Chemicals called _______________ control many of the processes in the body. The concentration of sugar in the blood is monitored by the _______________. If there is too much sugar in the blood the pancreas releases _______________. Excess glucose is stored in the _______________ as _______________. If there is too little sugar in the blood the pancreas releases _______________. If the pancreas does not release enough insulin, a person suffers from _______________.

**2** Two people, **A** and **B**, were given an identical meal containing large amounts of glucose. The concentrations of glucose and insulin in their blood plasma were measured at regular intervals over the next 150 minutes. The graphs show the results.

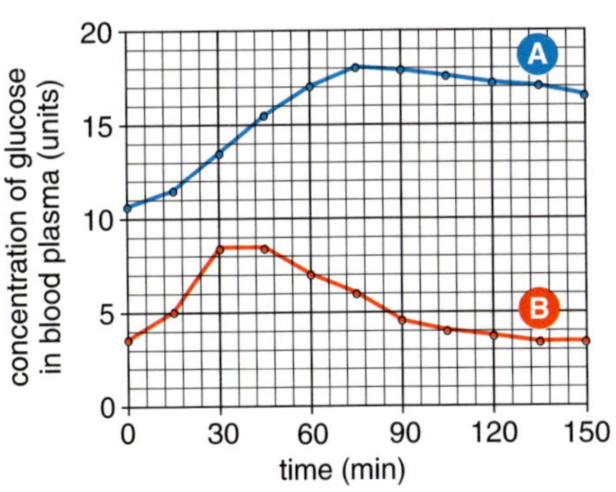


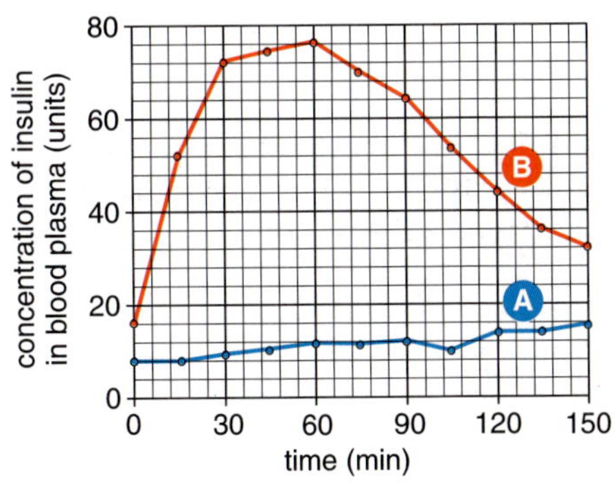


**a** Which person, **A** or **B**, had diabetes? Give the reason for your answer.

**b** Explain why the blood glucose concentration of person **B** rose for one hour after the meal, then fell.

### Key ideas

- *Insulin produced by the pancreas regulates the glucose concentration in the blood.*

# 8:6 Releasing and using energy

## Keeping going

During intense exercise you need lots of energy. This energy comes from glucose in your blood. Glucose is your body's main fuel.

When your muscles become short of glucose you start to feel tired and weak. This is why even very fit sportsmen and sportswomen use 'high energy' drinks or eat fruit during long periods of physical activity. They are making sure that their muscle are provided with enough glucose to keep up their energy levels.

Sportsmen and sportswomen use 'high energy drinks' to keep up their energy levels.

### Gasping for breath

As you become more active you breathe faster and deeper. This is to provide your muscles with the oxygen needed to release energy from glucose.

Oxygen and glucose react together in body cells to release energy. This process is **aerobic respiration**. Activities such as running need lots of energy from respiration. Aerobic respiration is summarised by the equation:

glucose + oxygen → carbon dioxide + water + energy

## Using energy

The energy that is released during respiration is used by the body to:

- build larger molecules from smaller ones, so that you can grow and repair damaged cells;
- enable muscles to contract so that you can move;
- keep your body temperature steady even when you are in colder surroundings.

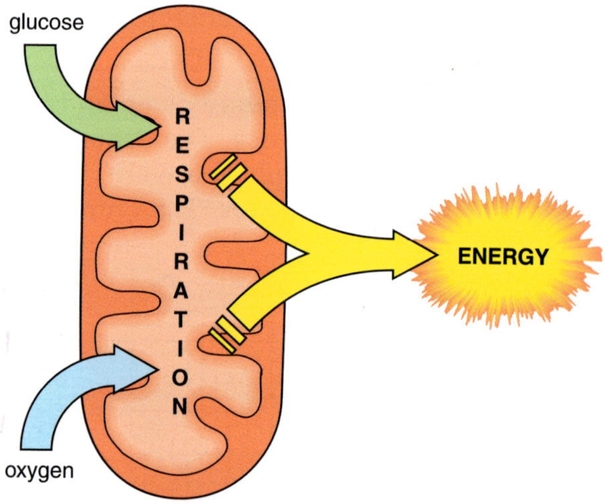


Mitochondria release energy from glucose to provide cells with energy.

### Respiration without oxygen

Sometimes your body cannot get enough oxygen. For example, during very strenuous exercise such as sprinting, your muscles are working so hard that they become short of oxygen.

To provide the energy that is needed, glucose is broken down without using oxygen. This process is called **anaerobic respiration**.

**Lactic acid** is produced as a waste product instead of carbon dioxide and water. Anaerobic respiration is summarised by the equation:

glucose → lactic acid + energy

**Getting into debt**

The lactic acid produced by anaerobic respiration causes muscles to become tired and they work less efficiently. The pain in the muscles is called **cramp**.

Lactic acid is removed using oxygen to break it down. After exercise you often keep breathing heavily to take in extra oxygen. The oxygen needed to break down lactic acid is called the **oxygen debt**.

lactic acid + oxygen → carbon dioxide + water + energy

## Questions

**1 The two pie charts show what two sports drinks contain.**

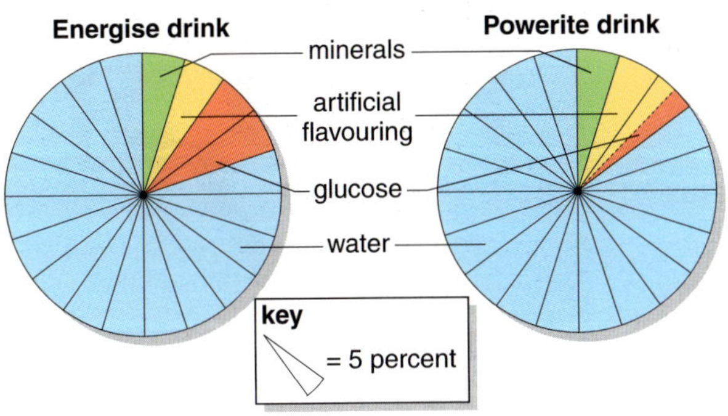


**a Copy and complete this table. Use data from the pie charts.**

| | Energise drink | Powerite drink |
|---|---|---|
| water | | |
| glucose | | |
| minerals | | |
| flavouring | | |

**b Which of the substances in the drinks provides energy to the body?**

**c Which of the two drinks is the best to take when resting during a sports match? Give a reason for your answer.**

**2 Copy and complete this table.**

| | Substances needed | Substances produced |
|---|---|---|
| aerobic respiration | glucose and ________ | water and ________ |
| anaerobic respiration | ________ | ________ |

**3 A marathon runner aims to get a balance between the oxygen taken in and the oxygen used in respiration. Why is this a good idea?**

### Key ideas

- *Aerobic respiration provides energy to grow and repair damaged cells, for work and to stay warm.*
- *In aerobic respiration glucose is changed into carbon dioxide and water, and energy is released.*
- *Anaerobic respiration takes place when there is not enough oxygen available for aerobic respiration.*
- *During anaerobic respiration glucose is changed into lactic acid and energy is released.*
- *Lactic acid in muscles produces cramp.*
- *Extra oxygen is needed to remove lactic acid.*

# Making the body work hard

## Britain is getting fatter

The health of most people living in Britain is now better than it used to be. One aspect of health that has become worse is the increase in the number of adults who are overweight. Britain is becoming a fatter nation.

Being overweight increases the risk of heart disease, high blood pressure and other illnesses.

Regular exercise helps to stop people becoming overweight. Despite the benefits of exercise nearly 20% of British adults do no or very little exercise. Activity levels of British youngsters still at school are very low. For example, half of primary schoolchildren do not take enough exercise.

**Did you know?**
The number of people who are obese in Britain has tripled over the past 20 years and continues to rise. At least 30 000 premature deaths can be linked to obesity.

Taking part in sport can be fun as well as improving health.

## Getting enough energy

When you are exercising your muscles need more energy. This energy is released from glucose during respiration.

When muscles are working harder more respiration takes place to release more energy.

The table below shows some of the changes in your body as you work harder.

| | Breathing rate (breaths per minute) | Pulse rate (beats per minute) |
|---|---|---|
| at rest | 18 | 65 |
| after 10 minutes strenuous exercise | 42 | 130 |

**a Using the table.**

**i** **Draw a bar chart to show pulse rate at rest and after 10 minutes exercise.**

**ii** **Compare the resting pulse rate with the pulse rate after exercise.**

**iii** **Explain why pulse rate and breathing rate both change during exercise**

## Improving fitness

Getting involved in regular exercise improves your fitness. This is because exercise has several effects on your body. When you exercise regularly your:

- heart muscles become stronger so that it pumps blood round your body more efficiently;
- rib muscles and diaphragm become stronger making your breathing system more efficient;
- muscles become larger and able to work hard for longer.

## Measuring pulse rates

Measuring pulse rate before and after exercise can show how fit you are. In a fit person the pulse rate is often low. When a fit person exercises his or her pulse rate increases and then it quickly returns to normal. When an unfit person exercises his or her pulse rate may become very high and return to normal only slowly.

## Questions

**1 The graph below shows the pulse rates of two girls. One of them takes part in sport and the other takes no exercise at all.**

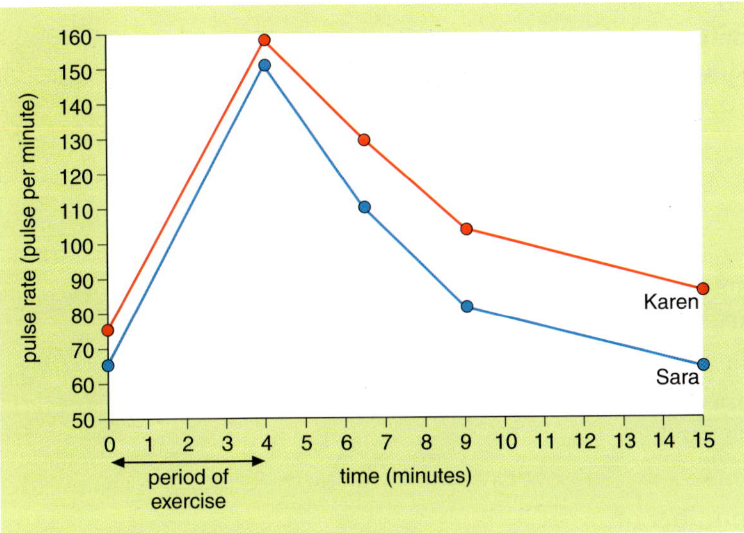


**a** **Which of the two girls is the fitter?**

**b** **What evidence is there on the graph to support your answer?**

**2 The effects of regular exercise on your body can be seen in this table.**

| | Before getting fit | After getting fit |
|---|---|---|
| amount of blood pumped out of the heart during each beat ($cm^3$) | 64 | 80 |
| heart volume ($cm^3$) | 120 | 140 |
| breathing rate (number of breaths per minute) | 14 | 12 |
| pulse rate (beats per minute) | 72 | 63 |

**Use the table to answer the following questions.**

**a** **Describe how pulse rate changed as the person became fitter.**

**b** **What evidence is there to show that regular exercise can make:**

**i** **heart muscles stronger**

**ii** **rib muscles and diaphragm stronger?**

## Key ideas

- *When you are active your body uses more energy.*
- *To provide more energy the rate of respiration in cells increases.*
- *To increase their rate of respiration cells need more glucose and oxygen.*
- *To provide cells with more glucose and oxygen the heart beats faster and stronger and breathing becomes faster and deeper.*
- *When a person exercises the pulse rate increases. After exercise the pulse rate returns to normal. With a fit person the return to normal is faster than with an unfit person.*

# 8:8 Misuse of steroids

## Boosting performance

**Getting an advantage**
There is nothing new about wanting to win.

Wrestlers in ancient Greece used to eat huge amounts of meat to build up their muscles.

The first athletes to be charged with using drugs and nonfood substances were swimmers in Amsterdam in the 1860s. Athletes tried everything from caffeine to heroin in an attempt to improve performance.

Once some athletes started to use these substances, others would copy.

**a Why do other athletes take these drugs?**

Drug taking became more important when scientists made testosterone in the laboratory in the 1930s. This started to be used by athletes in the 1940s and 1950s.

The Russian weightlifting team in 1952 won many medals in the 1952 Olympic Games. Later they were found to have used testosterone.

By 1958 American chemical firms had produced a number of similar materials called **steroids**.

**What are steroids?**
Steroids are substances related to male sex **hormones** such as testosterone. They were developed as important treatment for males who did not naturally produce enough testosterone. A healthy male produces between two and ten milligrams of testosterone each day. Females only produce trace amounts of this hormone.

This hormone helps the body keep protein in the body, thus aiding growth of muscles, bones and skin. Doctors and sports coaches report that people using steroids have more muscle mass, strength and endurance.

For the person in the photograph building up muscles is important.

**b What happens to excess protein in the body?**

Testosterone also has other effects. It promotes the growth of body hair, deepening of the voice and can make a person more aggressive.

All international sports bodies such as the International Olympics Committee have banned these substances.

After competing in sports events athletes have to take a urine test.

**c** **What is this test for?**

**d** **Why do scientists have to keep developing new tests for drugs?**

**e** **What happens to an athlete who tests positive?**

What are the effects of taking steroids?

| | **Effects of taking steroids** |
|---|---|
| in males | ◆ reduced sperm production |
| | ◆ shrinkage of testicles |
| | ◆ impotence |
| | ◆ balding |
| | ◆ breast enlargement |
| in females | ◆ deepening of voice |
| | ◆ excessive body hair |
| in males and females | ◆ increased risk of liver cancer |
| | ◆ blood clotting, high blood pressure and cholesterol changes that can lead to heart attacks |

Doctors do prescribe steroids for some patients, e.g. treating men with low testosterone levels and for patients with body wasting conditions such as with AIDS.

Steroids can be taken as tablets, as ointments rubbed into the skin and injected. Addicts using shared needles run the risks of contacting HIV.

**Steroid abuse**

Steroids cannot be obtained without a prescription from a doctor. However, people can obtain these substances illegally.

It is not just athletes who take steroids.

It is estimated that in the United States there are hundreds of thousands of adults using steroids illegally. Most of these are males but there are a growing number of females.

## Questions

**1** **Tariq is a young man who wants to be a successful weightlifter.**

**a** **Write down *three* reasons why taking steroids might endanger his health.**

**b** **Why despite all these risks might he be tempted to take steroids?**

**c** **What additional risks to his health does Tariq take buying his drugs illegally?**

**2** **Copy and complete these sentences. Use the words in this list.**

**advantage** **hormones** **muscle** **testosterone**

**Steroids are chemicals based on male ____________ such as ____________.**

**An athlete taking these drugs is trying to get an ____________ over other athletes.**

**The athlete is trying to build up more ____________.**

### Key ideas

- *Steroids are drugs that are related to male hormones such as testosterone.*
- *Taking these drugs can have serious effects to both young people and athletes.*
- *These include increased risks of liver cancer and heart attacks.*

# 8:9 Inherited disorders

## Inheriting illness

Most illnesses are caused when microorganisms get into your body.

Examples include:

- measles and flu – these are diseases caused by certain viruses that get inside your body.
- some forms of meningitis – these are diseases caused by bacteria inside your body.

**a How do viruses and bacteria enter your body?**

There are some diseases that are not caused by microorganisms.

Some health problems are caused by the genes passed on to children from their parents. These are called **inherited disorders**.

### Cystic fibrosis

One child in every 2000 is affected by an inherited disorder called **cystic fibrosis**.

The photograph shows a girl who suffers from cystic fibrosis.

Her body produces a thick, sticky mucus. The mucus blocks the air passages in her lungs. She will get a lot of chest infections due to this mucus.

She will also have difficulty digesting and absorbing food because a lot of mucus is produced by her digestive system.

Regular physiotherapy will help her cough up much of the mucus.

Antibiotics will help fight infections caused by bacteria.

Surgery may be used to clear obstructions especially in infancy.

Despite all this help the girl will become more and more ill.

There is no cure for cystic fibrosis yet.

*Inheriting faulty genes*

Cystic fibrosis is caused by a faulty recessive allele.

For a baby to have cystic fibrosis, both parents must have a recessive (or hidden) allele.

**Did you know?**

There was an early reference to cystic fibrosis in north European sayings.

'Woe to that child which when kissed on the forehead tastes salty. He is bewitched and soon must die'. This is a reference to the fact that children with cystic fibrosis commonly have excessive salt in their sweat. The disease was first identified in 1938.

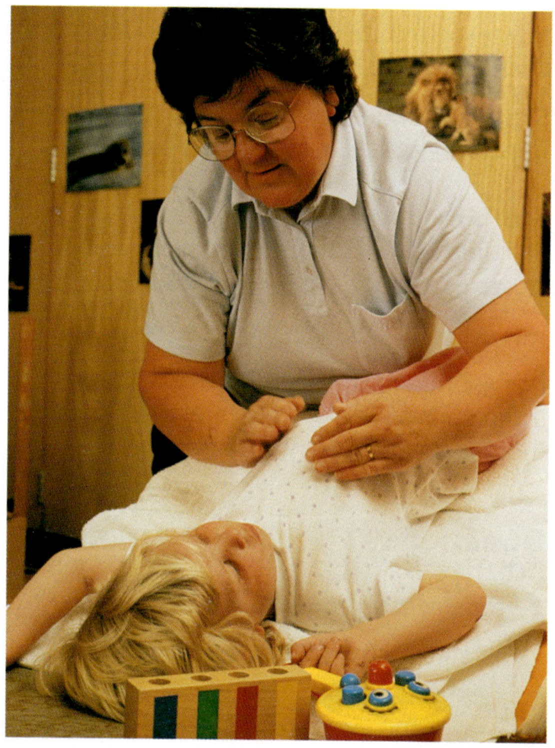

**Physiotherapy helps to shift the mucus from the lungs and unblock the air passages.**

There is then a one in four chance of it being passed on.

The faulty alleles must be passed on from both parents. The parents may be **carriers** of the disease without having the disease themselves.

### Huntington's disease

Huntington's disease is another inherited disease that damages the brain and other parts of the nervous system. People with the disease lose control of their movements and cannot remember things.

Sadly there is no cure and people with Huntington's disease need a lot of care and eventually die from the disease.

*Faulty dominant alleles*

Huntington's disease is caused by a faulty dominant allele, so only one allele needs to be present to give the disease.

It is passed on even if only one parent has the disease.

Because signs of the disease appear when people are 30–50 years-old they may have had children before finding out that they have a disease that can be inherited.

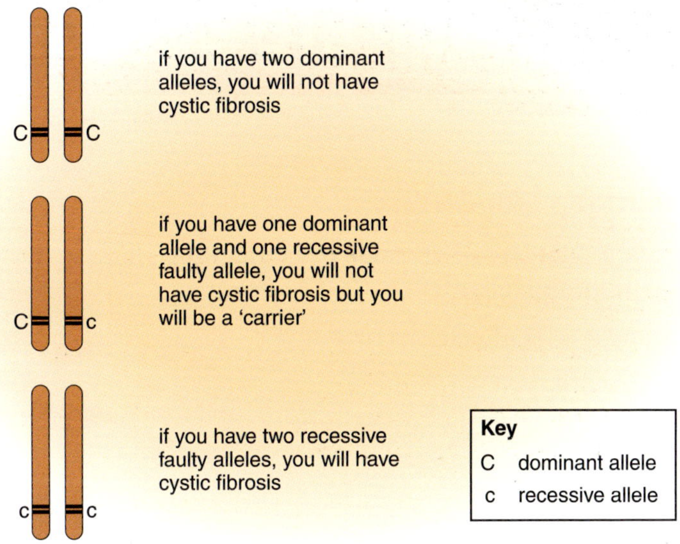


**If both parents are carriers, they may produce a child with cystic fibrosis.**

## Key ideas

- *Some diseases are caused by faulty alleles.*
- *These diseases can be inherited.*
- *Cystic fibrosis is caused by a faulty recessive allele.*
- *A person suffering from cystic fibrosis will have air passages in their lungs that block easily and will get a lot of chest infections. They will have difficulty digesting and absorbing food .*
- *Parents may be carriers of an inherited disease.*
- *Huntington's disease is caused by a faulty dominant allele.*

## Questions

**1** Copy and complete these sentences. Use words from this list.

**alleles carriers fibrosis inherited recessive**

Some diseases are passed on by genes or ______________. These are called ______________ diseases. An example is cystic ______________. This is caused by a faulty ______________ allele. Parents can pass on the faulty allele even though they do not have the disease. They are called ______________.

**2** Sue and Sam are expecting a baby. There is some history of cystic fibrosis in both the Sam's and Sue's families. Neither Sam nor Sue have cystic fibrosis.

**a** Is it possible for the baby to have cystic fibrosis? Explain your answer.

**b** Is it possible if only one is a carrier?

# 8:10 Sickle cell disease

## Blocking blood vessels

**Sickle cell disease** or **sickle cell amaemia** is an inherited disorder.

The disorder affects red blood cells, which carry oxygen from the lungs to all parts of the body. Anaemia occurs when people cannot get enough oxygen to the body organs.

People with sickle cell disease have red blood cells that are rigid and C-shaped (like a sickle). Healthy red blood cells can bend easily and have a doughnut shape.

Healthy red blood cells can bend to squeeze through small blood vessels such as capillaries. Rigid sickle red blood cells cannot get through small blood vessels. This causes blood vessels to become blocked and oxygen cannot get to where it is needed. Organs become damaged, causing a lot of pain.

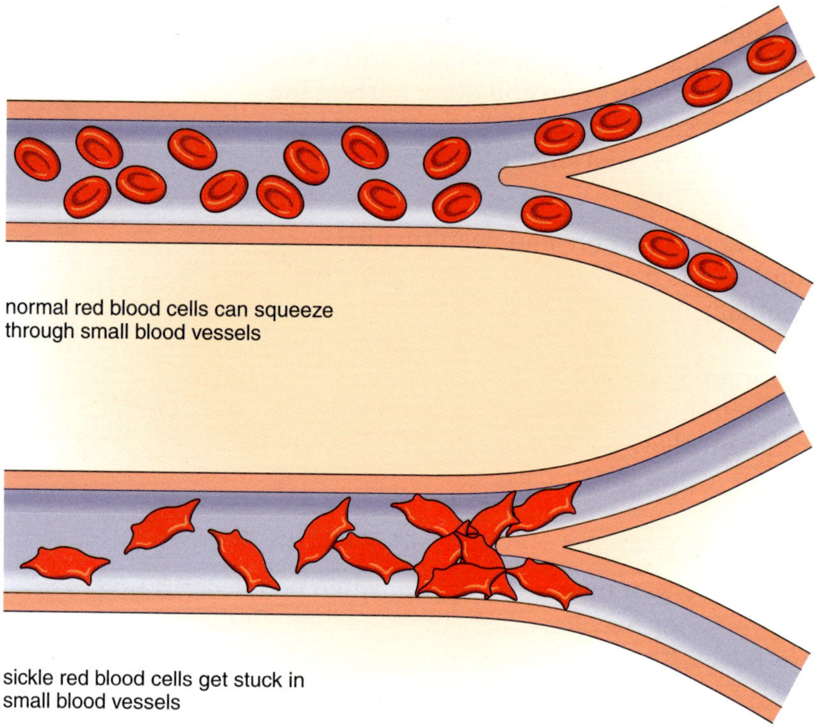


**The shape and stiffness of sickle red blood cells mean they clog up small blood vessels.**

**a What is the job of red blood cells?**

**b What happens when red blood cells become faulty?**

### What are the symptoms of sickle cell disease

The symptoms of sickle cell disease include:

- fatigue;
- breathlessness;
- rapid heart rate;
- attacks of abdominal pain.

There is no known cure for the disease. The only treatments control the symptoms, e.g. bed rest to reduce use of energy and oxygen needs or antibiotics to fight infections that result.

### Inheriting sickle cell disease

Sickle cell disease is caused by a faulty allele.

People with sickle cell disease have two faulty alleles. This causes their red blood cells to be sickle-shaped.

People can inherit one faulty allele and one 'normal' allele. They will be **carriers** of the disease. They make enough normal haemoglobin to keep their red blood cells flexible. They do not usually have anaemia, but they have to be careful when they are doing an activity where there is less oxygen such as scuba diving and mountaineering.

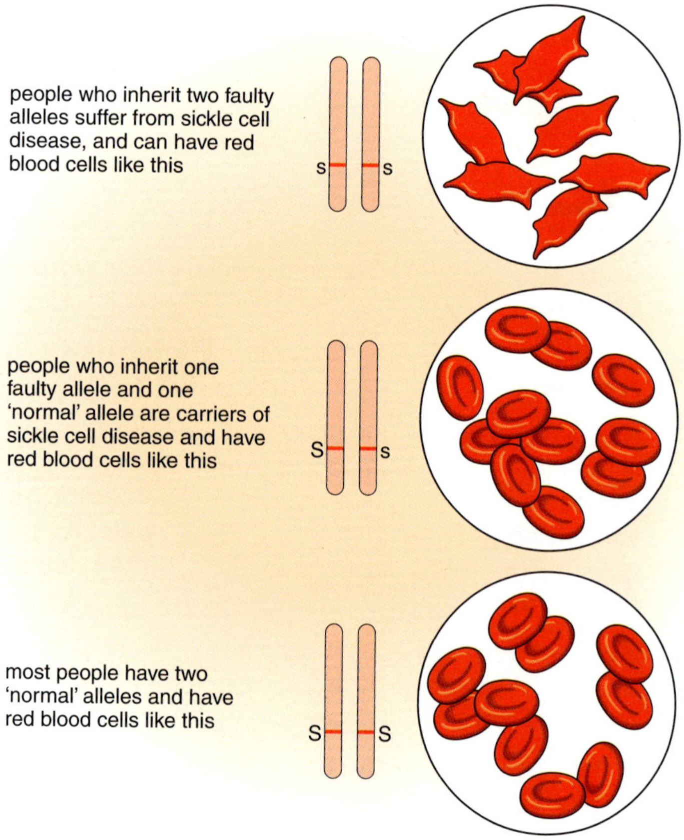


**Sickle cell disease is inherited.**

**c** Why do they have to be careful scuba diving or mountaineering?

**d** What is a 'carrier' of an inherited disease?

### A puzzling pattern

In parts of Africa more babies are born with sickle cell disease than in other parts of the world. Doctors could not explain this for many years. The maps opposite give an explanation.

The maps show that areas where sickle cell disease is common match areas where malaria is also common. Malaria is a disease that also affects red blood cells. Thousands of babies die from malaria every year.

People who are carriers of sickle cell disease do not have anaemia and they do not get malaria. In parts of the world where malaria is common it is an advantage to have the faulty allele.

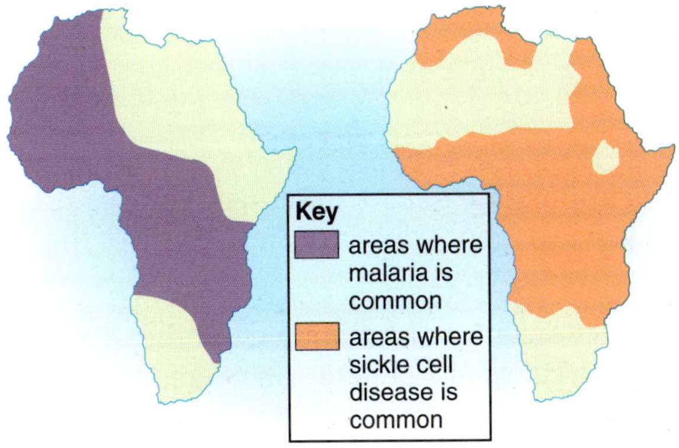


**In Africa, sickle cell disease is common where malaria is common.**

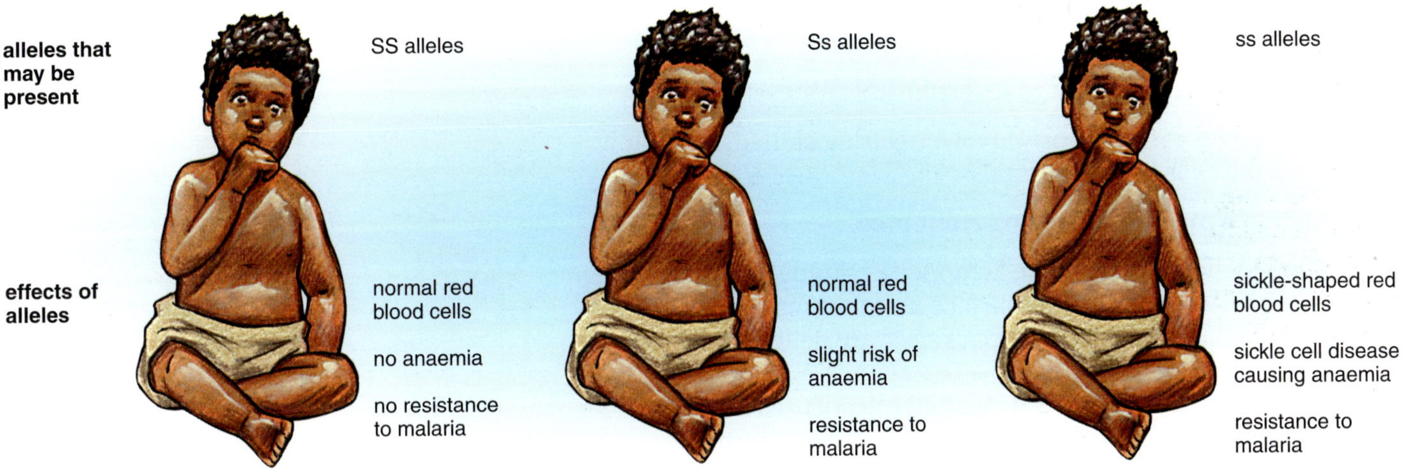


**In some circumstances, a 'faulty' gene can be helpful.**

## Questions

1. Why is it not possible to cure sickle cell disease by exchanging their blood with blood that does not contain sickle cells?

2. Copy and complete these sentences. Use words from this list.

   **carrier lungs malaria pain red blood cells respiration sickle tiredness**

   Oxygen is carried around the body by ______________ from the ______________ to the body organs. Here it is needed for ______________.

   A person with twisted red blood cells is said to suffer from ______________ cell disease.

   The symptoms that this person may show include ______________, breathlessness and abdominal ______________.

   A person with one allele for sickle cell disease will not show the disease but will be a ______________, This person is less likely to be affected by ______________.

## Key ideas

- *Sickle cell disease is an inherited disease that affects red blood cells.*
- *This disease reduces the ability of red blood cells to carry oxygen.*
- *The symptoms include tiredness, breathlessness and abdominal pains.*
- *It can be beneficial to be a carrier of this disease in countries where malaria is common.*

# 8:11 Gene therapy

## Potential of gene therapy

It is impossible to cure inherited diseases such as cystic fibrosis. However, it is possible to relieve some of the symptoms using **gene therapy**.

By 1946 scientists had worked out that cystic fibrosis was a disease caused by genetic disorders. They realised it was a recessive condition caused by the mutation of a single gene.

If the baby inherited a damaged copy of the gene from both parents, it would be unable to produce normal molecules of the protein specified by the gene. However, receiving a good copy from one parent and a damaged copy from the other, did not stop the gene producing the correct protein.

In 1989 scientists cloned the gene responsible for cystic fibrosis.

Gene therapy for cystic fibrosis involves getting cloned, healthy genes into the cells lining the lungs.

At present *two* methods are being attempted.

- Cloned, healthy genes are 'wrapped' in lipids that can be absorbed through the surface membranes into lung cells (the target cells). The 'packages' are delivered by aerosol spray.
- Cloned, healthy genes are inserted into viruses that normally infect the cells of the air passages of human lungs. The viruses are therefore very effective carriers, targeting those cells responsible for the problem. The viruses are sprayed into the lungs. (The viruses used are genetically modified so that they will still infect cells but not cause the diseases normally associated with them).

**a This is an example of genetic engineering. Many people think we should not do this as it amounts to changing nature. What do you think?**

This treatment is at present experimental but it could provide a big step forward in the treatment of cystic fibrosis.

### Prevention or cure?

This treatment, while it offers so much in relieving symptoms, will not prevent more babies being born with cystic fibrosis.

This can only be done by:

- studying the genetics of people planning to have children. This is called **genetic counselling**;
- devising tests for fetuses to detect potential genetic disorders. Then termination of pregnancy is still possible so these babies are not born.

### Other examples of genetic engineering

Genetic engineering is used to produce new materials but many people are against this sort of research.

It involves selecting a gene that gives a desirable product, e.g. human insulin. Then extracting it and putting it into another organism, e.g. a cow, to get a desirable product, e.g. human insulin that can be taken from its milk.

There are never enough hearts available for every person wanting a heart transplant.

Two ways of trying to overcome this shortage are:

- using a mechanical heart;
- using a heart from a pig.

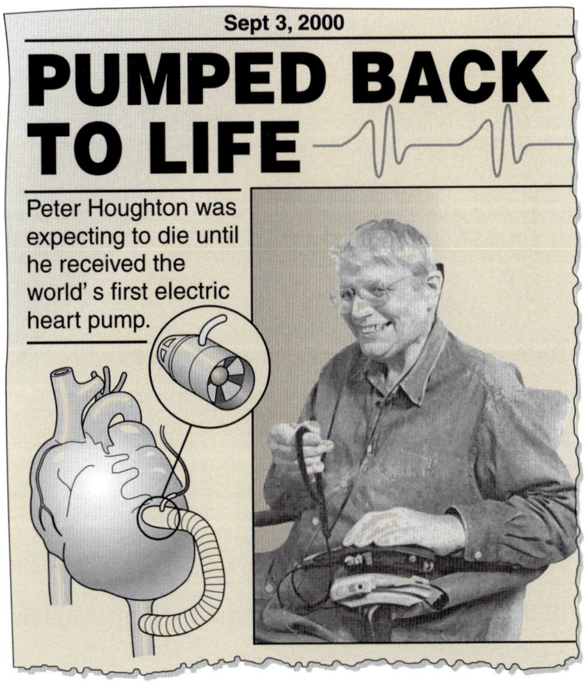


A heart from a pig is about the correct size to fit into a human. However, the biggest problem with a heart transplant is **rejection**. It is possible to breed pigs where one of the genes has been changed to avoid rejection.

**Did you know?**

Scientists have been able to cut up and rejoin DNA molecules since 1973.

In 1981 they became able to take genes from one organism and add them to another.

## Questions

**1** **Copy and complete this table. It gives advantages and disadvantages of using a heart from a pig rather than a human heart for a transplant.**

| | Heart of pig | Heart of human |
|---|---|---|
| availability | | |
| risk of rejection | | |
| chance of transferring unknown animal virus | | |

## Key ideas

- *It is possible that gene therapy may relieve some of the symptoms of cystic fibrosis but it cannot prevent the inherited disease.*

# End of module questions

## Low demand

**1** Which drug is an illegal drug?

**A** aspirin

**B** heroin

**C** paracetamol

**D** tobacco

**2** In the lungs gas exchange takes place. Which row is correct?

| | Transfers from air to bloodstream | Transfers from bloodstream to air |
|---|---|---|
| A | oxygen | nitrogen |
| B | oxygen | carbon dioxide |
| C | carbon dioxide | oxygen |
| D | nitrogen | carbon dioxide |

**3** Tim wants to become fitter. What should he do?

**A** put on weight

**B** smoke heavily

**C** drink alcohol

**D** take regular exercise

**4** Jo takes her pulse rate. She then exercises for 5 minutes and takes her pulse again. Finally she rests for 10 minutes and takes her pulse rate again.

Which row shows the pulse rates she measured correctly?

| | Pulse rate before exercise | Pulse rate after 5 minutes exercise | Pulse rate after 10 minutes rest |
|---|---|---|---|
| A | 70 | 110 | 70 |
| B | 70 | 110 | 110 |
| C | 110 | 70 | 110 |
| D | 110 | 110 | 70 |

**Questions 5–6**

The diagram shows a section through the chest.

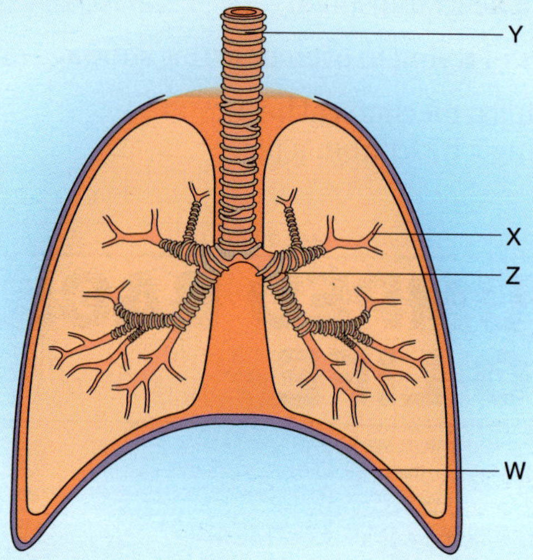


**5** Which letter represents a bronchiole?

**A** W

**B** X

**C** Y

**D** Z

**6** Which letter represents the diaphragm muscle?

**A** W

**B** X

**C** Y

**D** Z

**Questions 7–8**

The diagram shows a section through the heart.

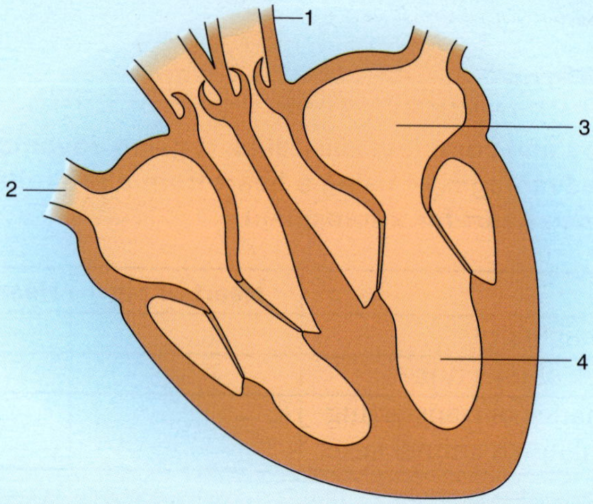

7 Which number is the correct label for a ventricle?

**A** 1

**B** 2

**C** 3

**D** 4

8 Which number is the correct label for a vein?

**A** 1

**B** 2

**C** 3

**D** 4

9 Blood from the heart passes through different types of blood vessels.

Which of the following is the correct order through which the blood passes?

**A** arteries, veins, capillaries

**B** arteries , capillaries, veins

**C** veins , capillaries , arteries

**D** capillaries, arteries, veins

10 A person with sickle cell anaemia

**A** cannot fight common diseases

**B** gets tired very easily

**C** bleeds very easily

**D** has a high blood pressure

11 Which row of the table describes what happens when you breathe in?

| | Ribs move | Diaphragm moves |
|---|---|---|
| **A** | out | up |
| **B** | in | up |
| **C** | out | down |
| **D** | in | down |

12 Steroid drugs are taken to

**A** remove pain

**B** build up muscle

**C** increase speed

**D** reduce blood pressure

## Standard demand

13 Which row shows the correct reactants and products during aerobic respiration?

| | Reactants | Products |
|---|---|---|
| **A** | oxygen and glucose | carbon dioxide, water and energy |
| **B** | oxygen, glucose and energy | carbon dioxide and water |
| **C** | oxygen and glucose | lactic acid and energy |
| **D** | glucose | carbon dioxide, water and energy |

14 Anaerobic respiration produces

**A** more energy than aerobic respiration

**B** lactic acid and energy

**C** carbon dioxide and energy

**D** water and energy

**Questions 15–18**

The graph shows the pulse rate of two girls measured before, during and after taking the same amount of exercise.

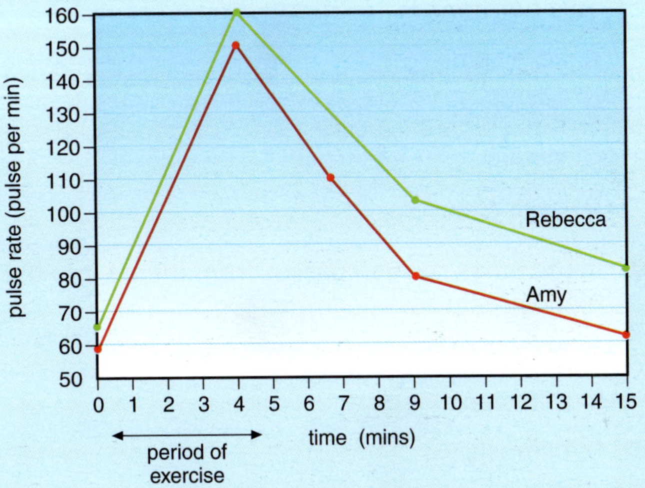


15 The pulse is measured by feeling

**A** an artery

**B** a capillary

**C** a muscle

**D** a vein

**16** Evidence that Amy is the fitter of the two girls is

**A** she has a lower pulse rate at rest

**B** her pulse rate gets back to normal more quickly

**C** her pulse rate goes high during exercise

**D** her pulse rate gets back to normal more slowly

**17** Pulse rate increases because

**A** the heart beats more rapidly

**B** each heart beat is stronger

**C** blood pressure is higher

**D** breathing rate increases

**18** The increase in pulse rate increases the supply of

**A** lactic acid to the muscles

**B** energy to the muscles

**C** heat to the muscles

**D** glucose to the muscles

**19** After a meal a hormone is released that reduces concentration of glucose in the blood.

This hormone is

**A** adrenaline

**B** glucagon

**C** insulin

**D** oestrogen

**20** In the lungs oxygen passes from the air into the bloodstream by

**A** breathing in

**B** diffusion

**C** osmosis

**D** respiration

**21** Blood from the heart goes to the lungs.

From which chamber does this blood get pumped?

**A** right atrium

**B** right ventricle

**C** left atrium

**D** left ventricle

**22** Blood returning from the lungs goes into the

**A** right atrium

**B** right ventricle

**C** left atrium

**D** left ventricle

**23** Smoking can make the alveoli less flexible. Gaseous exchange is not as good.

This condition is called

**A** bronchitis

**B** cancer

**C** emphysema

**D** heart attack

**24** A person is diagnosed with diabetes when the blood glucose level after a meal

**A** goes down

**B** goes up and then down again

**C** goes up and does not go down

**D** stays the same

# Module 9 – Chemicals and the Earth

This module is divided into eight parts.

1 The uses of some metals.

2 Metals are extracted from their ores. The method used depends on the reactivity of the metal. The extraction of iron (by reduction with carbon) and the extraction of aluminium (by electrolysis) are studied in detail.

3 The transition metals are a block of metals between groups 2 and 3 of the periodic table.

4 The alkali metals are a reactive family of metals in group 1 of the periodic table.

5 There are many chemical resources in the rocks of the Earth. Studying the structure of rocks and where they are found gives information about the history of the Earth.

6 The present Earth's atmosphere has evolved over millions of years. It is now kept in balance by processes such as respiration, combustion and photosynthesis.

7 Four-fifths of the atmosphere is an unreactive gas called nitrogen. This gas is important in manufacturing fertilisers. These are used because few plants can get the nitrogen they need directly from the atmosphere.

8 Helium, neon and argon are noble gases. They are present in the air in significant amounts. They now have a wide range of important uses.

Before you start, check what you can remember about the reactivity of metals. Try these questions first.

**The reactivity series is a list of metals in order of reactivity.**

**1** Which are the most reactive and least reactive metals in the list?

**2** Only three of the metals react with cold water. Which three metals?

**3** Which gas is produced when a metal reacts with cold water?

**4** What happens when a lighted splint is put into this gas?

Pieces of zinc, iron and copper were added to dilute sulphuric acid in three different test tubes.

**5** In which test tube will no bubbles of gas be seen?

**6** In which test tube will most bubbles of gas be seen?

**7** Copy and complete the word equation:

zinc + sulphuric acid → ______________ + ______________

**8** Calcium burns in oxygen. Write a word equation for this reaction.

potassium
sodium
calcium
magnesium
aluminium
zinc
iron
lead
copper
gold

# 9:1 Metals and their uses

## What a lot of metals!

Scientists have arranged the elements into a pattern of rows and columns called the periodic table. Elements with similar properties are found in the same column. These columns are called groups.

For example, all the elements in group 1 are very reactive metals. All the elements in group 7 are reactive non-metals.

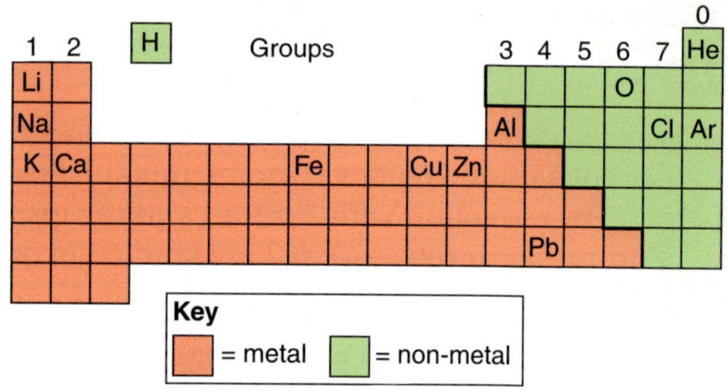


There is a full version of the periodic table on page 177.

**a Count up the number of non-metals shown in the outline periodic table. The rest of the elements are metals.**

There are many more metals than non-metals in the periodic table. More than three-quarters of all elements are metals.

**b Many elements have names ending in –ium. Most of these are metals. Find the names of non-metals with names ending in –ium.**

There are some properties that all metals have in common.

## Physical properties of metals

- Most metals are solids. The exception is mercury.
- Metals are shiny. Many are silvery, though some are yellow or brown.
- Most metals have a high density.
- Metals conduct heat.
- Metals conduct electricity.
- Many metals are hard and strong.
- Metals can be beaten into thin sheets. They are said to be **malleable**.
- Metals can be drawn into wires. They are said to be **ductile**.

## Chemical properties of metals

Metals burn in air or oxygen to form oxides. When water is added, the residue is either alkaline (pH value >7) or neutral (pH value = 7).

Making an element react with air or oxygen is the most reliable way of deciding whether it is a metal or a non-metal.

## Uses of metals

There are very few uses for pure metals. The photograph shows an electricity pylon. This supports cables that carry electricity. The cables are made of pure aluminium.

The electrical cables in our homes are made of pure copper.

Pure metals are very good **conductors** of electricity.

**c The metal cables are carrying electricity and the pylons are made of metal. Why does a person touching the bottom of the pylon not get an electric shock?**

**d Why is flying a kite close to electricity cables so dangerous?**

Most metals are used in mixtures of metals called **alloys**.

◆ Aluminium alloy is much stronger than pure aluminium. It is used for making the bodies of aeroplanes.

◆ Coins are made from copper alloys. Copper alloys are harder than pure copper.

◆ Steel is an alloy of iron. It is widely used for making car bodies, ships, bridges, etc.

## Questions

**1** **The table lists properties of a typical metal. Copy and complete the table, using the words high or low.**

| Property | High or low? |
|---|---|
| melting point | |
| boiling point | |
| conducting electricity | |
| density | |
| shine | |

**2** **The table gives some information about the properties of six metals.**

| Metal | Melting point (°C) | Density (g/cm$^3$) |
|---|---|---|
| sodium (Na) | 98 | 0.97 |
| aluminium (Al) | 660 | 2.7 |
| copper (Cu) | 1080 | 9.0 |
| iron (Fe) | 1540 | 7.7 |
| lead (Pb) | 327 | 11.3 |
| mercury (Hg) | –39 | 13.7 |

**a** **Suggest why aluminium rather than copper is used for overhead electricity cables.**

**b** **In Alaska the temperature can fall to –50°C. Why is it not possible to use a mercury thermometer in Alaska?**

**c** **Which metal floats on water? Explain your answer.**

**d** **Why are alloys of aluminium better than alloys of iron for panels of aeroplane wings?**

**e** **Fishing weights used to be made of lead. What property of lead makes it suitable?**

### Key ideas

- *Most of the known elements are metals.*
- *Metals are usually solid at room temperature.*
- *Metals are usually hard, shiny, higher density and good conductors of heat and electricity.*
- *Metals can be beaten into sheets (malleable) and drawn into wires (ductile).*
- *Metals burn in air or oxygen to form oxides that are alkaline or neutral when added to water.*
- *Metals have a wide range of uses. They are chosen for a particular use because they have suitable properties.*

# 9:2 Metals from the Earth

## Metals in the Earth

The rocks of the Earth contain all the metals we need, but they are not usually easy to get at.

- Some metals are common but others are rare.
- Most are locked up in chemical compounds.
- These compounds are mixed up in the rocks.

| Metal | Percentage of crust | First discovered |
|---|---|---|
| gold | 0.000 000 4 | 10 000 years ago |
| copper | 0.0045 | 7000 years ago |
| lead | 0.0015 | 6500 years ago |
| tin | 0.0002 | 6000 years ago |
| iron | 4 | 3000 years ago |
| zinc | 0.007 | 2000 years ago |
| aluminium | 7 | 170 years ago |
| magnesium | 2 | 130 years ago |
| sodium | 2.5 | 90 years ago |

**a Look at the table. What is the most common metal? What is the most rare metal?**

Fortunately, metal compounds called **minerals** are sometimes concentrated in rocks by natural processes. Rocks like this are called **ores**. It is easier and cheaper to get at the metals when they are concentrated in ores.

This table gives the names of some of the common metal ores:

| Metal | Name of ore | Formula of mineral in ore |
|---|---|---|
| sodium | halite | $NaCl$ |
| aluminium | bauxite | $Al_2O_3$ |
| iron | haematite<br>pyrites | $Fe_2O_3$<br>$FeS_2$ |
| zinc | zinc blende | $ZnS$ |
| copper | malachite | $CuCO_3$ |
| lead | galena | $PbS$ |

**b Which metals in the table are found in an ore containing a sulphide mineral?**

**Did you know?**

In the 1860s, Napoleon III used aluminum cutlery rather than gold to impress his guests. Aluminium was more expensive than gold.

## Discovering metals

The table at the top of the page shows when the different metals were discovered. You might have expected a common metal like iron to be discovered first. Instead it was gold – the rarest metal!

To understand why, you have to use the reactivity series.

## The reactivity series

Different metals react at different rates. You can list them in order of reactivity, from most reactive to least reactive.

The order of reactivity is the same, no matter what the reaction.

This list is called the **reactivity series** of metals.

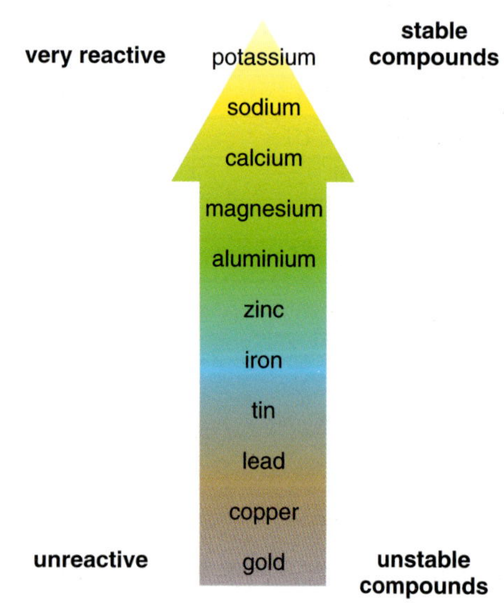

## How to extract a metal from it ore

- Metals high in the reactivity series (aluminum and all the metals above it) form **stable** compounds. A lot of energy is needed to extract these metals from their ores.
- This is supplied using electricity by a process called electrolysis (see page 72).
- Metals in the middle of the reactivity series are extracted by heating the ore with a reducing agent, often coke (carbon).
- Metals at the bottom of the reactivity series may be found unreacted (pure) in the Earth, or obtained just by heating the ore.

From left to right, these ores are malachite (a copper ore), galena (a lead ore) and pyrites (which could be used as an iron ore).

## Metal extractions are reduction reactions

To get a pure metal from its ore you need to reduce it. Reduction is the name given to a reaction where a compound loses oxygen.

If you heat copper oxide in a stream of hydrogen gas a reaction takes place.

copper oxide + hydrogen → copper + water (hydrogen oxide)

Copper oxide loses oxygen. This is called **reduction**.
Hydrogen gains oxygen. This is called **oxidation**.

## Questions

1 Copy and complete the sentences. Use words from this list.

**minerals** **ores** **reduction**

Most metals are found in compounds called ______________. These may be concentrated in ______________. These have to be broken down by ______________ to get the metal out

2 Lead oxide reacts with carbon monoxide to form lead. The other product is carbon dioxide.

a Write a word equation for the reaction.

b Explain the reaction using the words **oxidation** and **reduction**.

3 Three processes used for obtaining metals are:

A electrolysis of ore;

B reduction of ore with carbon;

C finding the metal unreacted in the Earth.

Which process is used to obtain:

a platinum (below gold in the reactivity series);

b sodium;

c tin;

d magnesium?

4 Choose from each pair of words to make the sentence correct.

**Reactive/Unreactive** metals form **stable/unstable** compounds that are **hard/easy** to break.

### Key ideas

- *Most metals are found as ores in the rocks of the Earth.*
- *The order of metals in the reactivity series can be used to predict the method used to extract a metal.*
- *Metal extraction processes involve reduction of metal ores.*

# 9:3 Displacement reactions

## Getting the metals out

Most metals are found locked up in chemical compounds, such as the metal oxide. These need to be broken apart to get the metal out. This cannot usually be done by heat alone. A suitable chemical reaction is needed.

**a You can break up mercury compounds by heating. Where would you expect to find mercury in the reactivity series?**

Iron forces the copper out of copper sulphate solution.

## Displacement reactions

If you dip a clean iron nail into blue copper sulphate solution, it comes out an orangey-brown colour. The nail has been copper-plated! Some of the iron atoms have swapped places with the copper ions in solution.

iron + copper ions → iron ions + copper
(solid) (in solution) (in solution) (solid)

This is called a **displacement reaction**. It happens because iron is more reactive than copper and so displaces it from solution.

## Displacement and reactivity

A less scientific view is that iron is a 'chemical bully', and pushes the weaker metal copper from its compound. Whichever way you choose to think of it, the rule is that a more reactive metal will be able to displace a less reactive one.

**b Which metal could bully iron out of its compound, magnesium or lead?**

## A spectacular displacement

Displacement reactions can also take place between solids.

Aluminium is more reactive than iron. If you mix aluminium with iron oxide and give it a kick-start of energy, the aluminium pushes the iron from its oxide. This is called the **thermit reaction**. It can be very spectacular, with sparks flying and molten iron left behind!

aluminium + iron oxide → aluminium oxide + iron

**c Aluminium is more expensive than iron. Why is this method not used to make iron industrially?**

**Did you know?**

This reaction is used to weld lengths of railway track together on site to produce continuous rails. These give a more comfortable journey.

Thermit reactions like that between aluminium and iron oxide are spectacular, but don't make economic sense as a way of making iron.

## The catch…

Displacement is a good way to get metals from their compounds, but there is a major catch. You need to use a more reactive metal to do it, which will be harder to get out of its compounds in the first place!

Fortunately, non-metals fit into the reactivity series too.

When metals fizz in acid, they are displacing the hydrogen from it and taking its place. Metals that react with acid like this must be more reactive than hydrogen. Copper never reacts in this way because it is less reactive than hydrogen.

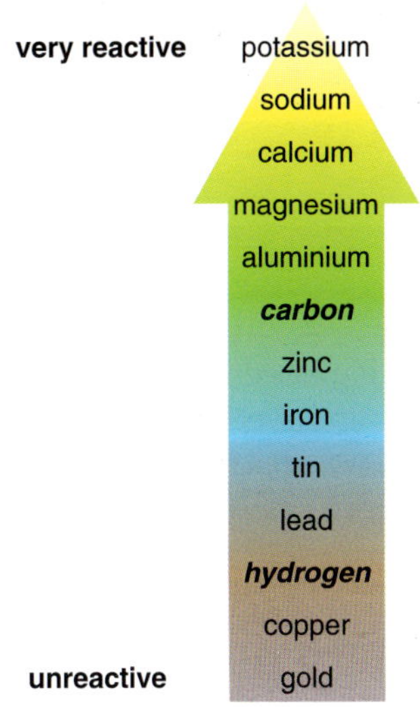


**d Use the reactivity series to list three metals that can displace hydrogen from acids.**

If you pass hydrogen over heated copper oxide, however, the copper is displaced from its compound.

copper oxide + hydrogen → copper metal + hydrogen oxide (water)

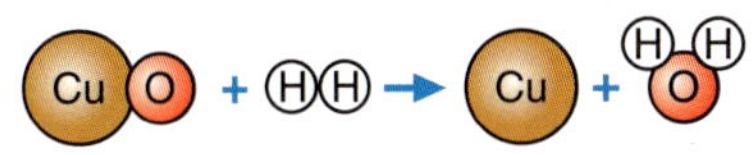


**e Use the diagram to help you write a symbol equation for this reaction.**

## Carbon to the rescue!

Even hydrogen is expensive to produce. What is needed is a cheap element, reactive enough to extract some important metals from their compounds.

The answer is carbon. Carbon fits into the reactivity series above zinc and so is quite capable of pushing lead, copper or iron from their compounds in a displacement reaction. It is usually used in the form of coke.

**f Could you use carbon to get aluminium from aluminium oxide?**

## Questions

**1 Which of these metals can push lead from a solution of lead nitrate?**

**iron copper zinc**

**2 This is the word equation for the reaction of zinc with silver nitrate:**

**zinc + silver nitrate → zinc nitrate + silver**

**Copy and complete the sentences about this reaction. Use words from this list:**

**displacement reactive silver**

**Zinc is more ____________ than silver. Zinc can act as a chemical bully and push out the metal ____________ from silver nitrate. The reaction is an example of a ____________ reaction.**

### Key ideas

- *A more reactive element will displace a less reactive element from its compounds.*
- *Carbon can be used to displace some less reactive metals from their ores.*

# 9:4 Making iron

## The iron age

Iron can be displaced from its ores by carbon, but very high temperatures are needed to kick-start this reaction. Because of this, iron was not discovered until long after copper and lead. Today, more iron is used than all the other metals put together.

| Metal | Million tonnes per year |
|---|---|
| aluminium | 12.5 |
| copper | 8 |
| iron | 400 |
| lead | 3 |
| tin | 0.2 |
| zinc | 6 |

**a Arrange the metals in increasing production tonnage.**

**b Approximately what percentage of the total is iron? (Choose from: 9%, 19%, 49% or 90%.)**

## Reducing iron

In simple terms, iron is made from iron oxide ore by a displacement reaction with carbon. The carbon 'steals' the oxygen away from the iron.

When iron reacts with oxygen to form iron oxide, the process is called oxidation.

When oxygen is taken away like this, the process is called reduction. The production of iron in this way is often called **carbon reduction**.

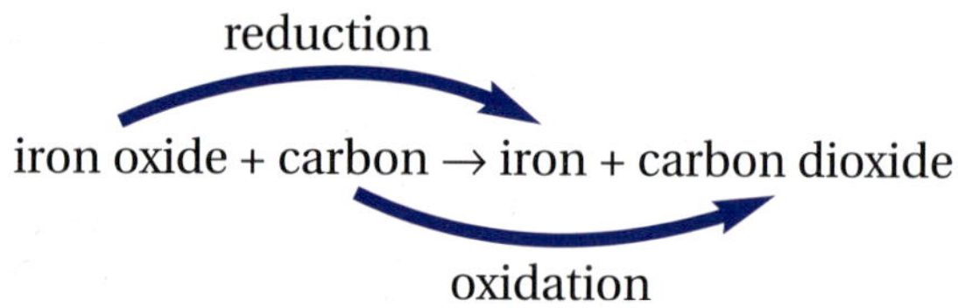


**c If the iron is reduced in this reaction, what is happening to the carbon?**

**d Lead oxide can be reduced to lead by carbon. Write a word equation for this reaction.**

## The raw materials

Iron is produced by carbon reduction in a **blast furnace**. For this, the following raw materials are needed.

- Iron ore – The commonest iron ore is haematite ($Fe_2O_3$).
- Coke – Carbon is needed to burn in the furnace to make it hot. It is also needed to reduce the oxide ore. Modern furnaces use coke. This is coal that has been heated to drive off oils and gases, leaving fairly pure carbon (C).
- Limestone – This is calcium carbonate ($CaCO_3$). It is added to remove acidic impurities.
- Oxygen – This is also needed for the carbon to burn. It is provided by blasting hot air into the furnace.

**e Why is this called a 'blast' furnace?**

A blast furnace in operation.

## How does the blast furnace work?

Iron is produced by a three-stage reaction.

- **Stage 1**
  The coke burns, giving off lots of heat.

  carbon + oxygen → carbon dioxide

- **Stage 2**
  The carbon dioxide reacts with more carbon.

  carbon dioxide + carbon → carbon monoxide

- **Stage 3**
  The carbon monoxide reduces the iron oxide.

  carbon monoxide + iron oxide → carbon dioxide + iron

**f Which stage of the reaction produces most heat energy?**

## What does the limestone do?

The main impurity in iron ore is silicon dioxide.

In the furnace, limestone is decomposed to produce calcium oxide.

calcium carbonate → calcium oxide + carbon dioxide

Calcium oxide (basic oxide) reacts with silicon dioxide (acidic oxide) to form calcium silicate, or slag.

calcium oxide + silicon dioxide → calcium silicate

Slag is a mixture of impurities. It is used to make road chippings and as a phosphorus fertiliser.

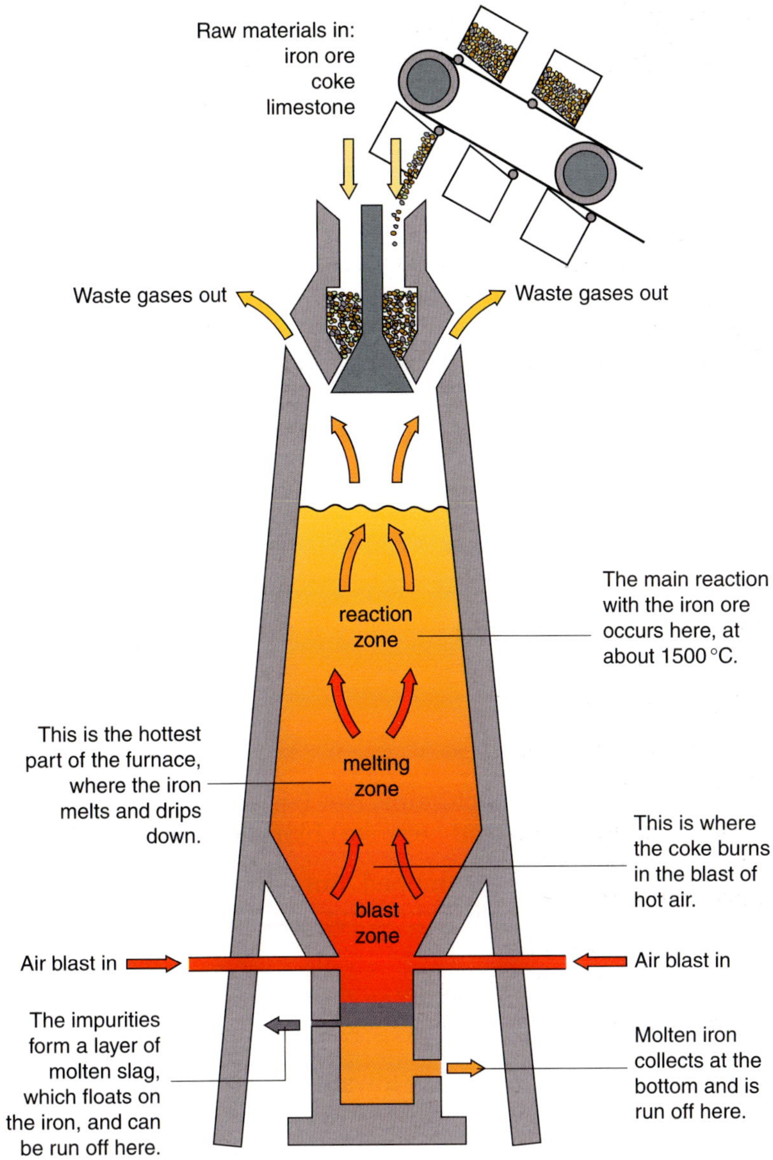


## Questions

**1** Copy and complete the sentences using these words.

**carbon dioxide limestone monoxide oxide slag**

Iron can be made from iron ore (iron ______________) by heating it with ______________. When coke burns in oxygen, carbon ______________ is first formed. This reacts with more carbon to form carbon ______________. Carbon monoxide reduces iron oxide to iron.

Calcium carbonate (______________) is added to the furnace. It removes the impurities as ______________.

**2** Reorder these sentences to describe the three-stage process that takes place in the blast furnace.

- Carbon dioxide and carbon react, forming carbon monoxide.
- Carbon monoxide reduces iron oxide.
- Coke burns in a blast of air to form carbon dioxide.

**3** Why is limestone added to the blast furnace?

### Key ideas

- *Iron oxide is reduced by carbon to iron.*
- *A very high temperature is needed before this reaction occurs.*
- *This is reached in a blast furnace.*
- *Iron ore, coke and limestone are added to the furnace.*
- *Impurities from the furnace are removed as slag. This can be used for road building and as phosphorus fertiliser.*

# 9:5 Electrolysis

## What about the reactive metals?

Carbon reduction is a relatively cheap and easy way to get the less reactive metals from their ores.

Unfortunately it does not work on the more reactive metals such as aluminium, which is above carbon in the reactivity series.

These metals have to be torn from their compounds using lots of electrical energy. That is a very expensive option and is only used when there is no other choice.

**a List four metals other than aluminium that cannot be made by carbon reduction.**

**b Iron and copper can be torn from their ores using electrical energy too. Why is this method not used in industry?**

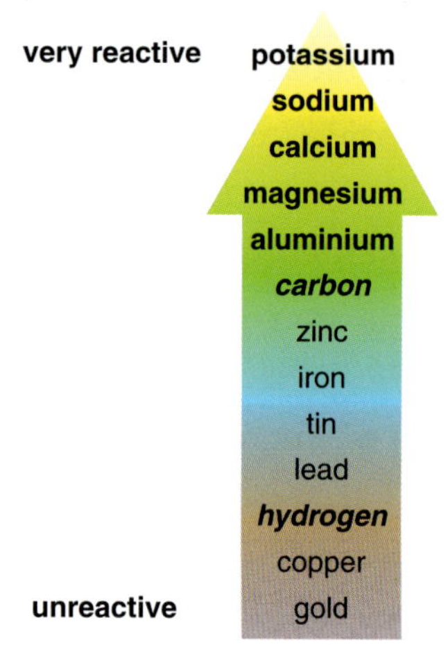


## Electrolysis of molten sodium chloride

Common salt (sodium chloride, NaCl) is an ionic compound of positive sodium ions and negative chloride ions.

In solid salt, the ions are trapped. But if the salt is melted or dissolved in water, the ions become free. They can be made to move.

If **electrodes** are put into molten sodium chloride, the ions move.

- The positive ions move towards the cathode (negative electrode).
- The negative ions move towards the anode (positive electrode).

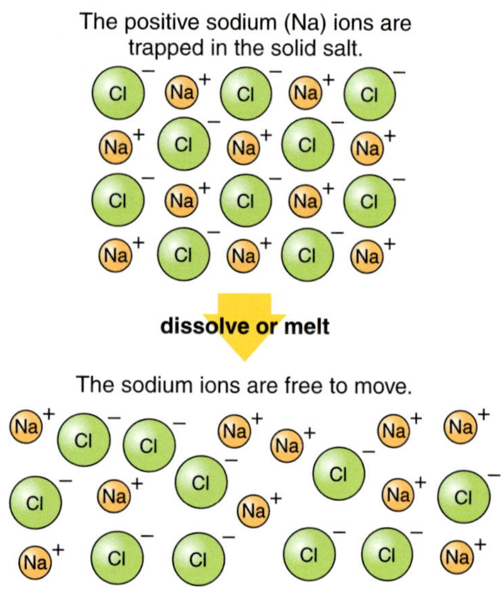


**c Which ion, sodium or chloride, moves towards the cathode (negative electrode)? Which ion moves towards the anode (positive electrode)?**

When the ions reach the electrodes the charges cancel out.

- The sodium ions form sodium metal at the cathode (negative electrode).
- The chloride ions form chlorine gas at the anode (positive electrode).

The splitting up of sodium chloride with electricity is called **electrolysis**.

**d Copy and complete the word equation for the electrolysis of molten sodium chloride.**

**sodium chloride → ______________ + ______________**

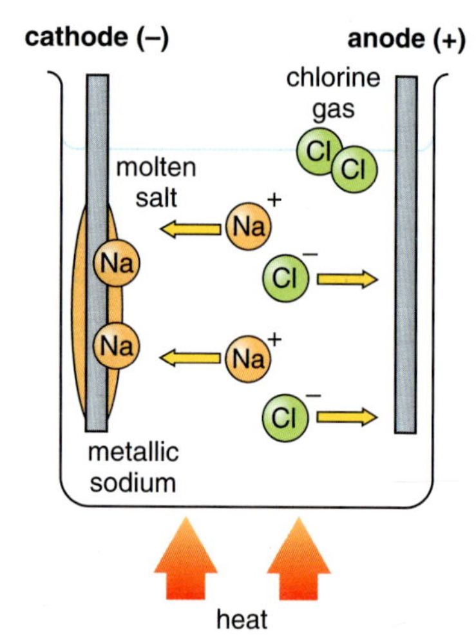


**Electrolysis of molten sodium chloride.**

## Copper from copper sulphate solution

Electrolysis also works in solution.

Copper has positive ions in copper sulphate. These ions give copper sulphate its blue colour. The ions are free to move.

If you put electrodes into copper sulphate solution, the positive copper ions are attracted to the cathode (negative electrode).

When they reach the electrode, the charges cancel out and they turn back to copper atoms. Metallic copper is deposited on the cathode.

**e Why are the copper ions attracted to the cathode (negative electrode)?**

**f What would happen to the colour of the solution if all the copper ions turned back to copper atoms at the electrode?**

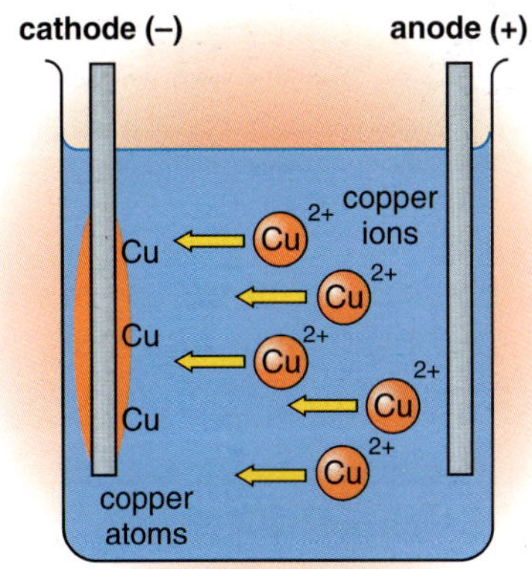


Electrolysis of copper sulphate solution.

## Electroplating

Electrolysis can be used to coat a metal with a thin layer of another metal.

For example, knives and forks made of steel can be electroplated with nickel and silver. The steel items are first coated with a layer of nickel to prevent rusting. Then they are coated with a very thin layer of silver for decoration. They are sometimes stamped with the letters EPNS, which stand for 'electroplated nickel silver'.

**g Why should objects that are silver plated in this way not be cleaned frequently with abrasive cleaners?**

**h The nose-cones of rockets are often gold plated. Why is this an advantage when the rocket comes back into the Earth's atmosphere?**

## Questions

**1** Copy and complete the sentences. Choose words from this list.

**anode cathode compounds electrolysis metal molten negative positive**

Reactive metals are split up from their ______________ using electricity in a process called ______________. For this to happen they have to be ______________ or in solution.

This works because ______________ metal ions are attracted to the ______________ electrode (called the ______________) . Here a ______________ is formed.

**2** Potassium can be made by electrolysing molten potassium chloride.

**a** Why does this have to be molten?

**b** Which ion is positive and which is negative?

**c** What is formed at each electrode?

### Key ideas

- *Reactive metals such as aluminium cannot be made from their ores by carbon reduction.*
- *They have to be torn from their ores using electricity.*
- *This process is called electrolysis.*
- *Electrolysis is the movement of charged ions to the anode (positive electrode) and the cathode (negative electrode).*
- *At the electrode the ions are discharged.*
- *The metal collects at the cathode (negative electrode).*
- *Electrolysis is expensive, so it is only used if other methods cannot work.*

# 9:6 Industrial electrolysis

Aluminium is the commonest of all the metals in the Earth's crust. You might expect it to be cheap to make. But as it is more reactive than carbon, it cannot be made by carbon reduction. This affects the cost of production.

**a Why might you have expected aluminium to be cheaper than iron? Why is that not the case?**

## Making aluminium

Aluminium is made by the electrolysis of aluminium oxide. The aluminium oxide is purified from its common ore, **bauxite**.

Aluminium oxide is a solid ionic compound. It has to be melted to free the ions before it can be electrolysed.

Unfortunately aluminium oxide has a very high melting point – over 2000°C. Electrolysis is already an expensive process. Having to reach such high temperatures would make it even more expensive.

Fortunately, the melting temperature can be lowered to just 950°C by adding small amounts of another aluminium compound called **cryolite**. Even so, this still takes vast amounts of energy.

**b Why does the aluminium oxide have to be molten for electrolysis?**

**c How does cryolite help to keep down the cost of making aluminium?**

## How it works

Electrolysis takes place in specially designed units. The raw materials are fed into the unit, where they melt.

- Positive aluminium ions are attracted to the cathode (negative electrode) – which in this case is the container itself. Here they turn into aluminium atoms. The molten aluminium is run off at the bottom.
- Negative oxygen ions are attracted to the anode (positive electrode), which is made of carbon blocks. There they turn back to oxygen gas. The carbon blocks burn away in the oxygen to make carbon dioxide gas. They have to be replaced regularly.

**d Why do the carbon blocks of the anode (positive electrode) have to be replaced regularly?**

Because of the high production costs, it is cheaper (per tonne) to make a lot rather than a little aluminium. This means that aluminium plants tend to be very large. A typical plant may have 300 electrolysis cells like the one shown, each making a tonne of aluminium every day.

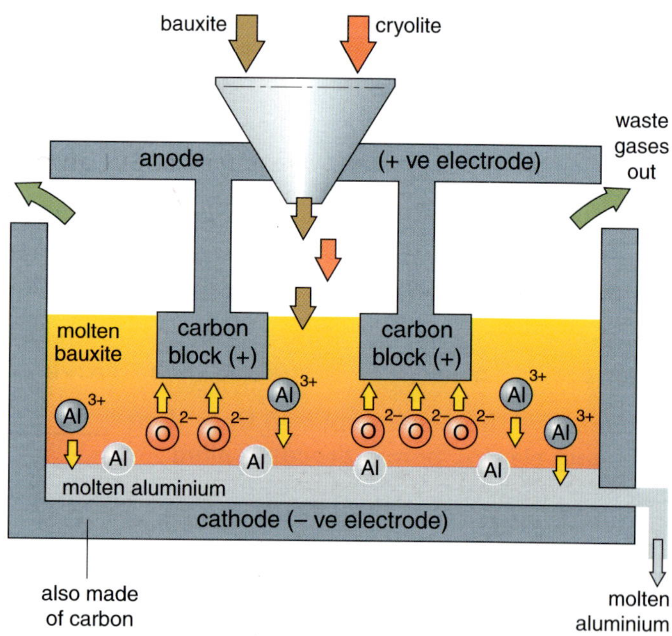


**Electrolysis of aluminium.**

Aluminium plants often need a power station of their own, as they use as much electricity as a small town. No wonder aluminium costs more than iron!

Scrap aluminium is collected and **recycled**. It is cheaper to do this than produce new aluminum from aluminium ore.

## Purifying copper

As copper is less reactive than carbon, it can be made by carbon reduction like iron. But the copper produced by the blast furnace has lots of impurities.

Electrolysis is then used to purify the copper. This is cheaper than you might expect. The ions involved can be freed by using the water in copper sulphate solution, without the expense of high temperatures.

A block of impure copper is connected up as the anode (positive electrode) in a solution of copper sulphate. A strip of pure copper is used as the cathode (negative electrode).

- When the current is switched on, the positive copper ions from the copper sulphate solution are attracted to the cathode (negative electrode) and deposited there as pure copper.
- Meanwhile, the copper atoms from the impure copper block become positive ions and go into solution to take their place.

The solution acts like a 'conveyor belt', moving the copper atoms across from the positive to the negative electrode. Eventually all of the copper ends up on the cathode (negative electrode) – as very pure copper.

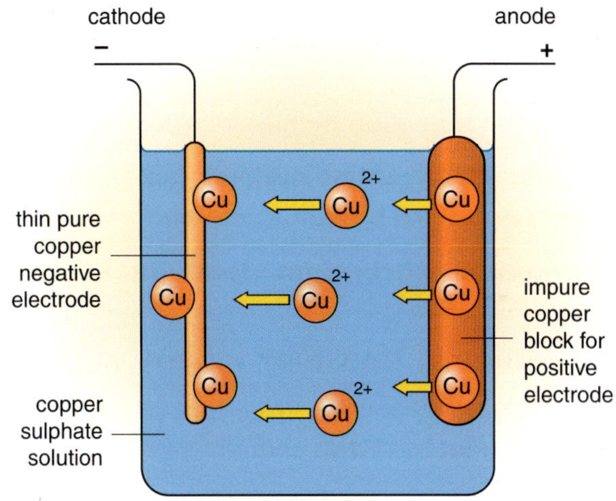

**Purifying copper by electrolysis.**

## Questions

1 Copy and complete the sentences about aluminum extraction. Use words from this list.

**aluminium bauxite cryolite dioxide oxide oxygen**

The common ore of aluminum is called ______________. Purification of this produces aluminum ______________.

Electrolysis of aluminium oxide dissolved in molten ______________ produces ______________ at the cathode (negative electrode) and ______________ at the anode (positive electrode).

The carbon anodes burn away to form carbon ______________.

2 Answer these questions about the purification of copper by electrolysis.

a What colour is copper sulphate solution?

b Where is copper deposited?

c Which electrode gets smaller?

d Why does the colour of the solution remain unchanged?

### Key ideas

- *Aluminium is made by the electrolysis of molten bauxite.*
- *Cryolite is added to lower the melting point.*
- *This is still an expensive process.*
- *Aluminium is produced at the cathode (negative electrode).*
- *Copper is purified by electrolysis using copper sulphate solution.*
- *Pure copper is deposited at the cathode (negative electrode). The impure copper anode gets smaller as copper goes into solution as copper ions.*

# 9:7 Transition metals

## Where are the transition metals in the periodic table?

The block of elements called **transition metals** are found between groups 2 and 3.

Two of the transition metals are iron and copper.

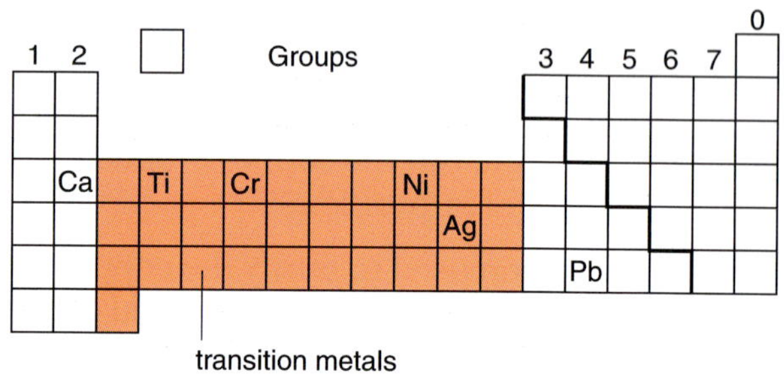


**a Look at the outline periodic table. Which of the elements in the list are transition metals?**

**calcium chromium lead nickel silver titanium**

## Properties of transition metals

The table compares the properties of iron and copper (transition metals) with sodium (not a transition metal).

| Metal | Melting point (°C) | Conductor of heat | Conductor of electricity | Density ($g/cm^3$) |
|---|---|---|---|---|
| iron | 1535 | good | good | 7.9 |
| copper | 1083 | good | good | 8.9 |
| sodium | 98 | good | good | 0.97 |

**b Suggest two ways sodium is similar to iron and copper. Suggest two ways it is different.**

## Transition metal compounds

On page 76 there are a some alkali metal compounds. These are usually white or colourless.

Transition metals also form a large number of compounds. These are often coloured. For example, you will probably have seen blue copper sulphate crystals.

The table gives the colours of some other copper compounds.

| Copper compound | Colour |
|---|---|
| copper sulphate | blue |
| copper nitrate | blue |
| copper carbonate | green |
| copper hydroxide | blue |
| copper oxide | black |

The photograph shows a copper roof that has been exposed to the atmosphere for many years.

**c Suggest the name of the copper compound that gives the roof its colour.**

**d What does this suggest about the reactivity of copper?**

## Transition metals as catalysts

Transition metals and transition metal compounds are often used as **catalysts**. A catalyst is a substance that speeds up a chemical reaction without itself being used up.

**e Catalysts are often expensive. Why is this not a serious problem in an industrial process?**

- Iron is used in the Haber process to produce ammonia from nitrogen and hydrogen (see page 86).
- Much of the ammonia produced is converted into nitric acid using platinum as a catalyst.
- In the laboratory, hydrogen peroxide is split up into water and oxygen using manganese oxide as the catalyst.
- Margarine is produced by passing an animal or vegetable fat or oil and hydrogen over a nickel catalyst.
- Catalytic converters fitted to cars contain platinum and rhodium catalysts. Carbon monoxide and nitrogen oxide are converted into carbon dioxide and nitrogen gases. These are less harmful to the environment.

Transition metal compounds are used to make paint pigments, pottery glazes and coloured glass.

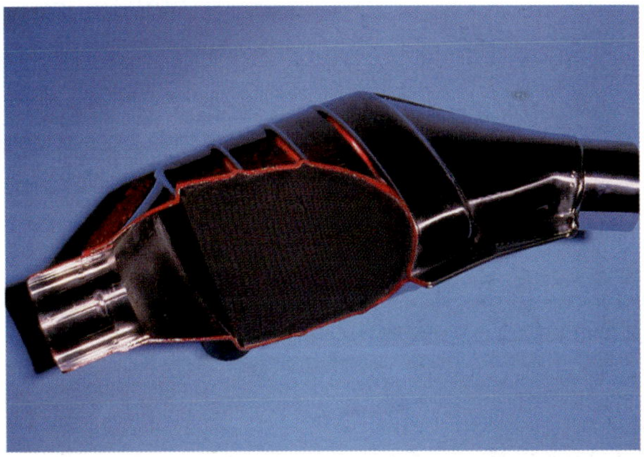

A catalytic converter contains the transition metals platinum and rhodium.

## Questions

**1 The table gives information about five elements A–E. These are not the chemical symbols.**

| Element | Melting point (°C) | Conductor of heat | Conductor of electricity | Density ($g/cm^3$) |
|---|---|---|---|---|
| A | 64 | good | good | 0.86 |
| B | 1240 | good | good | 7.2 |
| C | 44 | poor | poor | 1.8 |
| D | 1890 | good | good | 7.2 |
| E | 180 | good | good | 0.53 |

**a Which element in the table is not a metal?**

**b Which of the elements are transition metals? Explain your choice.**

**2 Potassium manganate (formula $KMnO_4$) is purple. Potassium chromate (formula $K_2CrO_4$) is yellow.**

**Suggest why these alkali metal compounds are coloured.**

**3 Copy and complete the sentences using these words:**

**copper electricity melting tough transition**

**The __________ metals are a family of useful metals, including __________ and iron.**

**Like the alkali metals, they conduct heat and __________ well.**

**Unlike the alkali metals, they are hard and __________ and have high __________ points.**

### Key ideas

- *The transition metals are a block of metals between groups 2 and 3 of the periodic table.*
- *Transition metals have high melting points and high densities.*
- *They are good conductors of heat and electricity.*
- *Many transition metal compounds are coloured.*
- *Transition metals and transition metal compounds are often used as catalysts for chemical reactions.*

# 9:8 The alkali metals

## Group 1

Group 1 of the periodic table contains a family of very reactive metals. They include lithium (Li), sodium (Na) and potassium (K).

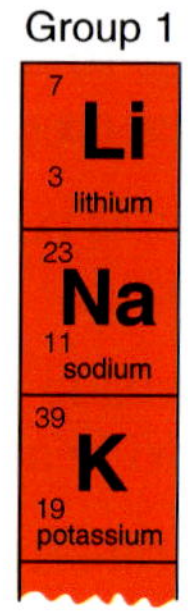


Like all metals, the metals in group 1:

- are good conductors of heat and electricity;
- are very shiny when fresh, though they tarnish rapidly in air.

But unlike most 'everyday' metals:

- they are very soft and can be easily cut with a knife;
- they have low densities and can float on water.
- they have relatively low melting and boiling points for metals.

**Sodium is a typical group 1 metal – very reactive and very soft.**

## Burning in air

The group 1 metals are very reactive. They are stored under oil to stop them reacting with air or water.

Group 1 metals react with the air to form the metal oxide. Lithium burns with a bright red flame.

lithium + oxygen → lithium oxide

**a Why might lithium compounds be put into fireworks?**

**Lithium burns in air with a bright red flame.**

## The alkali metals

Group 1 metals react with water. They form a metal hydroxide. Hydrogen gas is also given off in this reaction.

sodium + water → sodium hydroxide + hydrogen

Sodium hydroxide dissolves in water. The solution is a strong **alkali**.

**Did you know?**
All group 1 metals make strongly alkaline solutions in water. This is why group 1 metals are called **alkali metals.**

## Common salt

The alkali metals react with non-metals to form white compounds. These dissolve in water to give colourless solutions. Sodium reacts with chlorine to give sodium chloride – common salt.

**These compounds are different, even though they all look similar.**

## What's the trend?

| Metal | Melting point °C | Reaction with water |
|---|---|---|
| lithium | 180 | fizzes steadily |
| sodium | 98 | very rapid reaction |
| potassium | 64 | violent reaction |

**b** What pattern is there in melting points down group 1?

**c** The element below potassium is rubidium. Estimate the melting point of rubidium.

**d** What pattern do you see in the way the metals react with water as you go down group 1?

**e** Do you think it would be safe to put rubidium in water? Explain your answer.

Sodium reacts very rapidly with water.

## Electrolysis of sodium chloride

Electrolysis of molten sodium chloride (page 70) produces metallic sodium and chlorine gas.

Sodium chloride is found as rock salt (**halite**) in underground salt deposits, between layers of other rocks. It is pumped to the surface as a concentrated solution of sodium chloride (**brine**).

Electrolysis of sodium chloride solution (brine) produces sodium hydroxide, hydrogen and chlorine.

The table summarises some uses of the products of electrolysis of brine.

| Product | Uses |
|---|---|
| sodium hydroxide | making soap, bleach, paper and textile fibres |
| chlorine | killing bacteria in water; making bleach and PVC (a plastic) |
| hydrogen | as a fuel; making ammonia and margarine |

## Questions

**1** List three ways in which sodium is a typical metal, and three ways in which it is unusual.

**2** Copy and complete the sentences. Use words from this list.

**alkaline** **hydrogen** **reactive** **water**

The alkali metals are a family of soft, ____________ metals. They react with ____________, forming a strongly ____________ solution. The gas given off is ____________.

**3** Potassium reacts with water in the same way as sodium. Write a word equation for the reaction.

## Key ideas

- *Lithium, sodium and potassium are alkali metals (group 1 of the periodic table).*
- *These metals are soft and have low melting points.*
- *They are very reactive. They react with water to form the metal hydroxide and hydrogen gas.*
- *There is a pattern in reactivity down the group.*
- *Electrolysis of molten sodium chloride produces sodium and chlorine.*
- *Electrolysis of brine (sodium chloride solution) produces sodium hydroxide, chlorine and hydrogen.*
- *Sodium hydroxide is used for making soap, bleach, paper and textile fibre. Hydrogen is used for making ammonia and margarine. Chlorine is used to make bleach and PVC, and to kill bacteria in water.*

# 9:9 Making and changing rocks

## New rocks from old

We make 'new rock' every time we mix concrete. Broken rock fragments are stuck together by the cement and set rock-hard in hours. Nature does this too, but it takes millions of years.

Existing rocks are broken down by wind and rain.
↓
Fragments of rock are washed into rivers and carried to the sea.
↓
The fragments are dumped and form layers.
↓
The layers press down on lower layers. Minerals in the water crystallise and cement the fragments together.
↓
New sedimentary rock is formed.

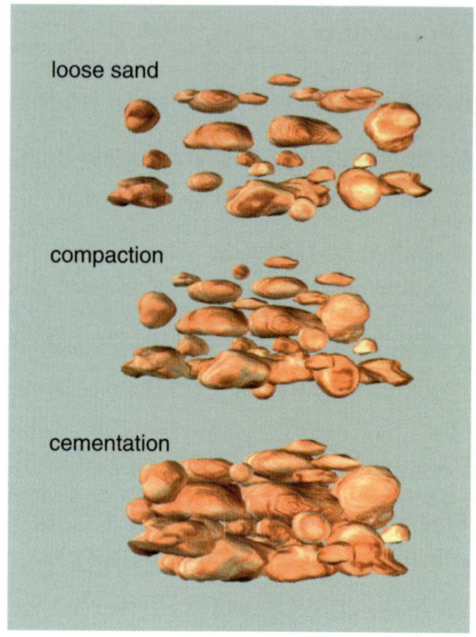

Sedimentary rock formation.

**a The fragments of rock that are broken off existing rocks have sharp edges. The fragments cemented together in sedimentary rocks do not. Why? (Hint: Think about what happens in the river.)**

## Sedimentary rocks

Rocks made from broken fragments are usually **sedimentary rocks**.

- Pebbles form conglomerate.
- Sand forms sandstone.
- Clay forms mudstone or shale.
- Limestone is made of calcium carbonate – often from broken shells.

**b Which sedimentary rock looks just like concrete?**

Sedimentary rocks are formed in layers. The older the rock, the lower down it is. Geologists call the order in which the rocks were deposited a **succession**.

Conglomerate

Sandstone

Sedimentary rock is formed in layers.

## Metamorphic rocks

If sediment is buried deep enough, the high temperature and pressure makes it change. The rock recrystallises. Rocks that have changed (or 'metamorphosed') like this are called **metamorphic rocks**.

Limestone turns into marble when it is metamorphosed. Evidence for this is that limestone and marble are both forms of the same chemical – calcium carbonate.

Any fossils in the limestone are distorted or lost as the calcium carbonate changes.

Limestone

Marble

## Fossils

**Fossils** are the remains of living creatures found in sedimentary rock or metamorphic rock. They can tell us about how the rock was formed. For example, a limestone with fossil corals must have formed in the sea. Shale with fossil ferns must have formed in a swamp.

Life has evolved and changed over time. So fossils can also help to tell us how old a rock is.

- Young rocks contain fossils of animals and plants similar to those today.
- Older rocks show strange fossils of creatures that are not alive today, such as the coiled shells of ammonites or the older trilobites.

**c What fossils might you find in 500 million year old shale?**

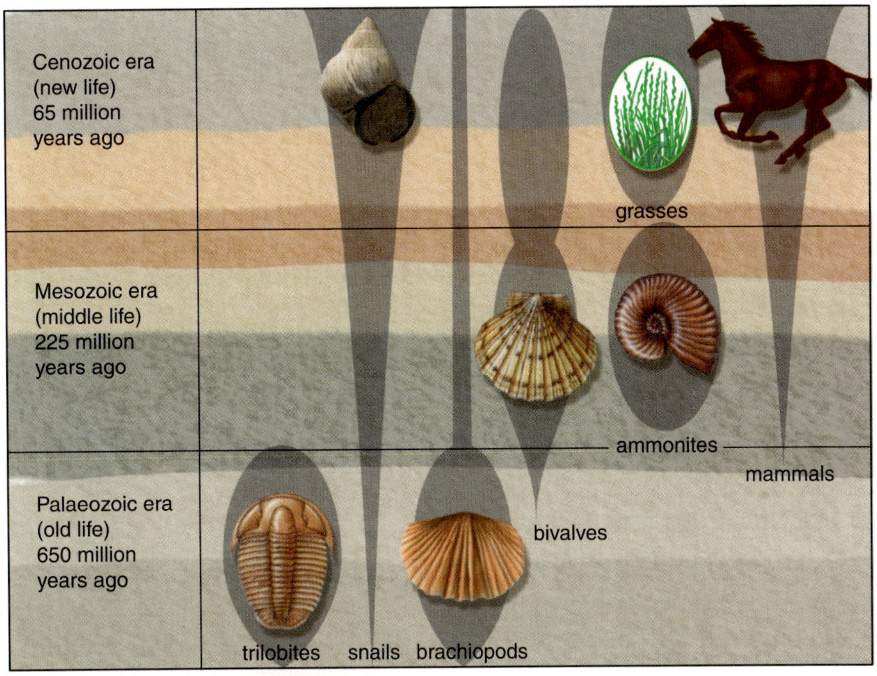


**The age of fossils can be used to date rocks.**

## Questions

**1** Copy and complete the sentences. Use words from this list. You can use words more than once.

**age cemented deposited fossils heat pressure**

Sedimentary rocks are formed from fragments of existing rocks that are ______________ and then ______________ together under ______________.

Metamorphic rocks are made by the action of ______________ and high ______________ on existing rocks.

The remains of animals and plants are found in rocks as ______________. The type of fossil present in a rock gives an indication of its ______________.

**2**

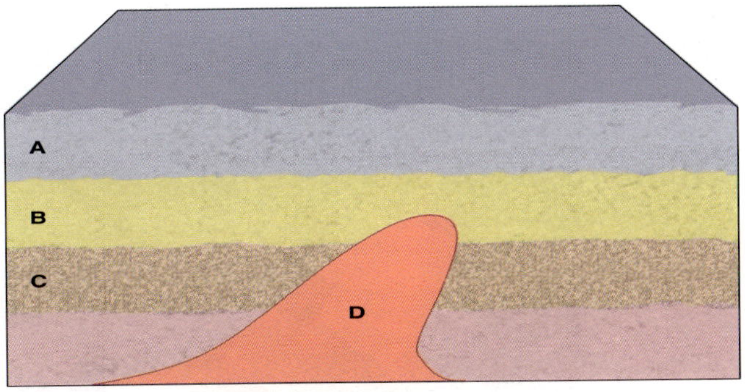


**a** Which is an igneous rock?

**b** Which are sedimentary rocks?

**c** Which is the oldest sedimentary rock? Explain your choice.

**d** Where will metamorphic rocks form?

## Key ideas

- *Sedimentary rocks were formed from broken fragments of other rocks.*
- *Sedimentary rocks contain fossils. The age of fossils can be used to date rocks.*
- *Sedimentary rocks are found in layers. The deeper the layer, the older the rock.*
- *Metamorphic rocks are formed by the action of heat and pressure on existing rocks.*
- *Metamorphic rocks have the same composition as other rocks. This is evidence for their formation from these rocks.*

# 9:10 Igneous rocks

## Hot rocks

It is very hot deep inside the Earth – hot enough to melt rock in places. The rock here is called **magma**. When magma cools and solidifies it forms **igneous rock**.

Igneous rocks are made of crystals arranged randomly. The type of igneous rock formed depends on how and where it cools and sets.

## Volcanoes

In some places on the Earth, molten rock bursts out through the crust.

Sometimes it flows out as molten lava. This cools and solidifies to form a hard igneous rock such as **basalt**.

At other times it explodes out under enormous pressure, spraying droplets of magma into the air. These solidify and fall back to the earth as volcanic ash.

Lava and volcanic ash set to form igneous rocks. They often build up in layers to form a cone-shaped **volcano**.

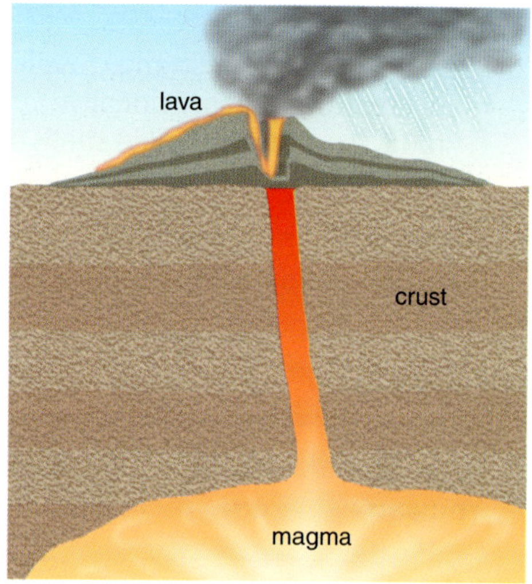


**a** **Volcanic ash is an igneous rock. But in what way is it similar to a sedimentary rock?**

**b** **Lava pouring from a volcano flows downhill like a river. Why doesn't it all end up in the sea?**

## Deep down in the crust

Deep down below an active volcano there is usually a great chamber full of molten rock – often tens of kilometres across.

This feeds magma up to the volcano when it erupts. But not all of the magma reaches the surface. A lot of it stays within the crust, where it slowly cools and sets to form an igneous rock such as **granite**.

**c** **If granite forms deep in the crust, how can you find it at the surface in Scotland and Cornwall?**

## Looking closely at granite

Magma is a mixture of chemicals, rich in the elements silicon, oxygen, aluminium and iron. When it cools and sets, different chemicals crystallise out. These are the **minerals** that make up the rock.

Granite has large crystals.

Because the crystals grow from liquid, they are free to grow in any direction. The different crystals usually end up dotted at random throughout the rock. When the rock sets completely, the crystals interlock tightly with one another. This makes a very hard rock.

A rock that has randomly arranged interlocking crystals is usually igneous. Granite shows these features clearly.

**d Look at the photograph of basalt through a microscope. What features tell you it is an igneous rock?**

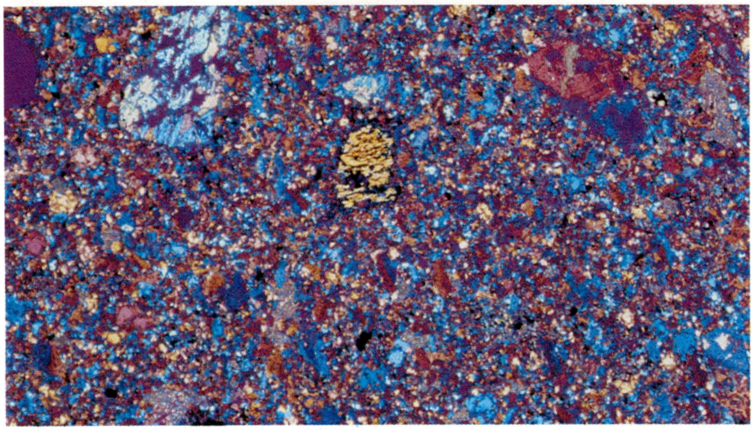

**Basalt has tiny crystals.**

## Why does basalt have tiny crystals?

Basalt lava is a hard, black and often featureless rock. But if you look at it through a microscope you can see the randomly arranged interlocking crystals that show it is an igneous rock. But why are the crystals so small?

Basalt magma pours out of a volcano at about 1000°C and flows over the cold rocks. It cools quickly, solidifying within minutes. Rapid cooling like this means that you get lots of crystals starting to form, but they have little time to grow before the rock sets. These rocks usually have tiny crystals, too small to see without a microscope.

Granite magma, however, stays trapped deep within the hot rocks. It may take hundreds of years to cool down. This means that the crystals have much longer to grow, and can end up large enough to see clearly. Rocks formed inside the Earth usually have large crystals like this.

## Questions

**1 Copy and complete the following sentences. Use words from the list.**

**basalt black granite igneous magma small large**

**Inside the Earth the ______ crystallises and forms ______ rocks.**

**If the crystallising takes place quickly on the surface of the Earth, ______ crystals are formed. These are often ______ in colour. An example of this type of rock is ______.**

**If the crystallising takes place inside the Earth the cooling is slow and ______ crystals are formed. An example of this type of rock is ______.**

**2 a Describe granite and basalt.**

**b In what ways are they the same?**

**c In what ways are they different?**

**d Account for the differences.**

## Key ideas

- *Igneous rocks are formed when molten rock (magma) crystallises.*
- *Igneous rocks do not contain fossils.*
- *Igneous rocks have interlocking crystals arranged randomly.*
- *Basalt is formed when the magma crystallises quickly, so tiny crystals are formed.*
- *Granite is formed when the magma crystallises slowly, so large crystals are formed.*

# 9:11 The atmosphere

The **atmosphere** is a blanket of air wrapped around the planet Earth. Dry air is a mixture of two main gases: oxygen (the gas we need to breathe) and nitrogen (an unreactive gas).

The proportions are approximately:

- one-fifth oxygen (20%)
- four-fifths nitrogen (80%)
- small amounts of carbon dioxide and some unreactive gases (noble gases).

The apparatus in the diagram can be used to find the percentage of oxygen in the air.

**Did you know?**

At the end of the 19th century scientists thought that air was a single substance. Lavoisier, a French scientist, experimented by heating mercury in air. Whenever he did this, only one-fifth of the air was used up and a red powder was formed. He concluded that air was a mixture of gases, and the gas used up he called oxygen.

Lavoisier was a rich and powerful man in France. He was guillotined in the French Revolution.

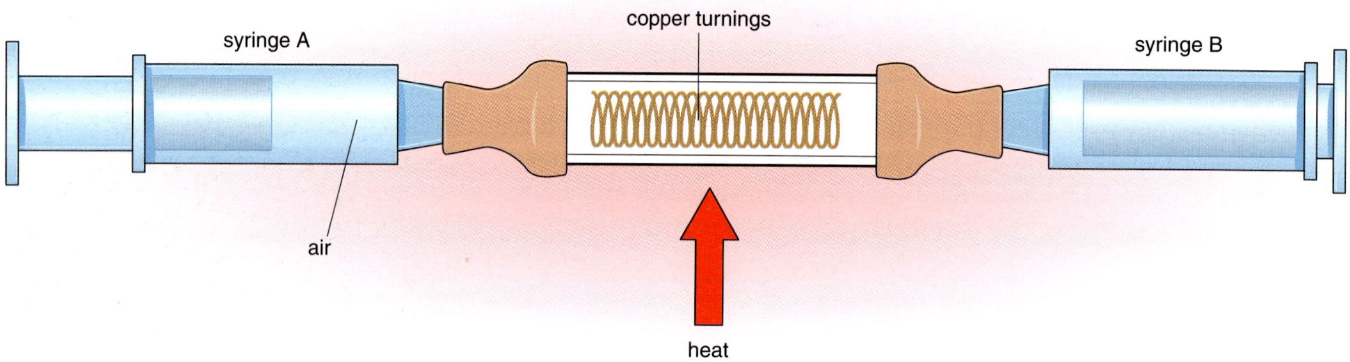


## The first atmosphere

The atmosphere has been more or less the same for about 200 million years. But when the Earth first formed, $4\frac{1}{2}$ billion years ago, things were very different.

The Earth was molten at first, and any original atmosphere (probably hydrogen and helium) boiled away into space.

When the surface rocks cooled and hardened, a new atmosphere formed from gases blasted out of volcanoes – carbon dioxide, steam, and some ammonia and methane.

**a Near Naples in Italy there is a cave known as 'the mouth of hell' that fills up with volcanic gas. Any dogs that wander in die by suffocation. What gas causes this?**

The Earth 4.5 billion years ago.

In time, the Earth cooled enough for the steam to condense back to water, forming the oceans. But for the first billion years the atmosphere was very different to that of today, with no free oxygen.

The main gas in the atmosphere was probably carbon dioxide, just like on Mars and Venus today. Other gases such as nitrogen, hydrogen and carbon monoxide were present.

Simple forms of life evolved on Earth in this oxygen-free environment. Then about 3 billion years ago simple plants evolved and they literally changed the world.

**b Where can you find organisms that live without oxygen today?**

The Earth 3 billion years ago.

## The first pollutant on Earth

Plants make oxygen as a by-product of **photosynthesis**. To all the other life forms at the time, oxygen was as poisonous as chlorine would be to you! So the growth and spread of simple plants led to massive pollution of the world's oceans – with oxygen!

By 2 billion years ago, other life forms were wiped out, or restricted to oxygen-free environments such as deep ocean mud or stagnant pools.

The Earth 2 billion years ago.

## Questions

1 Copy and complete the following sentences. Use words from the list.

**plants   polluted   oxygen   atmosphere**

The Earth's first ______________ was mostly carbon dioxide, with no ______________. Oxygen only appeared after ______________ evolved. Oxygen ______________ the oceans, killing off much of the early life.

2 If you pass 100 $cm^3$ of a sample of air over heated copper, black copper oxide is formed . The volume of air is reduced to 79 $cm^3$.

a What is the exact percentage of oxygen in this sample of air?

b Write a word equation for this reaction.

3 a What was the red powder formed in Lavoisier's experiments?

b Write a word equation for the reaction.

c Why is no more than one-fifth of the air used up each time?

## Key ideas

- *The present atmosphere of the Earth consists of about 80% nitrogen and 20% oxygen.*
- *There are smaller amounts of other gases, including carbon dioxide and noble gases.*
- *Volcanic activity produced gases such as carbon dioxide, steam, methane and ammonia.*
- *The percentage of oxygen increased when primitive plants produced oxygen by photosynthesis.*

# 9:12 Keep it in balance

## What do plants do for us?

Plants changed the Earth's atmosphere, killing off early life forms with toxic oxygen. But animal life has since evolved to rely on this same gas for **respiration**. You couldn't live unless plants produced the oxygen you need to breathe.

$$\underset{\text{(free in air)}}{\text{carbon dioxide}} + \text{water} \xrightarrow{\text{photosynthesis}} \underset{\text{(trapped carbon)}}{\text{glucose}} + \text{oxygen}$$

**Plants use glucose to grow, so the carbon is trapped in their tissues.**

**a What else do we need plants for, apart from oxygen?**

## What else do they do for us?

Plants put oxygen into the air – but they also take out carbon dioxide. This is important, as the amount of carbon dioxide in the air helps to control the temperature of the Earth.

If there is too much carbon dioxide in the air, the Earth gets hotter as more of the Sun's energy is trapped. This process is known as the **greenhouse effect**. It results in **global warming**. It makes the seas expand and also melts the ice caps at the poles – so the sea level rises.

**b Why does it matter if the sea level rises?**

Plants take carbon dioxide out of the air during photosynthesis.

carbon dioxide + water → glucose + oxygen

The carbon is locked up in plant tissues while they are alive. When they die, some is released but some stays trapped in fossil fuels (coal, oil and gas).

**c How do plants help to prevent global warming?**

## Shellfish, too

Plants have had help removing carbon dioxide from the atmosphere – from shellfish!

Many sea creatures such as shellfish and corals build shells from calcium carbonate. They get this from calcium salts in seawater and carbon dioxide. When they die, their remains eventually form limestone rock. Vast amounts of carbon dioxide are locked up in limestone.

$$\underset{\text{(soluble)}}{\text{calcium salts}} + \text{carbon dioxide} \rightarrow \underset{\text{(insoluble)}}{\text{calcium carbonate}}$$

**Shellfish remove carbon dioxide from seawater.**

## Tipping the balance

Over the last 200 millions of years, our atmosphere has kept itself more or less in balance. But over the last 200 years we have burnt vast quantities of fossil fuel, pouring extra carbon dioxide into the atmosphere.

Some of this carbon dioxide has been taken in by plants and shellfish, as before. Some has simply dissolved in the sea, forming soluble salts such as calcium hydrogencarbonate or magnesium hydrogencarbonate.

But these natural processes have not been able to keep up, so the carbon dioxide level has risen steadily.

The problem is the rate at which we are producing extra carbon dioxide. We are burning fossil fuels a million times faster than they form. So the natural recycling of carbon is unbalanced.

**Burning fossil fuels releases carbon dioxide into the atmosphere.**

## Questions

**1** **Copy and complete the following sentences. Use words from the list.**

**dioxide limestone photosynthesis rocks shellfish**

**Plants take carbon ____________ out of the atmosphere during ____________.**

**____________ take carbon dioxide out of the atmosphere to make their shells. Some of this carbon remains trapped in ____________ as fossil fuels and ____________.**

**2** **Look at the graph.**

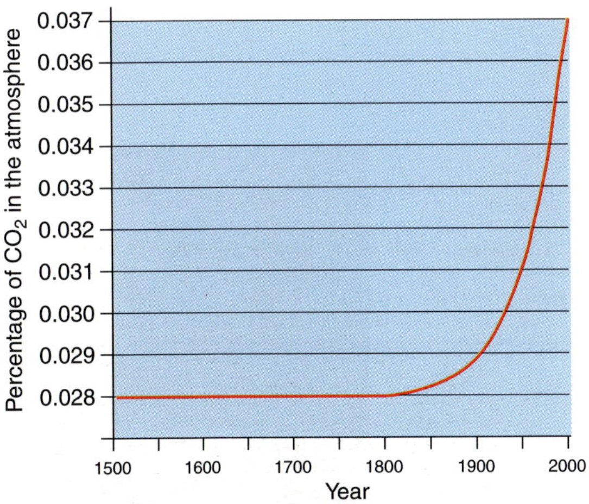


**a** **What does this graph show?**

**b** **What might have caused the rise since 1800?**

**c** **What effect has this had on the global temperature?**

**3** **Large quantities of methane are trapped inside ice in the ice caps. It will be released if the ice caps melt. Methane is a greenhouse gas. What effect might this have?**

### Key ideas

*The present Earth's atmosphere is kept in approximate balance because:*

- *photosynthesis produces oxygen in the presence of sunlight;*
- *respiration and burning of fuels use up oxygen and produce carbon dioxide;*
- *carbon dioxide is used up by plants and absorbed by seas and oceans.*

# 9:13 The Haber process

## Reversible reactions

Most chemical reactions are one-way processes. For example, if you burn wood you get the products carbon dioxide and water. But you cannot get the reactants wood and oxygen back again.

Some reactions are reversible. For example, blue copper sulphate has water molecules chemically bound into the crystal structure. These can be driven off by heating, leaving a white powder called anhydrous copper sulphate. If water is added to this powder, the water recombines with the copper sulphate and the blue colour reappears. This is the chemical test for the presence of water.

$$\text{hydrated copper sulphate (blue)} \underset{\text{water added}}{\overset{\text{water driven off by heat}}{\rightleftharpoons}} \text{anhydrous copper sulphate (white)} + \text{water}$$

The water test with copper sulphate – a reversible reaction.

**a Anhydrous means 'without water'. What do you think hydrated means?**

With a reversible reaction, it is possible to set up a **dynamic equilibrium**. Then the quantities of reactants and products remain unchanged. This suggest the reaction has stopped, but this is not so:

the rate of the forward reaction = the rate of the reverse reaction

The sign used to show an equilibrium is $\rightleftharpoons$.

## Ammonia for fertilisers

Plants need nitrogen to grow well, but they cannot use the vast amount of nitrogen in the atmosphere directly. Fortunately, nitrogen can be made to react with hydrogen to form ammonia. Ammonia can be used to make nitrogen-providing **fertilisers** for plants:

$$\text{nitrogen} + \text{hydrogen} \underset{\text{back reaction}}{\overset{\text{forward reaction}}{\rightleftharpoons}} \text{ammonia}$$

Unfortunately this reaction is very slow and is reversible, so some of the ammonia that forms breaks down to form nitrogen and hydrogen again.

The first attempts to make ammonia in this way gave just a few percent of ammonia. Something had to be done to increase the percentage **yield** of ammonia before the process could be used commercially.

## The Haber process

In theory, to get the highest possible yield, ammonia should be made at low temperature and very high pressure. But in practice, the reaction would be far too slow and the equipment needed would be far too expensive to make this work commercially.

The solution to the problem was finally worked out 100 years ago by Fritz Haber.

Fritz Haber – the father of fertilisers.

In the **Haber process** the reaction is run at moderately high pressure, but also at a moderately high temperature to make it go faster. Even so, an iron catalyst is needed to speed things up further. This is not a perfect solution in terms of yield, but Fritz Haber came up with a final trick.

Ammonia has a boiling point of –33°C. Haber realised that ammonia could be cooled and liquefied easily and so removed from the system. The unreacted gases could then be recycled in a continuous process, turning all the nitrogen and hydrogen into ammonia.

**b A typical Haber plant may run at 450°C and 200 atmospheres pressure. Use the graph to work out the percentage yield.**

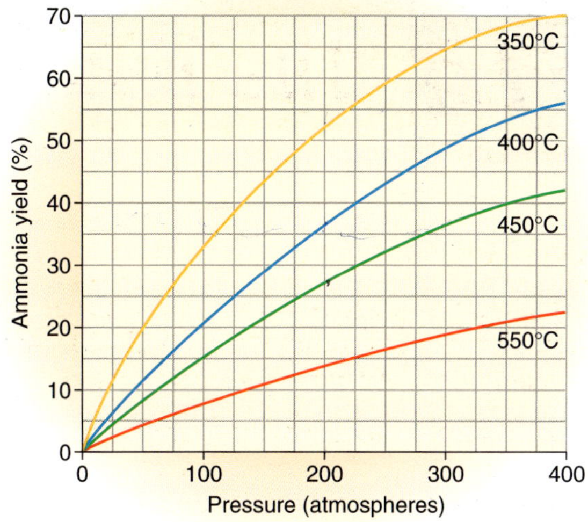


**How yield varies with temperature and pressure.**

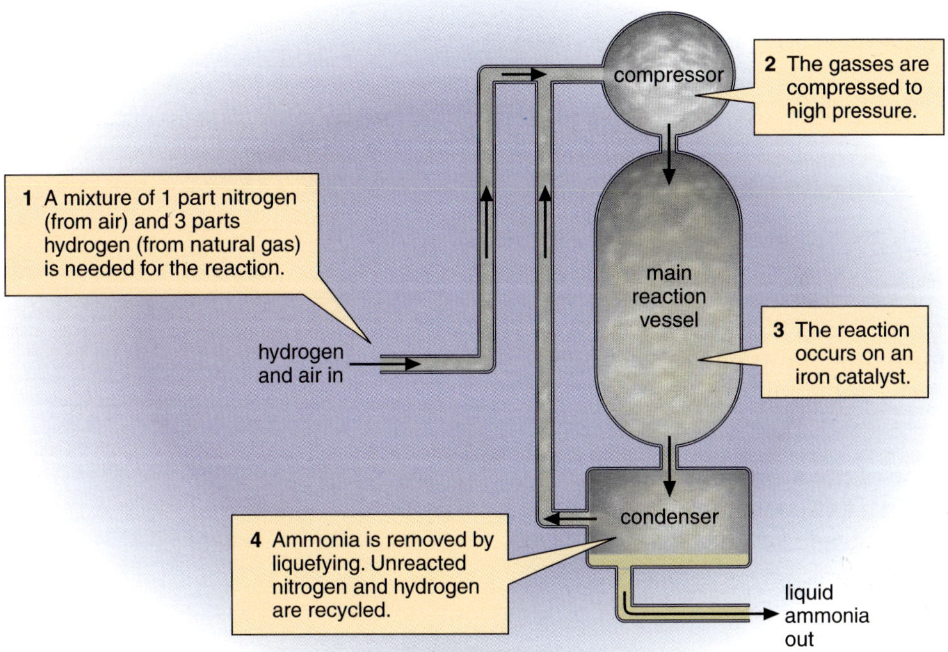


## Questions

**1 Copy and complete the following sentences. Use words from the list.**

**catalyst combine hydrogen iron liquefies nitrogen pressure recycled**

**Ammonia is manufactured from ____________ and ____________, extracted from the air.**

**The gases are compressed to a high ____________ and passed over a heated ____________ made of the metal ____________.**

**Some of the gases ____________ and the ammonia is removed by cooling until the ammonia ____________. The unreacted gases are ____________.**

## Key ideas

- *The Haber process is an important industrial process.*
- *Nitrogen from the air and hydrogen are combined to form ammonia.*
- *The best conditions are low temperatures and high pressures with a catalyst of iron.*

# 9:14 The importance of fertilisers

Plants need nitrogen to make proteins and so to grow. But they are unable to use directly the nitrogen that makes up 80% of the air. Instead, they have to get it from chemicals in the soil.

There is rarely enough usable nitrogen available naturally in the soil to grow crops on the scale demanded by modern farming.

In the past, farmers used natural materials rich in nitrogen to improve the soil – animal manure and vegetable compost. Today, some farmers are trying to go back to this method of farming, as 'organic' food becomes popular.

But most farmers throughout the world still have to use industrially produced nitrogen fertilisers to give the high crop yields that are needed to feed the world's growing population.

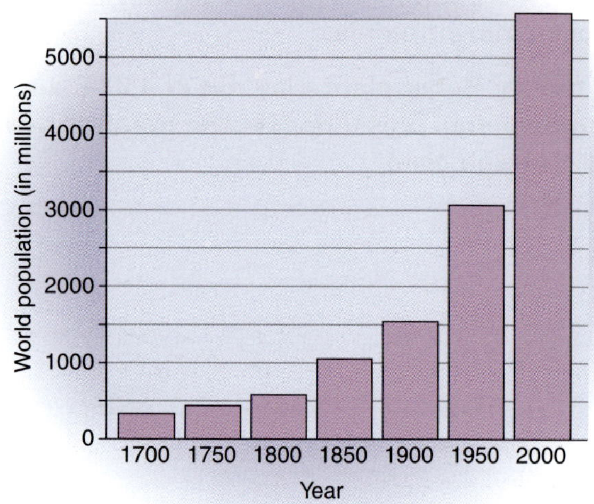


**a Why did the need for fertilisers grow dramatically over the last 100 years?**

## Nitric acid

Fertilisers must contain nitrogen in a form that plants can take in and use. Compounds of ammonia ($NH_3$) and compounds of nitric acid ($HNO_3$) are suitable.

Nitric acid can be made by oxidising some of the ammonia made by the Haber process. This is done in a two-stage process. Apart from ammonia, air and water are also used.

## Ammonium nitrate fertiliser

The most commonly used 'nitrogen' fertiliser is ammonium nitrate ($NH_4NO_3$). This is made by dissolving ammonia in water and then combining it with nitric acid in a neutralisation reaction.

ammonia + water → ammonium hydroxide

ammonium hydroxide + nitric acid → ammonium nitrate + water

The solution is then evaporated to give ammonium nitrate crystals.

**b Ammonium sulphate is produced when ammonium hydroxide reacts with sulphuric acid. Write a word equation for this reaction.**

## Nitrate problems

Manufactured fertilisers have worked wonders on crop production, raising yields and keeping food prices down. But there are problems. If fertilisers wash into rivers, they can upset the natural balance and make algae grow out of control.

These algae block sunlight from all but the top few centimetres of the water. Plants further down cannot photosynthesise, and so they die.

When these plants die and decompose they use up oxygen in the water. The fish in the river then die.

This process is called **eutrophication**.

Another serious problem can be caused by fertiliser nitrates getting into drinking water. This occurred recently in East Anglia, where vast wheatfields are heavily sprayed with fertiliser to keep the crop yields high.

The problem is that the nitrates ($NO_3^-$) are converted to nitrites ($NO_2^-$), which can react with the iron in blood haemoglobin. This affects the blood's ability to carry oxygen. In its extreme form it causes **blue baby syndrome**, in which a baby turns blue due to lack of oxygen.

**c East Anglia also has a problem with its lakes and rivers. Many parts of the Norfolk Broads are now covered by thick algal growths that have killed the fish. What might have caused this?**

These fish died because algal bloom caused a lack of oxygen in the water.

## Questions

**1** Copy and complete the following sentences. Use words from the list.

**ammonia    ammonium nitrate    nitric**
**sulphate    sulphuric acid    water**

Much of the ______________ produced by the Haber process is converted into ______________ acid. This involves a process using air and ______________.

Ammonia and nitric acid react together to form ______________. The reaction of ammonia with ______________ produces another fertiliser called ammonium ______________.

**2** The stages in the pollution of water by fertilisers are given below. They are in the wrong order. Copy them out in the correct order.

- Fish and waterlife die, and the water becomes stagnant.
- Fertilisers are dissolved in rainwater and washed into rivers.
- Plants die and use up dissolved oxygen.
- Plants deep in the water cannot photosynthesise.
- Green algae grow on the surface of the water.

### Key ideas

- *Many farmers use nitrogen fertilisers to promote growth in plants and so increase crop yields.*
- *These fertilisers are made by neutralising ammonia with nitric acid or sulphuric acid.*
- *Fertilisers can cause problems if they get in lakes or drinking water.*

# 9:15 The noble gases

Group 0 of the periodic table contains the spectacularly unreactive family of **noble gases**. These are typical non-metals in many ways:

- they have very low melting/boiling points;
- when solid they are soft and crumbly;
- they do not conduct electricity.

You may think that such unreactive gases will not be of much use, but sometimes their very inactivity is just what is needed.

Group 0

| Group 0 |
|---|
| 4 He 2 helium |
| 20 Ne 10 neon |
| 40 Ar 18 argon |
| 84 Kr 36 krypton |

## Uses of the noble gases

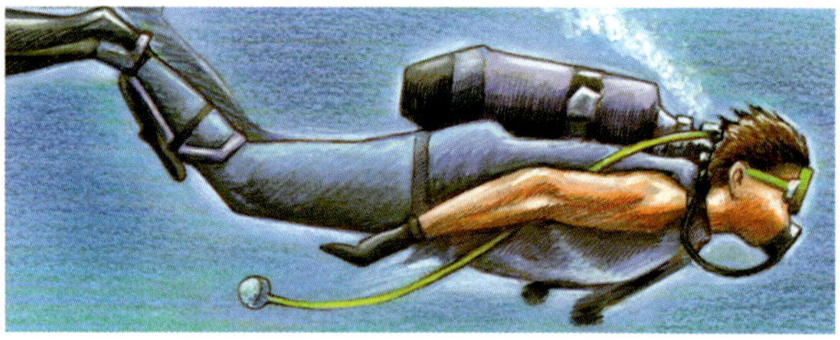

**Helium**
Helium is not very soluble in water, even under pressure. This makes it an excellent substitute for nitrogen in the 'air' that deep-sea divers breathe. Nitrogen bubbling out of the blood can cause the 'bends' on surfacing. Helium doesn't do this, but does have the side-effect of making you sound like Donald Duck when you talk!

**Neon**
Neon is most commonly used for another property. It glows if an electrical discharge is passed through it. These discharge tubes can be coloured, making them ideal for flashy neon signs.

**Argon**
This is the cheapest of the noble gases to produce, as it makes up 1% of the air. Argon is used inside ordinary lightbulbs, to stop the filament from burning. It is also used to give an unreactive atmosphere for welding, which could be dangerous in air.

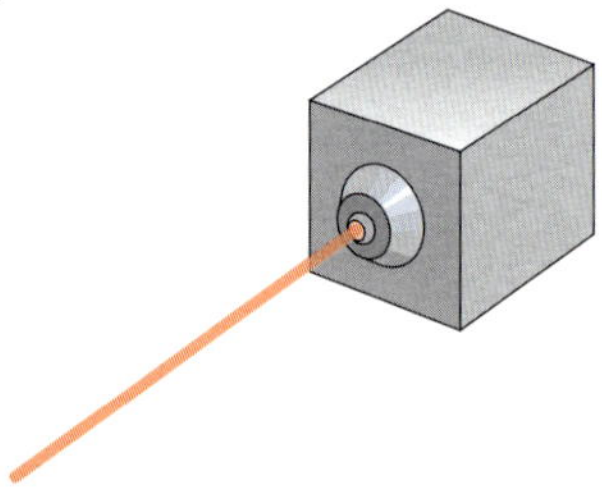

**Krypton**
Krypton is used in lasers, for example in hospitals.

**a** **Noble gases used to be called rare gases. Why is this an incorrect name for all these gases?**

**b** **Where do you use noble gases at home?**

## Helium versus hydrogen

Airships used to be filled with hydrogen, which is a light but highly flammable gas. Like hydrogen, helium has a very low density – much less than that of air. This makes it a safe alternative to hydrogen for modern airships – or party balloons.

But helium does have a higher density than hydrogen.

**c** **Give one advantage and one disadvantage of helium for airships compared to hydrogen.**

The Hindenburg airship disaster of 1937.

## Why are they so unreactive?

The atoms of all the noble gases have full outer electron energy levels. This gives the atoms great stability – they will not try to lose, gain or share electrons. This means that they will not form chemical bonds.

Because of this, the noble gases always exist as single atoms – they are **monatomic gases**. This is unlike the other gases in the atmosphere, which form molecules such as $N_2$ and $O_2$.

**d** Spot the noble gas in this close up picture of air. How can you tell?

**e** Radon is also found in group 0. Draw a diagram showing a close-up view of pure radon gas.

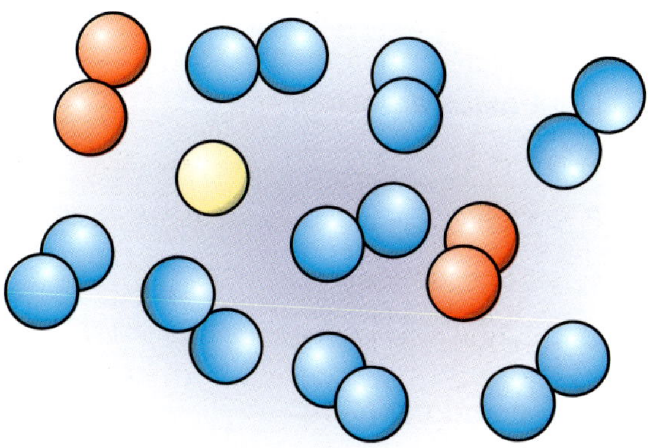

**Did you know?**

Noble gases were not discovered in the Earth's atmosphere until 1892. It was because of their lack of reactivity that they remained 'hidden'.

Scientists believed that noble gases did not react with any other elements to form compounds.

In 1962 scientists showed that noble gas compounds were possible. Xenon tetrafluoride ($XeF_4$) was the first of such compounds.

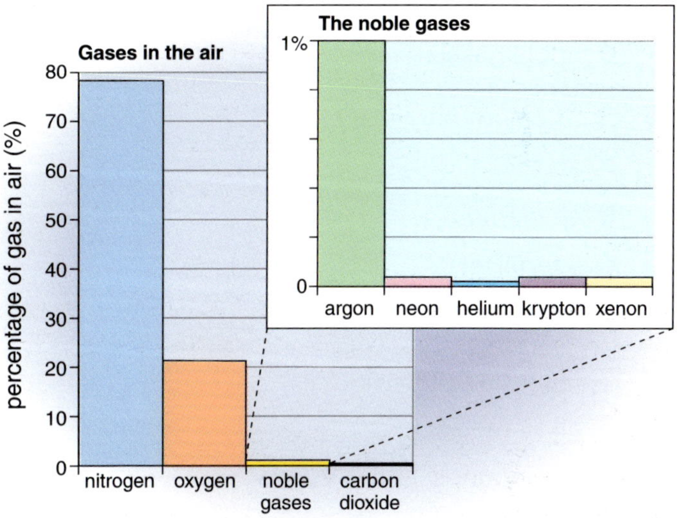


**The noble gases make up 1% of the air – but most of that is argon.**

## Questions

**1 a** If a lightbulb were filled with air rather than argon, what would happen when it was switched on?

**b** Why is argon used rather than helium in lightbulbs?

**2** Write down the name of a noble gas used for:

**a** filling light bulbs;

**b** filling lighting tubes for airships;

**c** filling weather balloons;

**d** making lasers.

**3** Nitrogen and oxygen form diatomic molecules but argon is a monatomic gas. Explain the terms 'diatomic' and 'monatomic'.

## Key ideas

- *Group 0 of the periodic table contains the unreactive noble gases.*
- *Noble gas atoms have full outer shells, which makes them stable and unreactive.*
- *Noble gases exist as single atoms.*
- *The noble gases have other properties that make them useful.*

# End of module questions

## Low demand

1 Light bulbs are filled with
- **A** air
- **B** argon
- **C** carbon dioxide
- **D** oxygen

2 Argon and neon are
- **A** alkali metals
- **B** compounds
- **C** halogens
- **D** noble gases

3 Ammonium nitrate is
- **A** an acid
- **B** an element
- **C** a fertiliser
- **D** a weedkiller

4 Sodium and potassium are
- **A** alkali metals
- **B** compounds
- **C** halogens
- **D** noble gases

5 The most reactive gas in the air is
- **A** argon
- **B** carbon dioxide
- **C** nitrogen
- **D** oxygen

6 In the extraction of iron, iron ore is heated with
- **A** sand
- **B** sand and limestone
- **C** coke and limestone
- **D** coke and sand

7 Transition metals
- **A** are usually liquids
- **B** have low densities
- **C** form coloured compounds
- **D** do not conduct electricity

8 Marble and limestone
- **A** are both forms of calcium carbonate
- **B** are both sedimentary rocks
- **C** do not fizz when acid is added
- **D** are both crystalline

9 Metals are made from
- **A** plants
- **B** the atmosphere
- **C** ores
- **D** crude oil

10 Electrolysis is used to extract
- **A** aluminium
- **B** iron
- **C** lead
- **D** gold

11 If a reaction is reversible
- **A** it forms more than one product
- **B** it is slow
- **C** it does not turn all the reactants into products
- **D** it is of no useful purpose

12 Rock salt is
- **A** a metal
- **B** a pure substance
- **C** an impure form of salt
- **D** used to make sweets

## Standard demand

**13** The percentage of oxygen in air is

**A** less than 1%

**B** 4%

**C** 20%

**D** 79%

**14** Nitrogen and hydrogen are used in the Haber process to make

**A** ammonia

**B** nitric acid

**C** plants

**D** plastics

**15** Which row of the table gives where nitrogen and hydrogen come from for the Haber process?

| | Nitrogen comes from | Hydrogen comes from |
|---|---|---|
| **A** | air | crude oil |
| **B** | crude oil | water |
| **C** | air | air |
| **D** | water | crude oil |

**16** Rocks that are found on the surface of the Earth and are made up of small black crystals are

**A** sedimentary

**B** metamorphic

**C** igneous formed by slow crystallisation

**D** igneous formed by rapid crystallisation

**17** Sodium reacts with cold water to form

**A** sodium oxide and hydrogen

**B** sodium oxide and oxygen

**C** sodium hydroxide and hydrogen

**D** sodium hydroxide and hydrogen

**Sodium reacts very rapidly with water.**

**18** Electrolysis of concentrated sodium chloride solution produces

**A** sodium hydroxide and hydrochloric acid

**B** sodium hydroxide, hydrogen and oxygen

**C** sodium hydroxide , hydrogen and chlorine

**D** sodium oxide, chlorine and hydrogen

**19** In the electrolysis of copper sulphate solution using copper electrodes

**A** pure copper is deposited on the cathode (negative electrode)

**B** copper from the cathode (positive electrode) goes into solution

**C** the colour of the copper sulphate solution fades

**D** pure copper is deposited on the anode and the cathode

**20** Which of the following increases the amount of oxygen in the atmosphere?

**A** combustion of fuels

**B** respiration of animals

**C** photosynthesis in plants

**D** rusting of iron

**21** Rubidium is an alkali metal below potassium in group 1 of the periodic table.

Rubidium

**A** has a lower melting point than potassium

**B** is less reactive than potassium

**C** forms oxygen when reacted with water

**D** forms ions with a single positive charge

22 Which of the following is a reduction reaction?

**A** copper oxide + hydrogen → copper + water

**B** copper + oxygen → copper oxide

**C** copper oxide + sulphuric acid → copper sulphate + water

**D** copper nitrate → copper oxide + nitrogen dioxide + oxygen

23 Aluminium is extracted from aluminium oxide by

**A** heating strongly

**B** heating strongly with carbon

**C** electrolysis of a melt

**D** electrolysis of an aqueous solution

24 Copper is purified by

**A** electrolysis of copper sulphate solution

**B** electrolysis of a molten copper salt

**C** heating copper sulphate with carbon

**D** heating copper sulphate

**Bauxite (aluminium oxide ore).**

# Module 10 – Understanding chemical reactions

This module is divided into four parts.

1 Atoms of the same element may not all be exactly the same. Most elements exist as mixtures of isotopes.

2 Atoms are held together by chemical bonds. Two types of bonding are ionic bonds and covalent bonds.

3 Chemical reactions are often accompanied either by energy given out or by energy taken in.

4 Chemical reactions can be used to predict reactions. Relative formula masses can be calculated from relative atomic masses.

Before you start, check what you can remember about atoms. Try these questions first.

1 Write down the names of the elements combined in sodium chloride.

2 Write down the names of the elements combined in sodium nitrate.

3 Write down the names of the elements combined in potassium hydroxide.

4 Write down the names of the three particles in a carbon atom.

5 Which of these particles is not usually present in a hydrogen atom?

6 Where are the protons and neutrons found in an atom?

7 Where are electrons found in an atom?

8 Which particles must always be present in equal numbers in an atom?

9 Nitrogen is in group 5 and period 2 of the periodic table. What is the electron arrangement in a nitrogen atom?

10 What is special about the electron arrangement in a noble gas atom?

# 10:1 Atoms and isotopes

All atoms of the same element contain the same number of protons and the same number of electrons.

It is possible, however, for atoms of the same element to contain different numbers of neutrons.

Atoms of the same element containing different numbers of neutrons are called **isotopes**.

## Atomic number and mass number

The **atomic number** tells you the number of protons in an atom. The atomic number will be the same as the number of electrons in the atom. This is because an atom has no overall positive or negative charge.

The **mass number** tells you the number of **nucleons** (protons and neutrons) in the nucleus of the atom.

This information is shown in the periodic table.

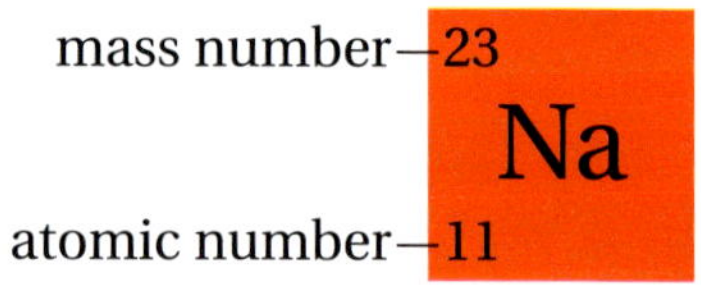


For example, sodium has an atomic number of 11 and a mass number of 23.

This means an atom of sodium contains:

- 11 protons
- 11 electrons
- 12 neutrons (23 – 11)

**a How many nucleons are there in a sodium atom?**

**b Find the mass number and atomic number of aluminium. Use the periodic table on page 177.**

**c Work out the number of protons, neutrons and electrons in an aluminium atom.**

> **Did you know?**
> Nearly every element exists as a mixture of two or more isotopes. The element tin is made up from ten different isotopes.

## Isotopes of hydrogen

The diagrams show the three isotopes of hydrogen.

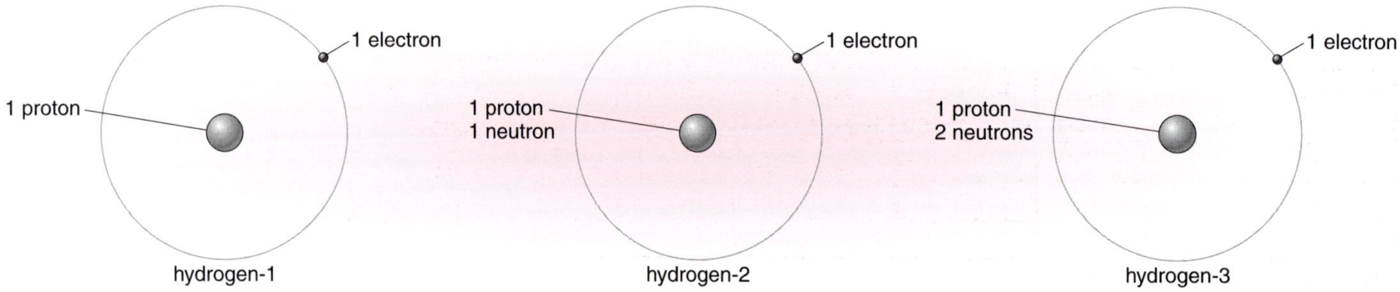


- Hydrogen-1 is the most common hydrogen atom. It contains 1 proton and 1 electron, as all isotopes of hydrogen must. It contains no neutrons.
- Hydrogen-2 (sometimes called deuterium) contains 1 proton and 1 neutron in the nucleus.
- Hydrogen-3 (sometimes called tritium) contains 1 proton and 2 neutrons in the nucleus.

All isotopes have identical chemical properties but different physical properties.

Heavy water looks like the water that comes from your tap, but its molecules contain the isotope hydrogen-2 (deuterium).

**Did you know?**
Deuterium burns in oxygen to form deuterium oxide. This is sometimes called 'heavy water'.

## Isotopes of carbon

Carbon is made up from three different isotopes – carbon-12, carbon-13 and carbon-14.

In a sample of carbon, most atoms are carbon-12.

Carbon-14 is radioactive and breaks down to produce nitrogen-14. Carbon-14 used in archaeology to date objects.

**d** Carbon has an atomic number of 6. How many protons, neutrons and electrons are there in each isotope of carbon?

**e** Chlorine can exist as two isotopes, chlorine-35 and chlorine-37. Chlorine has an atomic number of 17. Work out the number of neutrons in chlorine-35 and chlorine-37.

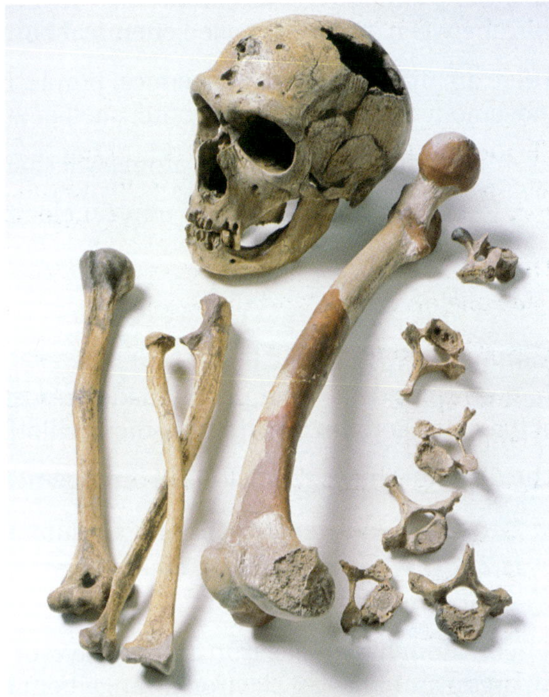

The radioactive isotope carbon-14 in these bones helps scientists work out how old they are.

## Questions

**1** Copy and complete the following sentences. Use words from the list. You can use words more than once.

**electrons   neutrons   nucleons   nucleus   protons**

An atom of an element contains protons and __________ packed together in a positively charged __________. The nucleus is surrounded by rapidly moving __________.

The atomic number is the number of ______________ in the nucleus.

The mass number is the number of ______________ in the nucleus.

Two isotopes of the same element contain the same number of ______________ and electrons but different numbers of ______________.

**2** Copy and complete the table.

| Isotope | Atomic number | Mass number | Number of protons | Number of electrons | Number of neutrons |
|---|---|---|---|---|---|
| lithium | 3 | 7 | | | |
| nitrogen | 7 | 14 | | | |
| calcium | 20 | 40 | | | |
| fluorine | 9 | 19 | | | |
| boron | 5 | 9 | | | |

**3** Oxygen (atomic number 8) can exist as three isotopes: oxygen-16, oxygen-17 and oxygen 18. Describe similarities and differences between these isotopes in the numbers of protons, neutrons and electrons.

## Key ideas

- *All atoms of the same element have the same number of protons.*
- *The atomic number is the number of protons (and the number of electrons).*
- *The mass number is the number of nucleons (protons + neutrons) in the atom.*
- *Isotopes of the same element contain the same number of protons and electrons but different numbers of neutrons.*

# 10:2 Joining atoms together

## Chemical bonds

The gases in the last column of the periodic table (group 0) are called the noble gases. These are gases such as helium, neon and argon. They are made up of single atoms.

All other elements and all compounds involve atoms joining together. The joins between atoms are called **chemical bonds**.

There are different kinds of chemical bonds. Each type involves the movement of electrons in the outer shell of atoms.

- Sometimes two or more atoms will share electrons.
- At other times atoms will transfer electrons over to other atoms.

## Ionic bonding

**Sodium chloride, NaCl**
Sodium chloride is a compound made from atoms of the metal sodium and the non-metal chlorine.

The diagram shows their electron arrangements.

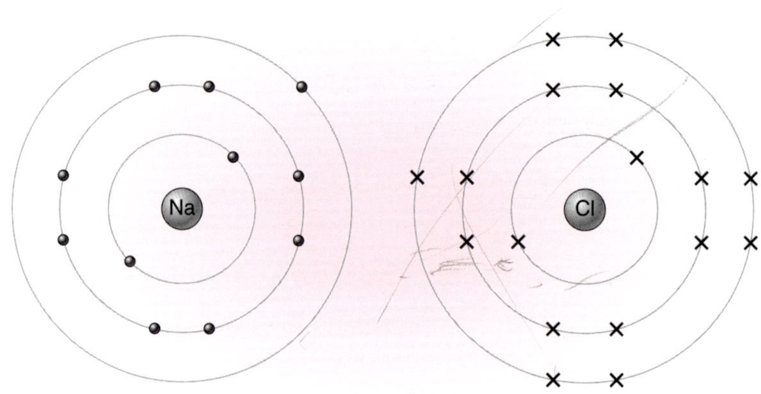

sodium atom    chlorine atom

**a The electron arrangement of a sodium atom is 2,8,1. What is the electron arrangement of a chlorine atom?**

A neon atom has an electron arrangement of 2,8. An argon atom has an electron arrangement of 2,8,8. These are stable arrangements, because they have full outer shells of electrons.

In a reaction, atoms tend to lose or gain electrons to make them as stable as noble gases.

A sodium atom has one more electron than a neon atom. A chlorine atom has one fewer electron than an argon atom. So when sodium reacts with chlorine to form NaCl:

- each sodium atom loses one electron to form a sodium **ion** with a single positive charge;
- each chlorine atom gains one electron to form a chloride ion with a single negative charge.

Following the reaction, strong **electrostatic forces** hold the ions together.

The formula of sodium chloride is NaCl. This does not mean that just one sodium atom combines with one chlorine atom. It does mean that a crystal of sodium chloride contains equal numbers of sodium and chloride ions.

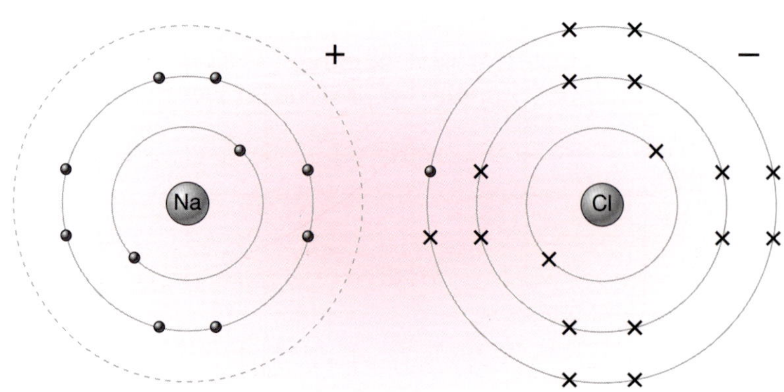

sodium ion    chloride ion

**Magnesium oxide, MgO**

Magnesium oxide is a compound of magnesium (a metal) and oxygen (a non-metal). This is another example of **ionic bonding**.

**b** **What are the electron arrangements of a magnesium atom and an oxygen atom?**

**c** **How many electrons are there in the outer shell of a magnesium atom? (Hint: in which group of the periodic table is magnesium placed?)**

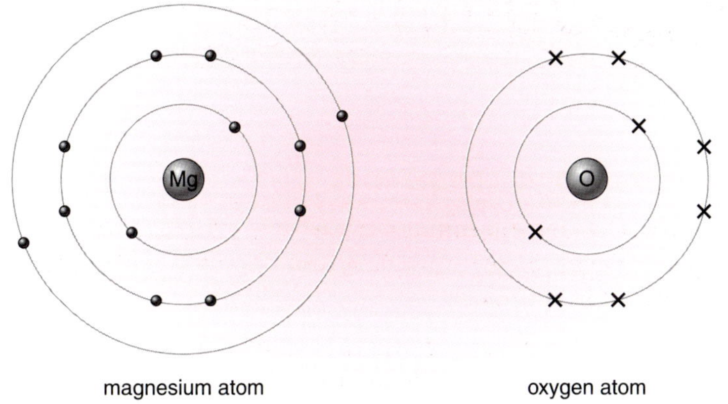


A magnesium atom has two more electrons than the stable neon atom.

Since the outer electron shell of a magnesium atom is only partly full, these two electrons can be lost. A magnesium ion is formed with a 2+ charge.

The oxygen atom needs two electrons to achieve a stable electron arrangement like that of neon.

Each oxygen atom gains two electrons and forms an oxide ion with a 2– charge.

This is summarised in the diagram.

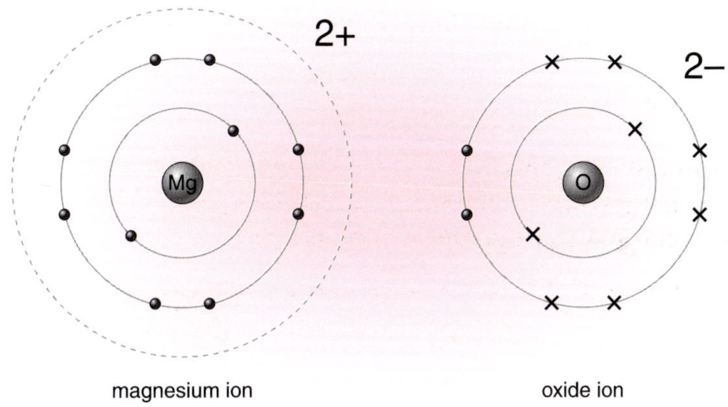


## Questions

**1** Copy and complete the sentences. Use words from the list. You can use words more than once.

**argon** **electron** **electrostatic forces** **ion** **neon**

A sodium atom has one more ______________ than an atom of the noble gas ______________.

A chlorine atom has one fewer electron than an atom of the noble gas ______________.

Each sodium atom loses one electron and forms a sodium ______________.

Each chlorine atom gains an electron and forms a chloride ______________.

The ions are held together by strong ______________.

**2** In lithium fluoride the bonding is ionic.

**a** Write down the electron arrangements in a lithium atom (Li, atomic number 3) and a fluorine atom (F, atomic number 9).

**b** Write down the charges on the two ions formed.

**c** Describe the electron changes that take place when lithium and fluorine combine.

### Key ideas

- *An ion is an atom or a group of atoms with a positive or negative charge.*
- *Ionic bonds are formed when a metal combines with a non-metal.*
- *Ionic bonding involves a complete transfer of electrons from metal to non-metal.*
- *Ions are formed, and these are held together by strong electrostatic forces.*

# 10:3 More about ionic compounds

## Properties of ionic compounds

Compounds with ionic bonding have certain properties in common.

Ionic compounds usually:

- are solid;
- have high melting points because of strong forces between ions;
- are not good conductors of electricity;
- do not dissolve in organic solvents such as petrol.

**a A compound has a melting point of 50°C and dissolves in hexane. Does it have ionic bonding?**

**b Sodium chloride contains ionic bonding. Write down three properties of solid sodium chloride.**

Sodium chloride (common salt) is made up from an arrangement of sodium and chloride ions. This arrangement is called a **lattice**.

This is shown in the diagram.

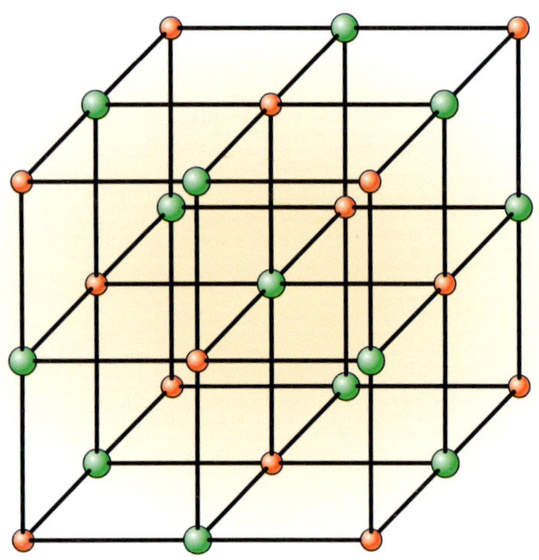

Sodium chloride lattice structure.

Crystals of sodium chloride.

**c What shape does a crystal of sodium chloride have?**

**d Look at the ion in the centre of the lattice. How many ions are there around it?**

The diagram shows only a small part of the structure and it extends in the same way in all directions. A structure that extends in all directions like this is called a **giant structure**.

Sodium chloride forms a **crystal** when the particles in it are regularly arranged. This happens when:

- a hot saturated solution is allowed to cool;
- a **molten** compound is left to cool and crystallise.

Before sodium chloride can melt, all of the bonds between ions have to be broken. As the forces holding the ions together are strong, a large amount of energy is needed to melt sodium chloride. This is why sodium chloride has a very high melting point.

## When do ionic compounds conduct electricity?

Solid sodium chloride does not conduct electricity. The lattice contains ions, but the ions are not free to move.

If you heat sodium chloride to its melting point, the lattice breaks down and the ions are free to move. This is how the solid crystal becomes a liquid.

You can also break the bonds by dissolving sodium chloride in water. Again, the lattice breaks down and ions are free to move.

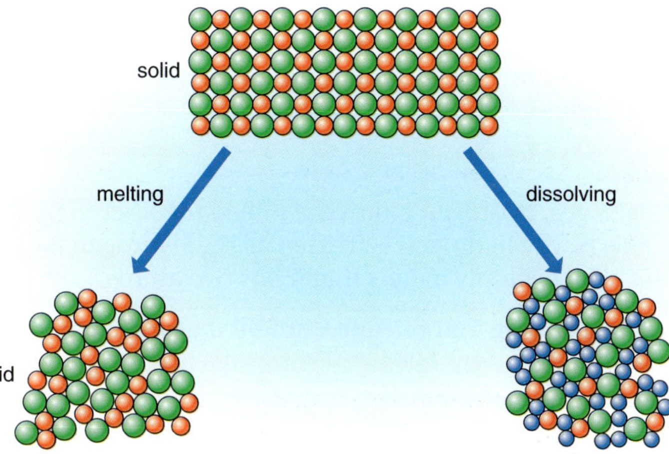


**Sodium chloride can melt and dissolve.**

## Questions

**1** Copy and complete these sentences. Use words from the list.

**dissolving electricity lattice melting molten solids**

Most compounds with ionic bonding are ________________.

The ions are held together tightly in a ________________.

This is broken down by ________________ or ________________ in water.

These compounds will conduct ________________ when ________________ or in solution in water.

**2** The table gives the properties of five compounds, A–E.

| Compound | Melting point in °C | Solubility in water | Conductivity of molten compound | Solubility in organic solvent |
|---|---|---|---|---|
| A | 900 | good | good | poor |
| B | 2200 | poor | poor | poor |
| C | 90 | poor | poor | good |
| D | 630 | good | good | poor |
| E | 140 | good | poor | good |

Which compounds are likely to have ionic bonding? Explain your choice.

## Key ideas

- *A sodium chloride lattice consists of a regular arrangement of positively charged and negatively charged ions.*
- *The ions are held together by strong electrostatic bonds.*
- *The lattice has a high melting point.*
- *The lattice breaks down by melting or dissolving in water.*

# Covalent bonding

## The covalent bond

Ionic bonding occurs when metal and non-metal atoms join together. Bonds between two non-metal atoms cannot be ionic. This is because neither non-metal atom can give away one or more electrons.

The type of bonding used to join two non-metal atoms is called covalent bonding.

### Hydrogen

In hydrogen gas, hydrogen atoms are joined together in pairs of atoms. This is why hydrogen is written as $H_2$. Hydrogen is **diatomic**, which simply means that it has two atoms.

**a Oxygen, chlorine and nitrogen are all diatomic. How would you write the formulae for molecules of oxygen, chlorine and nitrogen?**

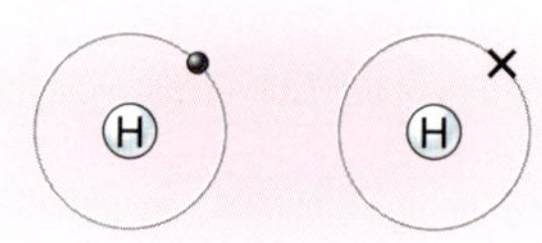


Two hydrogen atoms.

The diagram above shows two hydrogen atoms.

- Each hydrogen atom has a single electron. One electron is shown as a dot and one as a cross.
- Each hydrogen atom has one fewer electron than a helium atom (a stable electron arrangement).

The two hydrogen atoms can share a pair of electrons (one from each hydrogen atom). Together they make a hydrogen molecule.

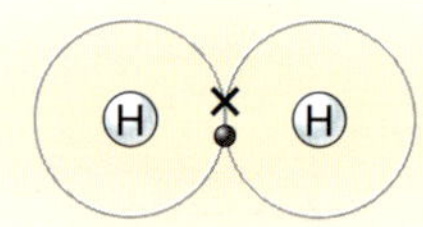


A hydrogen molecule.

In this way, each hydrogen atom becomes stable. The two atoms each have a share of two electrons.

The shared pair of electrons is called a **covalent bond**.

It is often shown as:

$$H{-}H$$

### Chlorine

Chlorine gas also consists of pairs of chlorine atoms bonded together by covalent bonding.

The electrons of one atom have been shown as dots and the other as crosses.

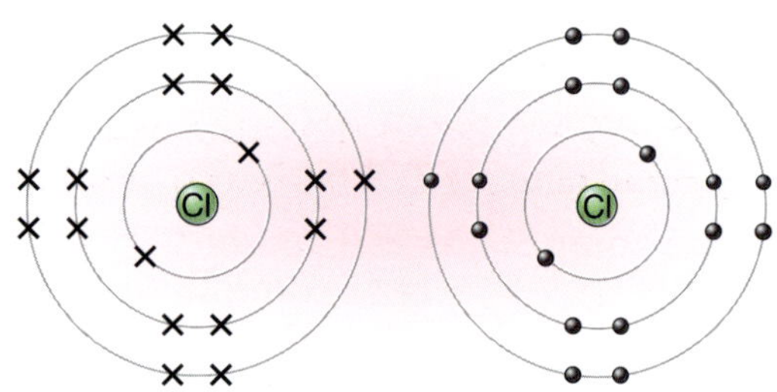


Two chlorine atoms.

Each chlorine atom is one electron short of the stable electron arrangement of argon. Again, each chlorine atom gives one electron and the pair of electrons is shared to form a covalent bond.

**b How many electrons does each chlorine atom now have in its outer shell?**

**c For each chlorine atom, how many electrons in the outer shell are not involved in bonding?**

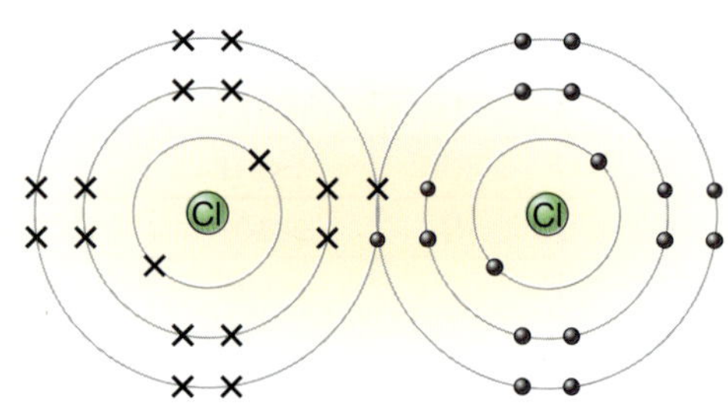


A chlorine molecule.

### Oxygen

Oxygen exists in the gas as pairs of atoms ($O_2$).

Each oxygen atom has six electrons in the outer shell – two electrons short of the stable electron arrangement of a neon atom.

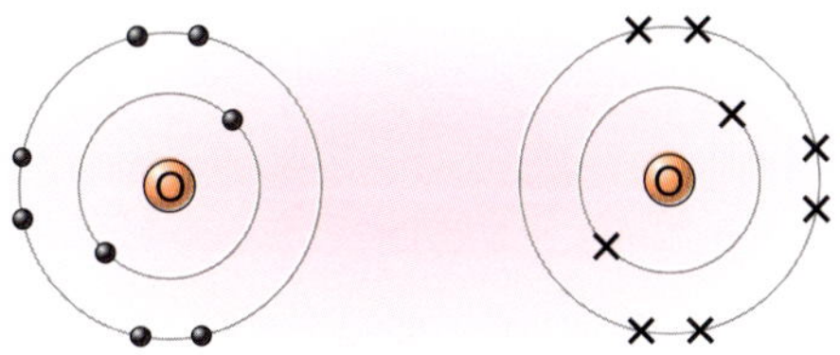


Two oxygen atoms.

Each oxygen atom gives two electrons to be shared. There are two pairs of electrons shared, so this makes two covalent bonds. Each covalent bond involves two electrons.

This is shown as:

$$O{=}O$$

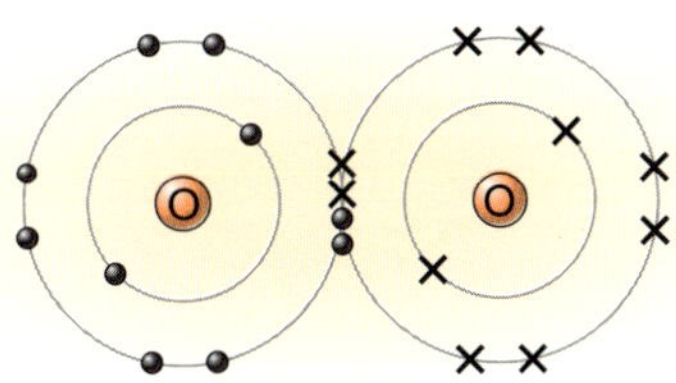


An oxygen molecule.

**Did you know?**

You can show electron arrangements and covalent bonds in different ways.

- Show just the outer shell of electrons.

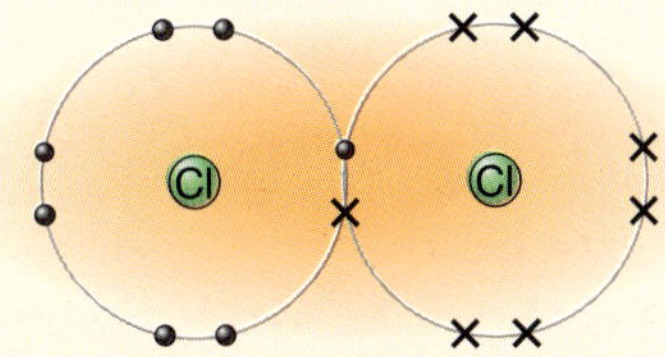


- Use just dots and crosses.

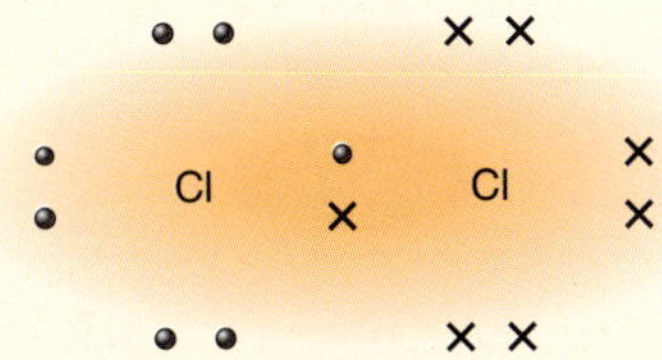


- Use lines to represent the bonds.

Cl — Cl

### Hydrogen chloride

Hydrogen chloride is different from hydrogen, chlorine and oxygen molecules as it is a compound. But it still has covalent bonding between the atoms.

The diagram shows an atom of hydrogen and an atom of chlorine.

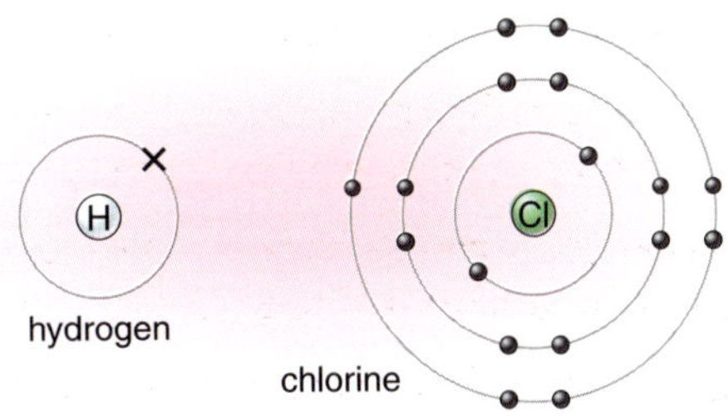


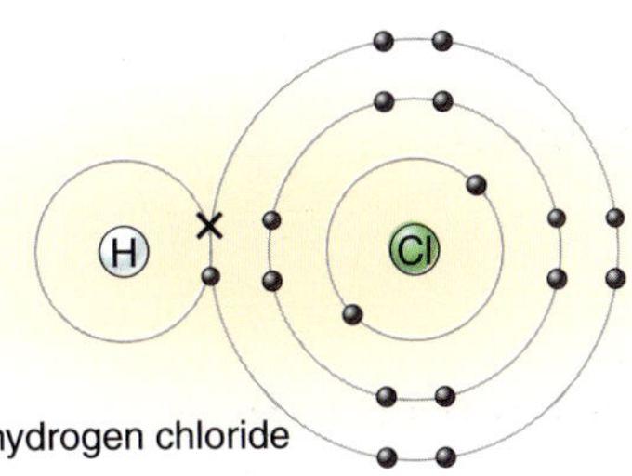


Both hydrogen and chlorine are one electron short of a stable electron arrangement. A hydrogen atom has one electron fewer than a helium atom. A chlorine atom has one electron fewer than an argon atom.

Each atom gives one electron to form a pair that is shared between the two atoms. This is a covalent bond.

## Questions

**1** A fluorine atom has an electron arrangement of 2,7.

- **a** Draw a diagram of a fluorine atom.
- **b** Draw a dot and cross diagram of a fluorine molecule.

**2** Nitrogen is also diatomic. A nitrogen atom has an electron arrangement of 2,5.

- **a** Draw a diagram of a pair of nitrogen atoms bonded together.
- **b** How many electrons are shared?
- **c** How do we show three bonds between the two nitrogen atoms? (We call this a triple covalent bond.)

## Key ideas

- *Covalent bonds are formed between non-metal atoms.*
- *Examples of covalent bonding are found in hydrogen, nitrogen, oxygen, chlorine and hydrogen chloride.*

# 10:5 More covalent bonding

## More compounds with covalent bonding

Three other examples of covalent bonding are water, ammonia and methane.

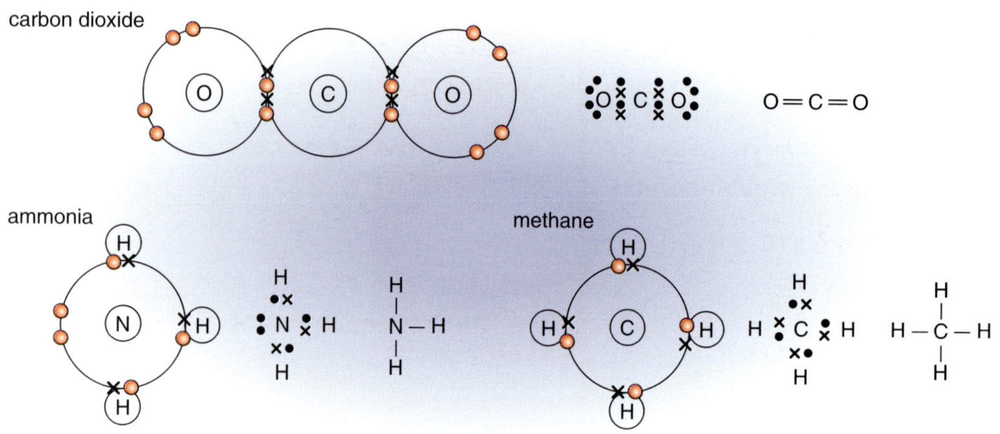


**a Carbon dioxide, ammonia and methane are all compounds. Which elements are combined in each of these compounds?**

## Properties of compounds with covalent bonding

All of the examples of covalent bonding used so far involve two, three, four or five non-metal atoms bonded together to form a **molecule**.

A molecule is a group of atoms bonded together.

**b Ethane is a compound with a formula $C_2H_6$. How many atoms are there in a molecule of ethane?**

## Properties of compounds made up of molecules

Compounds made from molecules have certain properties:

- they are usually gases;
- their melting points are very low;
- they are poor conductors of electricity;
- they do not dissolve easily in water (except HCl);
- they dissolve well in organic solvents.

The bonds within covalent molecules are very strong. But the particles have no electrical charge, so there are only very weak forces between the molecules.

This explains why substances made up of molecules have low melting and boiling points. Small molecules form gases at room temperature. Larger molecules may be liquids or soft solids.

**c Sulphur reacts with oxygen to form small sulphur dioxide ($SO_2$) molecules. Is this likely to be a solid, liquid or gas?**

## Large molecules

So far, the examples of covalent bonding you have seen involve small molecules. But there are larger molecules.

The photograph shows a molecule of carbon called fullerene, discovered by chemists accidentally in 1986. Each molecule is made up of 60 carbon atoms. It can be written as $C_{60}$.

Before 1986 the only forms of carbon were very large structures where millions of carbon atoms were joined together. It came as a great surprise when scientists made carbon molecules with only 60 carbon atoms joined together. These have opened new possibilities for carbon as a lubricant.

### Questions

1 Copy and complete the sentences. Use words from the list.

**compound covalent gas molecules**

Hydrogen sulphide ($H_2S$) is a ____________ of hydrogen (non-metal) and sulphur (non-metal). The compound is made up of ____________ containing ____________ bonding.

At room temperature hydrogen sulphide is a ____________.

2 Iodine exists as molecules ($I_2$). It is a solid with the iodine molecules packed together in a crystal. On gentle heating, iodine crystals turn to a purple vapour.

a Draw a diagram showing the arrangement of outer shell electrons in a molecule of iodine.

b What does the effect of heating suggest about the bond within the iodine crystal?

c Solid iodine is crystalline. What does this suggest about the arrangement of iodine molecules in the solid?

### Key ideas

- *Small molecules made from covalently bonded atoms are likely to form gases, because the forces between the molecules are weak.*
- *These substances are likely to be insoluble in water but soluble in organic solvents.*

# 10:6 Energy given out

## Getting warmer

It is not always easy to tell when a chemical reaction has taken place.

For example, if you mix cold dilute hydrochloric acid and sodium hydroxide solutions, you will not see any obvious change. Two colourless liquids just mix to form another colourless liquid.

But if you hold the tube, you will feel that something has happened. It will have got warmer.

**a How else could you tell a reaction had occurred? (Hint: this is a neutralisation reaction.)**

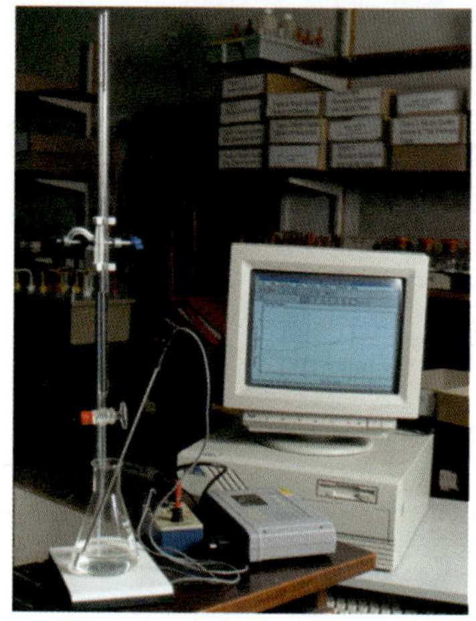

You can follow the rise in temperature during neutralisation with a temperature sensor connected to a computer.

Chemical changes are often accompanied by changes in temperature, as energy is transferred to or from the surroundings.

In this case, heat energy has been given out during neutralisation.

Chemical reactions that give out heat energy like this are called **exothermic** reactions.

acid + alkali → salt + water + energy

e.g. hydrochloric acid + sodium hydroxide → sodium chloride + water + energy

Many chemical reactions are exothermic like this – particularly reactions that start reacting as soon as the reactants are mixed. For example, metals reacting with acids:

metal + acid → salt + hydrogen + energy

e.g. magnesium + sulphuric acid → magnesium sulphate + hydrogen + energy

**b Name two other metals that would react in this way.**

## Combustion reactions

The combustion reaction of a fuel such as methane is also very exothermic. In fact, for fuels, the most important product is energy.

fuel + oxygen → waste gases + energy

e.g. methane + oxygen → carbon dioxide + water + energy

The difference is that fuels need a kick-start of energy before the reaction begins. This is true for most chemical reactions.

**c If fuels did not need a kick-start of energy before they reacted, what problems might this cause?**

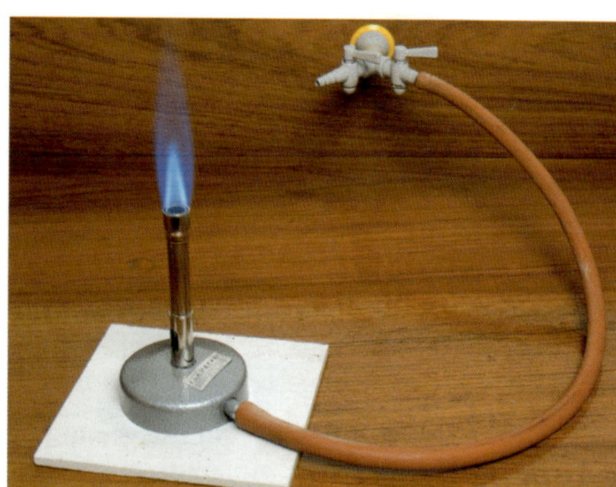

Fuels need a kick-start of energy to burn, but their combustion reactions are strongly exothermic.

## Breaking bonds

The reason that most reactions need a kick-start of energy to get them going is really quite simple. You need to break the existing bonds before new bonds can form. It takes energy to break bonds!

**d Where does the energy needed to break bonds come from, once the exothermic reaction has started?**

## Behind enemy lines

Some soldiers are behind enemy lines on a secret mission. They want hot food.

**e Why can they not light a fire to heat their food?**

Their food is in special packs. Alongside the food is a sachet that contains moist iron filings and salt mixed together, but no air. When the sachet is opened, air enters and the iron filings rust quickly. This reaction is exothermic and produces heat energy that heats the food.

The reaction can be summarised as:

iron + water + oxygen → rust + energy

Salt speeds up the reaction.

**Did you know?**

You can buy cans of coffee that heat themselves! Pressing a button under the can causes water to mix with a solid called soda lime. An exothermic reaction takes place that heats up the coffee.

A hot cup of coffee – wherever and whenever you want!

## Questions

**1** Sparklers are made from iron filings glued to wire. They can be difficult to light but, once alight, burn fiercely to form iron oxide.

**a** Write a word equation for this reaction.

**b** What else is produced during this reaction? (Hint: What type of reaction is this?)

**2** Sam measures some sodium hydroxide solution into an insulated cup with a lid. She measures the temperature of the sodium hydroxide solution. The temperature is 22°C.

She adds some dilute sulphuric acid and measures the temperature again.

**a** Why does she use an insulated cup?

**b** What are the products of the reaction?

**c** Which of the following temperatures is Sam most likely to measure after adding the acid?

15°C 18°C 22°C 27°C

Explain your choice.

### Key ideas

- *Temperature changes often accompany chemical reactions.*
- *Exothermic reactions give out thermal (heat) energy to the surroundings.*
- *A rise in temperature shows an exothermic reaction.*
- *Even exothermic reactions need an initial input of energy to break bonds and get the reaction started.*

# 10:7 Energy taken in

## Getting cooler

You can make a cool fizzy summer drink by adding a spoonful of baking soda to a glass of lemon juice. When you do this a chemical reaction occurs:

| | | | | | | | | |
|---|---|---|---|---|---|---|---|---|
| sodium hydrogencarbonate (baking soda) | + | citric acid (lemon juice) | → | sodium citrate | + | carbon dioxide | + | water |

**a What would you see happening that would suggest that a chemical reaction was occurring?**

If you were holding the glass as you stirred in the baking soda, you would also feel a change in temperature.

A temperature change is another indication that a chemical reaction is happening. But in this case, the temperature goes down.

**b You put a thermometer into the lemon juice. What would you notice when you added the baking soda?**

No ice needed for this summer drink!

## Take it in

Reactions that take energy in from their surroundings are called **endothermic** reactions. It is fairly rare for endothermic reactions to 'go on their own' like this. You usually need to pump energy into them to make them work.

The production of hydrogen and oxygen by the electrolysis of water is an endothermic reaction. You need to supply electrical energy to make the reaction happen (to 'kick-start' it).

water (hydrogen oxide) + electrical energy → hydrogen + oxygen

**c The hydrogen and oxygen ions are held together by strong bonds in water. What is the electrical energy doing in this reaction?**

Another similar process is involved in the extraction of aluminium.

aluminium oxide + electrical energy → aluminium + oxygen

You need to break bonds to electrolyse water into hydrogen and oxygen, so this reaction is endothermic.

### Did you know?

Scientists believed at one time that all reactions were exothermic. They believed that endothermic reactions could not take place. They thought this because they could not find examples of endothermic reactions. What a surprise when they found some!

## Energy changes in reversible reactions

You already know the word equation for respiration.

glucose + oxygen → carbon dioxide + water + energy

**d What does the word 'energy' on the right-hand side tell you about the reaction?**

The reverse reaction to this is found in photosynthesis.

carbon dioxide + water + energy → glucose + oxygen

**e What is the source of energy for this reaction?**

**f Is this reverse reaction exothermic or endothermic?**

Both exothermic and endothermic reactions take place in green plants.

Blue copper sulphate crystals turn white when they are heated. White anhydrous copper sulphate and water are produced.

The equation can be written as:

copper sulphate crystals + energy → anhydrous copper sulphate + water

**g Is this reaction exothermic or endothermic?**

**h Write down the word equation for the reverse reaction.**

**i Is this reverse reaction exothermic or endothermic?**

## Questions

1 Some dilute hydrochloric acid is added to a test tube.

The bulb of a thermometer is placed in the acid and the temperature reads 22.0°C.

Some sodium carbonate crystals are quickly added to the acid. The temperature on the thermometer is 19.5°C.

a What is the temperature change?

b Is the reaction exothermic or endothermic? Explain your answer.

2 In the Haber process the forward reaction is:

nitrogen + hydrogen → ammonia + energy

a Is the forward reaction exothermic or endothermic?

b Write down the word equation for the reverse reaction.

c Is this reverse reaction exothermic or endothermic?

3 The rusting of iron is an exothermic reaction. The metal is converted into a metal oxide. What does this suggest about the extraction of iron from iron oxide?

### Key ideas

- *Endothermic reactions take in more energy than they give out.*
- *You can recognise an endothermic reaction as it produces cooling.*
- *Electrolysis of water and photosynthesis are endothermic reactions.*

# 10:8 Chemical formulae

## Writing the formulae of chemical compounds

You will be used to seeing chemicals represented by **symbols** and **formulae**. It is important to write symbols and formulae correctly.

Remember, you can find the correct symbols for all the elements in the periodic table (see page 177).

Each symbol is either a single capital letter (e.g. C or H) or a pair of letters with the first letter a capital (e.g. Mg or Ca).

**a A student writes the symbol for an element as CO. Why is this confusing?**

Some elements have symbols you will never guess. You either have to know them or be able to look them up in the periodic table. The element iron, for example, has a symbol Fe. This is based on its Latin name *Ferrum*.

**b Which elements are represented by the following symbols? Look them up if you need to.**

| | | | |
|---|---|---|---|
| i | Na | v | Hg |
| ii | K | vi | Ag |
| iii | Pb | vii | Au |
| iv | Sn | viii | Sb |

You can write correct formulae using the list of ions in the table.

You can find the formula of a compound by ensuring that the numbers of positive and negative charges are the same.

**Example**
Sodium chloride is $Na^+Cl^-$.

The number of positive charges = the number of negative charges.

So the formula can be written as NaCl.
(Note: the charges are now missed out.)

| Positive ions | |
|---|---|
| $Na^+$ | sodium |
| $K^+$ | potassium |
| $Ag^+$ | silver |
| $NH_4^+$ | ammonium |
| $Ca^{2+}$ | calcium |
| $Mg^{2+}$ | magnesium |
| $Zn^{2+}$ | zinc |
| $Cu^{2+}$ | copper(II)* |
| $Fe^{2+}$ | iron(II)* |
| $Pb^{2+}$ | lead |
| $Al^{3+}$ | aluminium |
| $Fe^{3+}$ | iron(III)* |
| **Negative ions** | |
| $Cl^-$ | chloride |
| $Br^-$ | bromide |
| $I^-$ | iodide |
| $OH^-$ | hydroxide |
| $NO_3^-$ | nitrate |
| $HCO_3^-$ | hydrogencarbonate |
| $O^{2-}$ | oxide |
| $CO_3^{2-}$ | carbonate |
| $SO_4^{2-}$ | sulphate |

*Note: A number in roman numerals tells us the charge of the ions. For example, copper(II) is $Cu^{2+}$.

**Sodium sulphate, $Na^+SO_4^{2-}$**
The number of positive charges = half the number of negative charges.

To get equal numbers of positive and negative charges you need to have 2 $Na^+$. The formula has to be written as $Na_2SO_4$.

This formula tells us that there are 2 sodium ions to every sulphate ion. The ratio is 2:1.

**Aluminium sulphate, $Al^{3+}SO_4^{2-}$**
To get equal numbers of positive and negative charges, you need 2 aluminium ions and 3 sulphate ions. This will give 6 positive charges and 6 negative charges.

The formula is written as $Al_2(SO_4)_3$. The brackets show that there are 3 sulphates. The number 3 after the bracket refers to everything in the bracket.

**c** How many atoms of aluminium, sulphur and oxygen are there in the formula $Al_2(SO_4)_3$?

**d** What is the total number of atoms in the formula $Al_2(SO_4)_3$?

**e** Write the formulae of magnesium oxide, copper(II) oxide and potassium nitrate.

**f** Write down the formulae of potassium carbonate, iron(II) sulphate and iron(III) oxide.

**Did you know?**

Elements always combine in the same simple proportions. This was discovered by the English chemist John Dalton about 200 years ago. However, he did not know the combining ratios of different elements. He did not realise that water was $H_2O$ and not HO.

## Writing the formulae for other substances

The table shows some simple formulae you need to remember.

| | |
|---|---|
| $H_2$ | hydrogen |
| $O_2$ | oxygen |
| $Cl_2$ | chlorine |
| $N_2$ | nitrogen |
| $H_2O$ | water |
| $CO_2$ | carbon dioxide |
| $H_2SO_4$ | sulphuric acid |
| HCl | hydrogen chloride or hydrochloric acid |
| $HNO_3$ | nitric acid |

John Dalton.

## Questions

**1** Copy and complete the table.

| | $Cl^-$ | $O^{2-}$ | $OH^-$ | $NO_3^-$ | $SO_4^{2-}$ | $CO_3^{2-}$ |
|---|---|---|---|---|---|---|
| $Na^+$ | NaCl | | | | | |
| $Ca^{2+}$ | | | | | | |
| $Al^{3+}$ | | | | | | |

**2** Look carefully at the list of formulae. Some are correct and some are incorrect.

KCl KO $KNO_3$ KCl $KCO_3$

AgO AgCl $AgNO_3$ $PbCO_3$ $PbNO_3$ AlOH

Pick out the incorrect formulae and write them down correctly.

**3** Ammonium sulphate has the formula $(NH_4)_2SO_4$.

**a** Write down the names of the three elements in ammonium sulphate.

**b** Write down the numbers of each type of atom in the formula.

**Key ideas**

- *Elements and simple compounds can be represented by symbols and formulae.*

# 10:9 Chemical equations

## Writing chemical equations

Throughout your science course you will have become familiar with chemical reactions being represented by equations.

Even if you look at chemistry books from other parts of the world, you will still be able to recognise chemical equations. They look like ours!

These textbooks are written in Chinese and Slovenian, but the chemical symbols are the same in any language.

**Example**

**Step 1**
The first stage in writing chemical equations is to write a **word equation**. A word equation summarises a chemical reaction.

For example, sodium sulphate is formed when sodium hydroxide and sulphuric acid react. Water is also produced.

The word equation is:

sodium hydroxide + sulphuric acid → sodium sulphate + water

- The substances to the left of the arrow react together. They are called **reactants**.
- The substances to the right of the arrow are called the **products**.

**Step 2**
You then write the formulae of the reactants and products. This is called a symbol equation.

$$NaOH + H_2SO_4 \rightarrow Na_2SO_4 + H_2O$$

**Step 3**
Now you have to **balance** the equation.

This means there must be the same number of each type of atom on each side of the equation.

You must not change any of the formulae.

$$2NaOH + H_2SO_4 \rightarrow Na_2SO_4 + 2H_2O$$

On each side of the equation there are 2 sodium atoms, 4 hydrogen atoms, 1 sulphur atom and 6 oxygen atoms.

The equation is balanced.

**a** Write the symbol equation for the reaction of sodium hydroxide (NaOH) and hydrochloric acid (HCl) .

**b** Balance this equation:

$$H_2 + O_2 \rightarrow H_2O$$

**Another example**

The reaction of magnesium with hydrochloric acid produces magnesium chloride solution and hydrogen gas.

The word equation is:

magnesium + hydrochloric acid → magnesium chloride + hydrogen

Put in the formulae:

$Mg + HCl \rightarrow MgCl_2 + H_2$

Now balance the equation:

$Mg + 2HCl \rightarrow MgCl_2 + H_2$

Magnesium reacting with hydrochloric acid.

**c Write the symbol equation for the reaction of magnesium and dilute nitric acid.**

## Using state symbols

Sometimes symbols are used in equations to show the state of reactants and products.

These **state symbols** are:

(s) solid
(l) liquid
(g) gas
(aq) aqueous solution – water is the solvent.

So the equation of sodium hydroxide and sulphuric acid can be written as:

$2NaOH(aq) + H_2SO_4(aq) \rightarrow Na_2SO_4(aq) + 2H_2O(l)$

**d What would you see when this reaction takes place?**

$AgNO_3(aq) + HCl(aq) \rightarrow AgCl(s) + HNO_3(aq)$

**e Put state symbols into the equation for the reaction of magnesium and hydrochloric acid.**

## Questions

**1 a** Carbon can burn in oxygen to form carbon dioxide. Write a balanced symbol equation for this reaction. Include state symbols.

**b** Carbon can burn in oxygen to form carbon monoxide, CO. Write a balanced symbol equation for this reaction. Include state symbols.

**c** How do these equations show that less oxygen is needed to produce carbon monoxide?

**2** Calcium carbonate decomposes on heating to produce solid calcium oxide and carbon dioxide. Write a balanced symbol equation for this reaction. Include state symbols.

**3** Magnesium burns in oxygen ($O_2$) to form magnesium oxide (MgO). Write word and symbol equations.

### Key ideas

- *Chemical equations can be used to summarise chemical reactions.*
- *The same symbol equations are used throughout the world.*
- *State symbols are used to show the states of reactants and products.*

# 10:10 Using chemical formulae

## Common symbol equations

Throughout the course you will have met some reactions. You will have seen word equations.

Here are some of the common symbol equations.

**Remember**

A number in roman numerals tells you the charge of the ion. For example, copper(II) is $Cu^{2+}$.

sodium + chlorine → sodium chloride
$2Na(s) + Cl_2(g) \rightarrow 2NaCl(s)$

chlorine + sodium bromide → bromine + sodium chloride
$Cl_2(g) + 2NaBr(aq) \rightarrow Br_2(g) + 2NaCl(aq)$

magnesium + sulphuric acid → magnesium sulphate + hydrogen
$Mg(s) + H_2SO_4(aq) \rightarrow MgSO_4(aq) + H_2(g)$

calcium carbonate + hydrochloric acid → calcium chloride + carbon dioxide + water
$CaCO_3(s) + 2HCl(aq) \rightarrow CaCl_2(aq) + CO_2(g) + H_2O(l)$

sodium thiosulphate + hydrochloric acid → sodium chloride + sulphur dioxide + sulphur + water
$Na_2S_2O_3(aq) + 2HCl(aq) \rightarrow 2NaCl(aq) + SO_2(g) + S(s) + H_2O(l)$

hydrogen peroxide → water + oxygen
$2H_2O_2(aq) \rightarrow 2H_2O(l) + O_2(g)$

methane + oxygen → carbon dioxide + water
$CH_4(g) + 2O_2(g) \rightarrow CO_2(g) + 2H_2O(l)$

calcium hydroxide + carbon dioxide → calcium carbonate + water
$Ca(OH)_2(aq) + CO_2(g) \rightarrow CaCO_3(s) + H_2O(l)$

calcium carbonate → calcium oxide + carbon dioxide
$CaCO_3(s) \rightarrow CaO(s) + CO_2(g)$

calcium oxide + water → calcium hydroxide
$CaO(s) + H_2O(l) \rightarrow Ca(OH)_2(s)$

copper(II) oxide + hydrogen → copper + water
$CuO(s) + H_2(g) \rightarrow Cu(s) + H_2O(l)$

iron + copper(II) sulphate → iron(II) sulphate + copper
$Fe(s) + CuSO_4(aq) \rightarrow FeSO_4(aq) + Cu(s)$

carbon + oxygen → carbon dioxide
$C(s) + O_2(g) \rightarrow CO_2(g)$

carbon dioxide + carbon → carbon monoxide
$CO_2(g) + C(s) \rightarrow 2CO(g)$

carbon monoxide + iron(III) oxide → carbon dioxide + iron
$3CO(g) + Fe_2O_3(s) \rightarrow 3CO_2(g) + 2Fe(l)$

calcium carbonate → calcium oxide + carbon dioxide
$CaCO_3(s) \rightarrow CaO(s) + CO_2(g)$

calcium oxide + silicon dioxide → calcium silicate
$CaO(s) + SiO_2(s) \rightarrow CaSiO_3(l)$

lithium + oxygen → lithium oxide
$4Li(s) + O_2(g) \rightarrow 2Li_2O(s)$

sodium + water → sodium hydroxide + hydrogen
$2Na(s) + 2H_2O(l) \rightarrow 2NaOH(aq) + H_2(g)$

nitrogen + hydrogen ⇌ ammonia
$N_2(g) + 3H_2(g) \rightleftharpoons 2NH_3(g)$

hydrochloric acid + sodium hydroxide → sodium chloride + water
$HCl(aq) + NaOH(aq) \rightarrow NaCl(aq) + H_2O(l)$

hydrogen + oxygen → water
$2H_2(g) + O_2(g) \rightarrow 2H_2O(l)$

## Working out relative formula masses

You will know that the relative atomic mass of an element is the number of times an atom of the element is heavier than an atom of hydrogen (or $\frac{1}{12}$ the mass of a carbon-12 atom).

For example, magnesium has a relative atomic mass of 24. This means a magnesium atom is 24 times heavier than a hydrogen atom.

You can find the relative atomic masses in the periodic table (page 177). To help you on these pages, the common ones are shown in the margin.

You can work out the relative atomic masses of compounds by adding together relative atomic masses of the elements.

**Relative atomic masses**

| | |
|---|---|
| H = 1 | S = 32 |
| C = 12 | K = 39 |
| N = 14 | Ca = 40 |
| O = 16 | Fe = 56 |
| Mg = 24 | Cu = 64 |
| Al = 27 | Pb = 207 |

**Examples**

**Magnesium oxide, MgO**

The relative formula mass of magnesium oxide is 24 + 16 = 40.

**Sulphuric acid, $H_2SO_4$**

The relative formula mass of sulphuric acid
$= (2 \times 1) + 32 + (4 \times 16) = 98$.

**Calcium hydroxide, $Ca(OH)_2$**

The relative formula mass of calcium hydroxide
$= 40 + 2(16 + 1) = 74$.

## Questions

**1** Calculate the relative formula masses of the following:

**a** ammonia, $NH_3$;

**b** copper(II) oxide, CuO;

**c** potassium hydrogencarbonate, $KHCO_3$;

**d** sulphur dioxide, $SO_2$;

**e** iron(III) oxide, $Fe_2O_3$.

### Key ideas

- *The relative formula masses of simple compounds can be calculated by addition of relative atomic masses.*

# End of module questions

## Low demand

1. In a chlorine molecule two chlorine atoms are joined by
   - **A** a chemical bond
   - **B** electrostatic forces
   - **C** magnetic forces
   - **D** gravitational forces

2. Which of the following is an ion?
   - **A** $SO_2$
   - **B** $SO_3$
   - **C** $SO_4^{2-}$
   - **D** S

3. Sodium chloride contains
   - **A** sodium and chloride ions
   - **B** sodium and chlorine ions
   - **C** sodium chloride molecules
   - **D** sodium and chlorine atoms

4. What could you use to recognise an exothermic reaction?
   - **A** chemical balance
   - **B** measuring cylinder
   - **C** stopclock
   - **D** thermometer

5. Which of the following is a single compound?
   - **A** air
   - **B** hydrogen
   - **C** oxygen
   - **D** water

6. Atoms that join together are said to
   - **A** boil
   - **B** bond
   - **C** dissolve
   - **D** melt

7. When elements combine they form a
   - **A** compound
   - **B** mixture
   - **C** new element
   - **D** solution

8. Hydrogen is made up of molecules. It
   - **A** conducts electricity when solid
   - **B** conducts electricity when molten
   - **C** has a high melting point
   - **D** has a low boiling point

9. Which of the following is an element with covalent bonding?
   - **A** chlorine
   - **B** sodium
   - **C** sodium chloride
   - **D** water

10. Which of the following has a negative charge?
    - **A** atom
    - **B** electron
    - **C** neutron
    - **D** proton

11. A chemical reaction occurs in a car when the driver
    - **A** changes gear
    - **B** opens the driver's door
    - **C** starts the engine
    - **D** fills the car with petrol

12. Which of the following is a compound of two elements?
    - **A** carbon
    - **B** carbon dioxide
    - **C** calcium carbonate
    - **D** copper sulphate

## Standard demand

**13** Isotopes of the same element contain the same number of

**A** neutrons

**B** protons and neutrons

**C** protons and electrons

**D** electrons and neutrons

**14** The diagram shows a sodium chloride lattice.

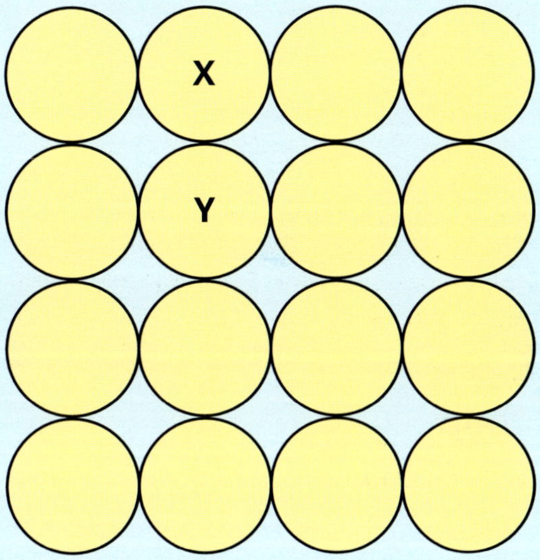


X and Y are

**A** atoms

**B** ions with the same charge

**C** ions with opposite charges

**D** molecules

**15** Hydrogen and oxygen combine to form water.

The correct symbol equation is

**A** $2H + O \rightarrow H_2O$

**B** $H_2 + O \rightarrow H_2O$

**C** $2H_2 + O_2 \rightarrow 2H_2O$

**D** $H_2 + O_2 \rightarrow H_2O$

**16** Calcium fluoride, $CaF_2$, contains ionic bonding.

The lattice contains

**A** equal numbers of calcium and fluoride ions

**B** calcium fluoride molecules

**C** twice as many calcium ions as fluoride ions

**D** twice as many fluoride ions as calcium ions

**17** Water is a compound of hydrogen and oxygen. Each molecule contains one oxygen atom bonded to two hydrogen atoms.

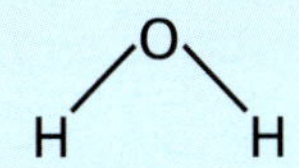


How many electrons are shared in covalent bonds in a molecule of water?

**A** 1

**B** 2

**C** 3

**D** 4

**18** Magnesium burns in nitrogen to form a compound called magnesium nitride.

The formula of magnesium nitride is

**A** $Mg(NO_3)_2$

**B** $Mg_3N_2$

**C** MnN

**D** $Mn(NO_3)_2$

**19** The reaction between sodium carbonate crystals and dilute hydrochloric acid is endothermic. The temperature of the acid before sodium carbonate crystals were added was 20°C.

Which temperature could be the temperature of the mixture after the reaction?

**A** 18°C

**B** 20°C

**C** 22°C

**D** 24°C

**20** In any exothermic reaction

**A** a black solid is formed

**B** a gas is produced

**C** energy is taken in

**D** energy is given out

**21** Which of the following contains covalent bonding?

**A** magnesium metal

**B** magnesium oxide

**C** oxygen gas

**D** magnesium chloride

**22** An aluminum atom has a mass number of 27 and an atomic number of 13.

Which row of the table contains the correct number of protons, neutrons and electrons in an aluminum atom?

| | Number of protons | Number of neutrons | Number of electrons |
|---|---|---|---|
| A | 13 | 13 | 14 |
| B | 14 | 13 | 14 |
| C | 14 | 14 | 13 |
| D | 13 | 14 | 13 |

**23** When an ionic bond is formed

**A** a metal atom loses one or more electrons

**B** a metal atom gains one or more electrons.

**C** a metal atom shares electrons.

**D** a non metal atom loses electrons.

**24** Isotopes of the same element

**A** contain the same number of protons

**B** same number of nucleons (protons + neutrons)

**C** have the same relative mass.

**D** have the same boiling point.

# Module 11 – Movement and change

For thousands of years, people have looked up at the night sky and watched the movement of the stars and planets. Physicists and astronomers such as Galileo, Newton and Einstein discovered how, by understanding forces, you can make sense of what you see in space, as well as how things move here on Earth. They showed that the same ideas about forces and motion work for giant stars and for the movement of everyday objects such as falling stones and moving cars.

In this module, you will find out about how forces affect movement. All movement requires energy, and you will learn how kinetic energy and potential energy are related to work.

Some forces are unpredictable, such as those that cause earthquakes and volcanoes. You will discover how these are caused by changes in the structure of the outermost layer of the Earth. In the final topic, you will learn about how measurements of radioactive decay are used to measure the age of some rocks and archaeological specimens.

Before you start this module, check that you can answer these questions about movement and forces.

1 What two measurements are needed to work out the speed of a moving object?
2 What type of force pulls objects towards the centre of the Earth, frictional, magnetic or gravitational?
3 When an object changes its speed, are the forces on it balanced or unbalanced?
4 What type of force opposes the motion of a child on a playground slide?
5 Are gravitational forces attractive, repulsive, or can they be either?

# 11:1 Distance–time graphs

Forces affect the way things move. You cannot see forces, but you can see how they change an object's speed.

This race doesn't seem very fair. Everyone has to travel the same distance, but the racing driver will get to the finishing line first.

The table shows how long each competitor took to travel 1000 m.

| Competitor | Time taken (s) |
|---|---|
| runner | 200 |
| cyclist | 100 |
| racing driver | 25 |

**a Work out the cyclist's average speed. (Remember, speed = distance travelled ÷ time taken.)**

## Plotting graphs

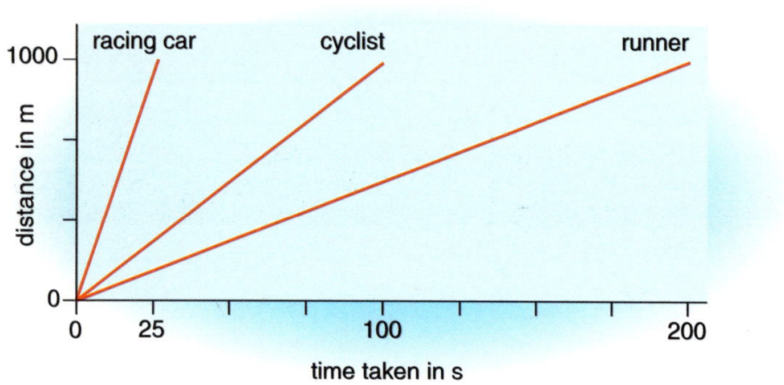


We can use the information in the table to draw a graph that shows how the competitors moved during the race. This is a **distance–time graph**.

**b Look at the graph. What quantity is shown on the horizontal axis? What quantity is shown on the vertical axis?**

A graph like this allows us to compare the speeds of moving objects.

- The graph for the racing driver is steepest, because his speed is greatest.
- The runner is slowest, so the slope of his graph is the least.
- The cyclist's speed is in between, so the slope of her graph is between the other two.

**Did you know?**

The first person to run a mile in less than four minutes was Roger Bannister.

He did it at Oxford in 1954.

## Speed from slope

The steeper the **slope** of a distance–time graph, the greater the object's speed. You can use the slope, or **gradient**, of a graph to calculate the speed of an object.

The graph shows part of a bus journey. You can see that it is in three sections, each one representing a different speed.

To calculate the speed on the last section:

- use the vertical scale to work out the distance travelled on this section;
- use the horizontal scale to work out the time for this section of the journey;
- divide the distance by the time: this is equivalent to working out the slope of the graph.

**c Use the graph to work out the speed of the bus on the first section of its journey.**

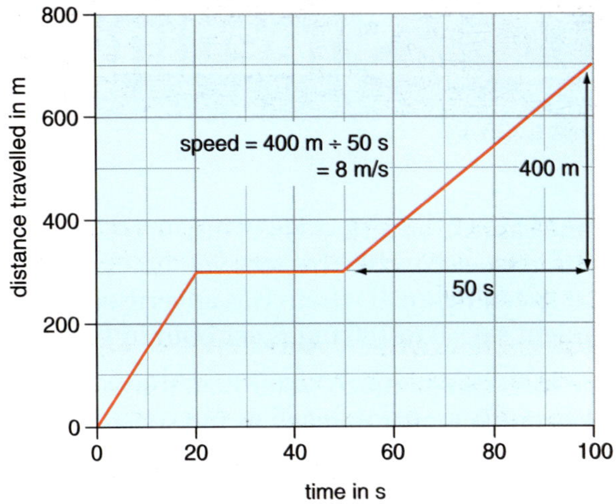


## Speed and velocity

Often you simply say how fast something is moving – its **speed**. Sometimes it is important to know the direction in which an object is moving. If you give speed and direction, this is its **velocity** – for example, 'The ball rolled towards the goal at 5 m/s.'

**d Who is stating the car's velocity, the driver or the police officer?**

## Questions

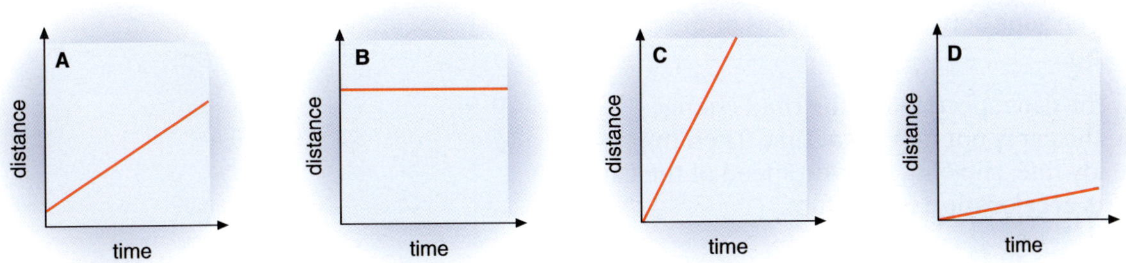


**1** **The graphs represent the motion of four different objects. Which graph is for:**

**a** **a stationary object;**

**b** **the fastest of the four?**

**2** **The table shows how far a train has travelled along its route during part of its journey.**

| | | | | | |
|---|---|---|---|---|---|
| **Distance travelled (m)** | 0 | 80 | 160 | 240 | 320 |
| **Time taken (s)** | 0 | 2 | 4 | 6 | 8 |

**a** **Draw a distance–time graph to show this data.**

**b** **Was the train running at a steady speed? How can you tell?**

**c** **Use the figures in the last column of the table to work out the train's speed.**

**3** **What *two* things must you know to describe a velocity?**

### Key ideas

- *A distance–time graph shows you how an object is moving.*
- *The steeper the graph, the greater the object's speed.*
- *Velocity means speed in a stated direction.*

# 11:2 Speeding up

Some cars are advertised like this: '0 to 60 miles per hour in 8.0 seconds!' This tells you how good the car is at speeding up. If a train was advertised like this, it might say: '0 to 180 miles per hour in 10 minutes!'

The train can go much faster than the car, but it takes much longer to reach its top speed. *Speeding up* is called *accelerating*. If the train accelerated like the car, passengers who were standing would be in danger of falling over as it set off.

People accelerate too. At the beginning of a race, an athlete accelerates away from the starting line.

**a When does a bus accelerate?**

## An accelerating car

The car in the picture is setting off. The picture shows its position each second. The gaps between the images of the car get longer as it speeds up.

The graph shows how the car's speed along the road changes. It starts at zero, because the car is not moving at first. Then the graph goes up at a steady rate, showing that the speed of the car is increasing steadily. Its **acceleration** is constant.

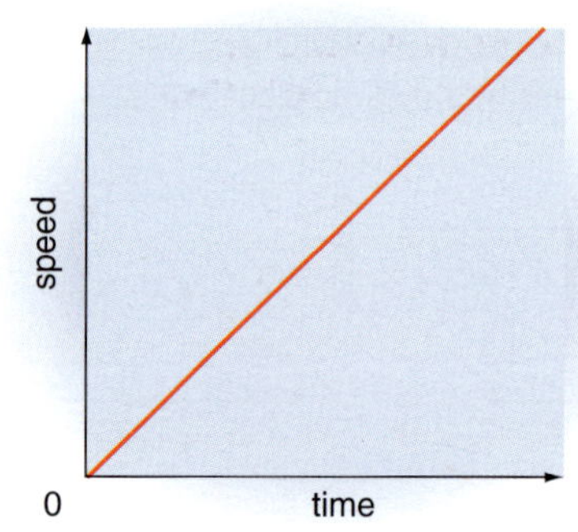


**b How would the pictures of the car look if the car was moving at a steady speed?**

## Speed–time graphs

Here is a **speed–time graph**. It shows you how the speed of a train changes as it leaves a station. Take care not to confuse this with a distance–time graph. Always check the labels on the axes.

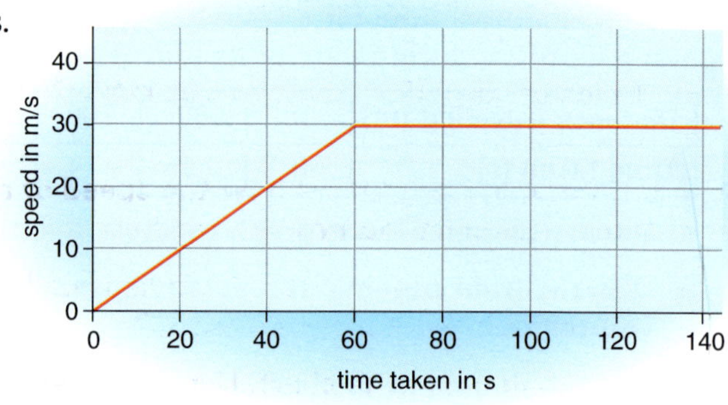


On a speed–time graph:

- the vertical axis represents speed and the horizontal axis represents time;
- the graph line can go down (showing a decrease in speed) as well as up (showing an increase in speed).

**c On a speed–time graph:**

**i Which axis is the same as that on a distance–time graph?**

**ii Which axis is different?**

The graph for the train is in two parts.

At first, it speeds up at a steady rate. It has constant acceleration. The graph is a straight line, sloping upwards. The steeper the slope, the greater the acceleration.

When it has reached its top speed, the train no longer accelerates. It moves at a constant speed. The graph is a horizontal straight line.

**d From the graph, find the speed of the train after 20 s. What is its greatest speed?**

**Did you know?**
In France some trains can run at speeds of over 300 mph.

## Spy in the cab

A lorry driver does a lot of driving each day. The lorry speeds up and slows down. Its speed is recorded by an instrument called a tachograph.

The tachograph makes a graph to show the lorry's speed. The line on the graph goes up and down as the lorry's speed changes.

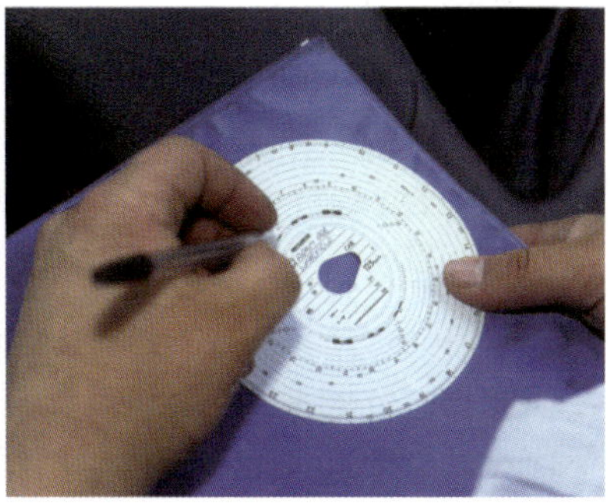

## Questions

**1** Give a single word that means the same as 'speeding up'.

**2** Here are four speed–time graphs.

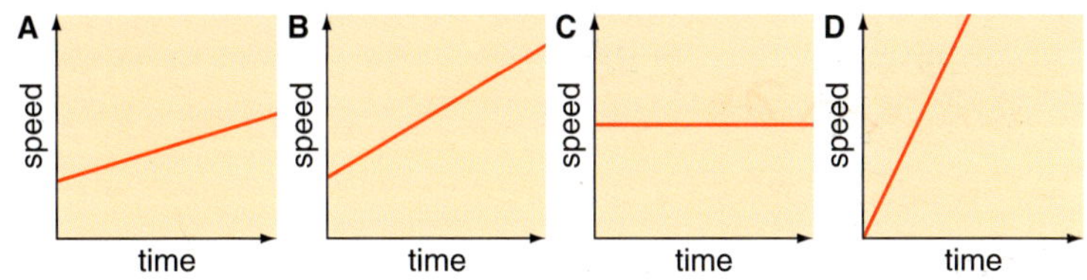


**a** Which graph represents a car travelling at constant speed?

**b** Which graph shows the greatest acceleration?

**3** The graph shows how the speed of two different cars changes with time.

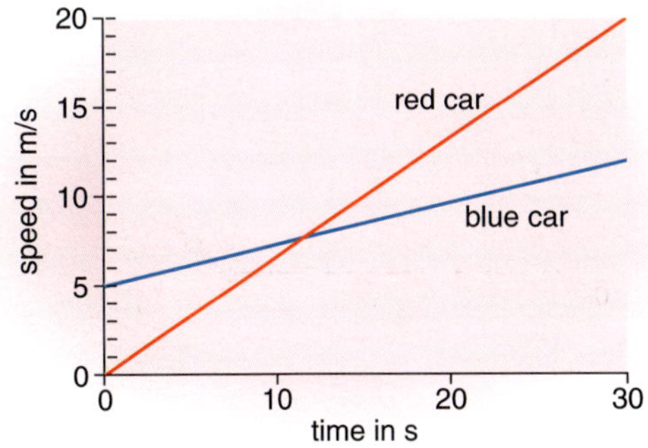


**a** Which car was not moving at the start of the graph?

**b** What was the speed of the other car at the start of the graph?

**c** Which car had the greater acceleration? How can you tell?

**4** A tachograph chart shows how the speed of a lorry changes during its journey.

**a** What does the graph look like when the lorry has been travelling at a steady speed?

**b** Police can check the chart. How can they tell if the driver stopped for a rest?

**c** Why do drivers sometimes call it 'the spy in the cab'?

### Key ideas

- *A speed-time graph shows how the speed of a moving object changes.*
- *The steeper the graph, the more rapidly the object's speed is changing – the greater its acceleration.*

# 11:3 Acceleration

Imagine you are at the start of a 100 m sprint race. If you are to win, you want to reach your top speed as quickly as possible. You need to accelerate rapidly. '**Acceleration**' means 'the change in speed each second'.

This can be written as:

Acceleration = change in speed ÷ time taken

Acceleration is measured in $m/s^2$ (metres per second each second). An acceleration of 1 $m/s^2$ means that the speed is changing by 1 m/s every second.

**a If your acceleration is 10 $m/s^2$, how much does your speed change in 1 s?**

Sprinters have to accelerate as much as they can at the start of a race.

**Did you know?**
If you fall out of a tree, you accelerate towards the ground at 10 $m/s^2$. This is known as 'free-fall' acceleration.

## Measuring acceleration

The model car in the photograph is freewheeling downhill. As it moves, it speeds up. It is **accelerating**.

The pupils in the photograph are using two infrared beams and a computer to measure the acceleration of the model car:

- each beam measures the time it takes for the car to travel a certain distance, the computer then works out the speed;
- beam 1 is used to measure the speed near the top of the slope, where the car is travelling slowly;
- beam 2 is used to measure the speed near the foot of the slope, where the car is travelling faster.

The computer then works out the acceleration of the car.

**b If the pupils make the ramp steeper, does the acceleration of the car increase or decrease?**

## Calculating acceleration

The computer needs three pieces of information to work out the acceleration of the car:

- the speed of the car at the top of the slope;
- the speed of the car at the bottom of the slope;
- the time interval between these measurements.

The example shows how it calculates the acceleration.

**Example**

*Step 1* Calculate the change in speed by finding the difference between the two speed measurements.

Increase in speed = 6.0 m/s – 1.0 m/s = 5.0 m/s

*Step 2* Divide by the time taken for this change.

Acceleration = 5.0 m/s ÷ 2.0 s = 2.5 m/s each second or 2.5 $m/s^2$

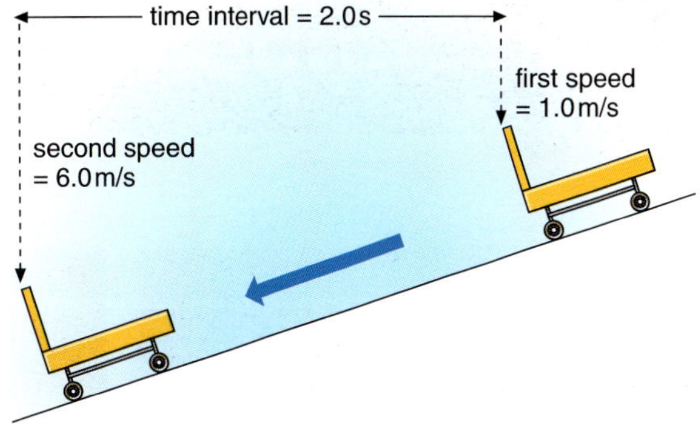


**How quickly is the car's speed changing?**

## Using a speed–time graph

The greater your acceleration, the faster you are speeding up. If your motion is plotted on a **speed–time graph**:

- a horizontal line shows no change in speed, there is no acceleration;
- a line sloping upwards shows an increasing speed, an acceleration;
- the steeper the slope, the greater the acceleration.

**c What does a downwards-sloping line show?**

The graph shows the motion of a racing cyclist. The acceleration is rapid at first, then becomes less and is zero on the third section of the graph.

The graph also shows how to work out the acceleration from the slope or gradient.

**d Calculate the acceleration of the cyclist on the first section of the graph.**

**e How can you tell that the acceleration on the third section of the graph is zero?**

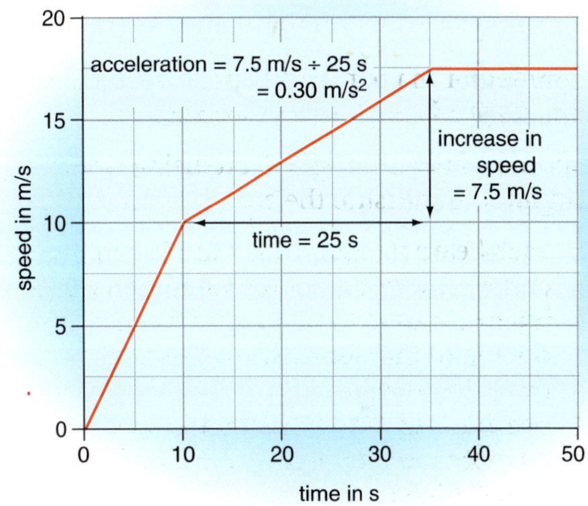


## Questions

**1** Look at the quantities in this list:

| | |
|---|---|
| **distance travelled** | **time taken** |
| **change in speed** | **maximum speed** |

**a** Which *two* of these quantities need to be measured to calculate acceleration?

**b** Write down the equation which shows how to calculate acceleration from these quantities.

**2** A car increases its speed from 0 m/s to 20 m/s in 10 s. What is its acceleration?

**3** The table shows how the speed of a car changes at the start of a journey.

| Speed (m/s) | 0 | 5 | 10 | 20 | 30 | 30 |
|---|---|---|---|---|---|---|
| Time (s) | 0 | 5 | 10 | 15 | 20 | 25 |

**a** Draw a speed–time graph that shows the change in speed of the car.

**b** Calculate the acceleration of the car on each section of the graph.

### Key ideas

- *The acceleration of a moving object is the change in its speed each second.*
  *Acceleration = change in speed ÷ time taken.*
- *Acceleration is measured in $m/s^2$.*
- *The slope or gradient of a speed–time graph represents acceleration.*

# 11:4 Stopping in time

Racing drivers need to be sure that their cars are in good condition before they go out on the track. A single misjudgement can lead to a nasty accident. Fortunately racing cars are designed to withstand strong impacts, so serious casualties are rare.

**a How is the racing car driver protected from injury if there is a collision?**

This driver crashed into the finishing post!

## Avoiding skidding

Stewart is driving along the road. Just in time, he notices the STOP sign ahead. He applies the brakes and comes to a halt at the junction.

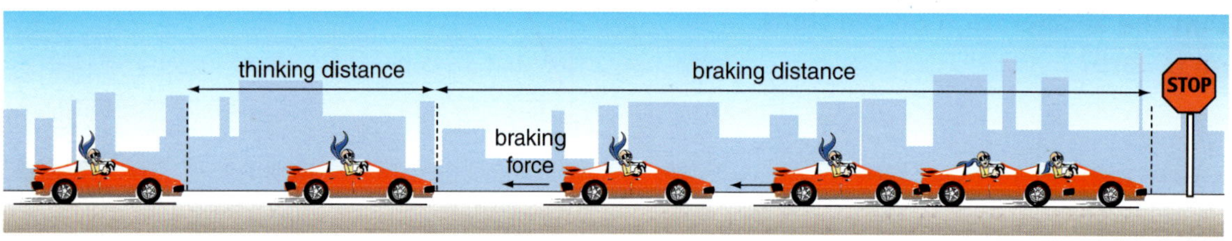


It takes a short time – about two-thirds of a second – for Stewart to react when he sees the sign. This is his **reaction time** (or thinking time). During this time, the car travels a short distance along the road. This is the **thinking distance**.

The brakes provide a backward force to slow the car. The brakes increase the resistance between the tyres and the road. The distance travelled by the car while the brakes are on is called the **braking distance**.

So the **stopping distance** is made up of these two distances:

Stopping distance = thinking distance + braking distance

If Stewart noticed the STOP sign a little later, he would have to press harder on the brakes. Then the friction force might not be great enough to stop the car in time; the car could go into a skid. You may have done this yourself, while riding a bike.

If visibility is poor (because of rain or snow, or because you are on a winding road) it is important to drive more slowly. You get less warning of the need to stop.

**Did you know?**
On modern cars, skidding is prevented by an *anti-lock braking system* (ABS). This senses if a wheel is about to lock and reduces the braking force to stop it from happening.

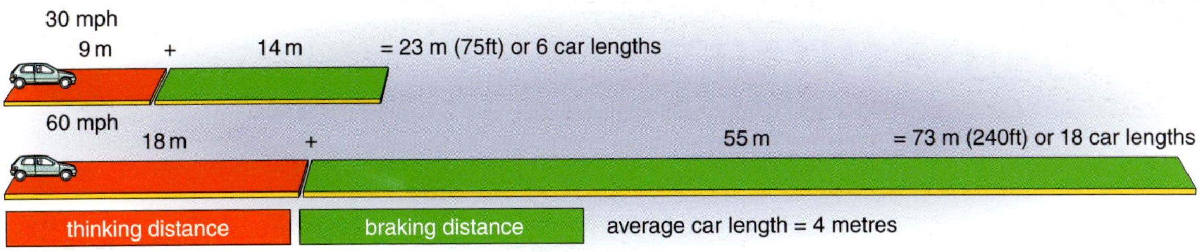


This diagram, from the Highway Code, shows the stopping distances for cars travelling in good conditions at two different speeds.

**b What happens to the thinking distance when the speed of a car is doubled?**

**c How is the pattern different for the braking distance?**

## Dangerous driving

Drivers need to think ahead, to make sure they are ready to stop safely if necessary. Several factors affect how quickly they can stop.

- How fast the car is moving.
  The faster the car is moving, the further it will travel before the force of the brakes can bring it to a halt.
- How quickly the driver can react.
  The driver may be tired, or under the influence of alcohol or drugs. A tired or drugged driver is slow to react, so the thinking distance is greater.
- The state of the road.
- The condition of the car.
  If the road is wet or icy, the driver has to apply the brakes gently, to avoid skidding. A smaller braking force takes longer to stop the car. If the car's brakes or tyres are worn, the braking force will again be reduced.
- The mass of the car.
  A car with a just a driver slows down more quickly than one that is fully loaded.

This man's driving has attracted the attention of the police.

**d Why do smooth tyres give a smaller braking force?**

## Questions

1 What *two* distances add together to make the stopping distance of a car?

2 The *reaction time* is the time it takes between when a driver sees the need to stop and the time when the brakes are applied. How might this be affected if the driver has been drinking alcohol, or is very tired from driving for a long time?

3 Look at the diagram from the Highway Code. It shows stopping distances when road conditions are good.

  a What road conditions might increase the stopping distance of a car?

  b What is the stopping distance for a car travelling at 30 mph?

  c Explain why the thinking distance is twice as much at 60 mph as at 30 mph.

  d A child steps out into the road, 80 m ahead of a car. The car is travelling at 60 mph. Can the driver be sure of stopping in time?

### Key ideas

- *Stopping distance is made up of thinking distance and braking distance.*
- *The stopping distance of a car depends on its speed, the driver's reaction time, the road conditions, and the condition and mass of the car.*

# 11:5 Balanced forces

When you are sitting comfortably in your chair, there are two forces acting on you:

- the Earth is pulling you down, this force is your weight;
- the chair is pushing upwards on you.

These two forces are **balanced**, and you stay on the chair. Without the upward push of the chair, you would fall onto the floor.

Now, if your chair turns out to be an ejector seat, it may give you an extra large upward push. There is an **unbalanced** force on you – more force upwards than downwards. The unbalanced force makes you accelerate upwards.

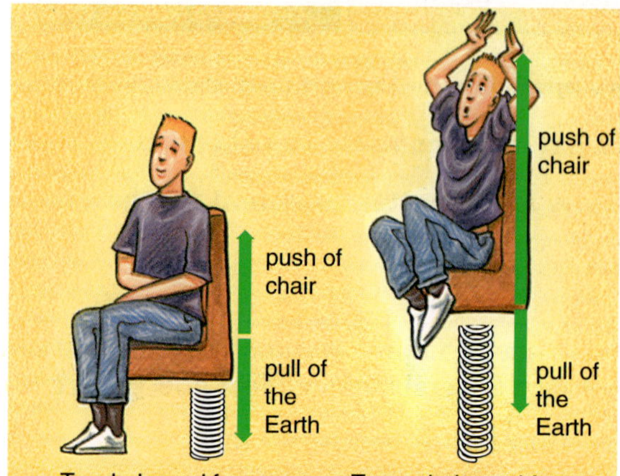

Two balanced forces Two unbalanced forces

**a The drawing shows two balanced forces. What can you say about the sizes of these two forces?**

## Balanced and unbalanced

Forces are represented by arrows. The arrow shows the direction of the force. The size of the force is given in newtons (N).

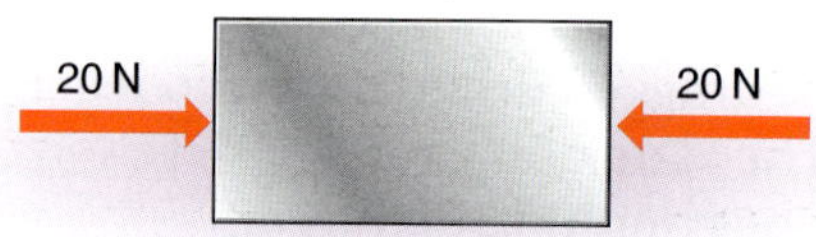

These forces are balanced

These forces are unbalanced. There is an unbalanced force of 10 N to the right

## The effects of balanced forces

If you give this book a short push, it slides along the desk before stopping. To keep it moving, you have to keep pushing it. Before the work of Galileo and Newton, scientists thought that a single force in the forwards direction acted on a moving object.

We now know that, unless the motion is in a vacuum, resistive forces such as friction and air resistance act backwards on a moving object.

To maintain motion at a constant speed, a forwards force is needed to **balance** the resistive forces.

**Did you know?**

Galileo spent the last ten years of his life imprisoned in his own house, by order of the Vatican. It took 350 years for the Vatican to admit that it had made a mistake.

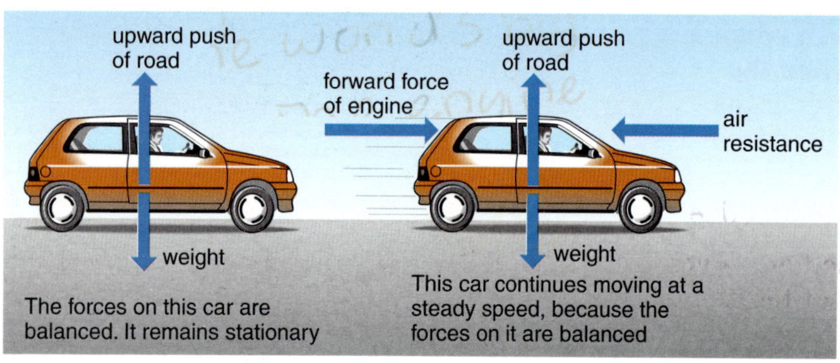

The forces on this car are balanced. It remains stationary

This car continues moving at a steady speed, because the forces on it are balanced

If the forces on an object are balanced, it either:

- does not move

or

- moves at a constant speed in a straight line.

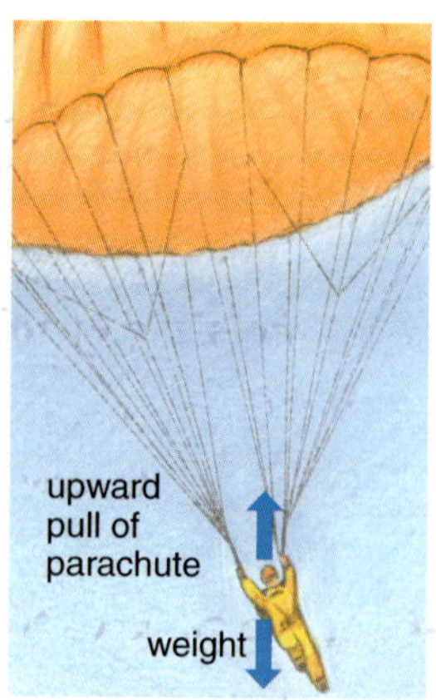


**b The parachutist in the picture is falling at a steady speed. Are the forces acting on her balanced or unbalanced?**

## Push meets shove

This car has crashed into a post. The car exerted a force on the post, and the post exerted a force on the car. The two forces were equal in size but opposite in direction. Unfortunately, the post was stronger than the car, and so the car was more badly damaged than the post.

You can feel the forces two objects exert on each other by holding two magnets close together, so that they repel each other. You can feel one magnet being pushed to the right while the other is pushed to the left. The two forces are equal in size but opposite in direction.

Whenever two objects interact, the forces they exert on each other are equal in size and opposite in direction.

**c If you held the magnets so that they attracted each other, what would you feel? What could you say about the forces they exert on each other?**

## Newton and gravitation

Newton realised that gravitational attractive forces act between all masses. Like other pairs of forces between objects that interact, the forces are equal in size and opposite in direction. So, although the Earth pulls you down, you pull the Earth up with the same size force.

## Questions

**1** For each of the following objects, decide whether the forces on it are balanced or unbalanced.

- **a** a book resting on a shelf
- **b** a car braking to a halt
- **c** a ball that has been thrown upwards
- **d** a cyclist moving at a steady speed in a straight line

**2** The student in the picture is standing on the floor. Two forces act on her: her weight, and the push of the floor.

- **a** Draw a diagram to show these two forces.
- **b** What can you say about the sizes of these forces?
- **c** Are these forces balanced or unbalanced?

**3** When you sit on a chair, you push downwards on the chair, and it pushes up on you.

- **a** What can you say about the sizes of these forces?
- **b** What can you say about their directions?

### Key ideas

- *Balanced forces do not affect an object's motion. If the forces on an object are balanced, it remains stationary, or continues to move at a steady speed in a straight line.*
- *When two bodies interact, the forces they exert on each other are equal in size and opposite in direction.*

# 11:6 Unbalanced forces

This oil tanker has hit the rocks.

**Did you know?**
An oil tanker starts to slow down when it is still several miles from port – its stopping distance is immense.

The world's biggest ships are oil tankers, up to 500 m long. They are very difficult to control.

The engines can provide a force to drive the ship forwards, backwards or sideways. The water exerts a resistive force in the opposite **direction**.

The crew must control these forces carefully. A giant super tanker takes a very long time to slow down, and a small mistake in the timing can result in a disastrous collision.

**a When should a tanker's engines be put into reverse, to provide a backwards push?**

A SeaCat ferry rises out of the water. This reduces the resistive force on it.

## Steady as she goes

The ferry captain can control the ship's speed by changing the force of the engine. To change the ferry's speed, the forces on it must be unbalanced.

For most of its journey, the ferry maintains a steady speed. The engines give a forward push to balance the resistance of the water.

If the captain wants to go faster, the force of the engines must be increased so that it is greater than the resistance of the water.

To go slower, the force of the engines must be reduced. The resistance of the water slows the ferry down.

**b You are rowing a boat across a lake. You stop rowing and quickly come to a halt. What force causes you to stop?**

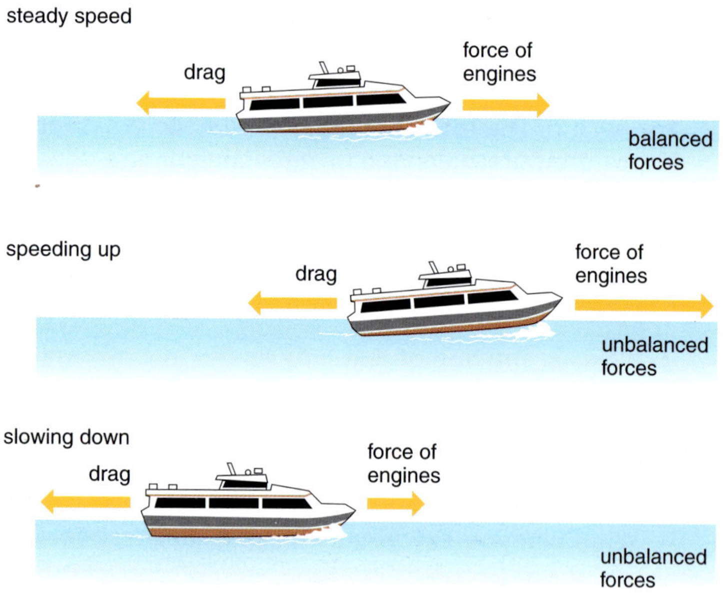

## Changing direction

The forces must be unbalanced to change an object's *speed*. Unbalanced forces may also change the *direction* in which an object is moving.

When a ferry comes into dock, it must change its direction in order to reach its berth. An unbalanced sideways force is needed to make it change direction.

## Masses large and small

A large ferry has a large **mass** – millions of kilograms – so it needs a big unbalanced force to make it accelerate. A speedboat has a much smaller mass. It needs a much smaller unbalanced force to give it the same acceleration. That is why the motor of a speedboat is so much smaller than a ferry's large engines.

The larger an object's mass, the greater the force needed to give it a particular acceleration.

**c Alex has filled the back of his car with sacks of cement. When he drives off, he finds that it takes a long time to get up to speed on the main road. Explain why this is.**

## Questions

**1** Copy the table. In the second column, write whether the forces must be balanced or unbalanced.

| | |
|---|---|
| **Speeding up (accelerating)** | ______________ forces |
| **Steady speed** | ______________ forces |
| **Slowing down** | ______________ forces |
| **Changing direction** | ______________ forces |

**2** This car is travelling fast along the road. The diagram shows the forces on the car. Will the car speed up, slow down or carry on at the same speed? Why?

**3** These two cars are waiting at the traffic lights. When the lights change, they will accelerate away. Which will have the greater acceleration? Explain your answer

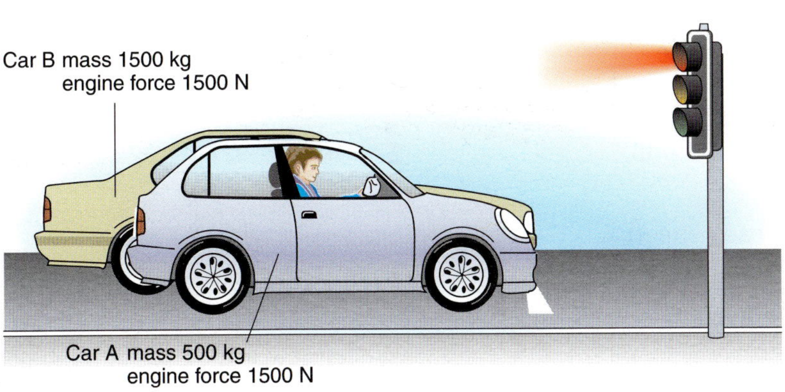


### Key ideas

- *An unbalanced force affects an object's motion.*
- *It may start the object moving, speed it up, or slow it down.*
- *The greater the unbalanced force, the greater the acceleration it produces.*
- *Increasing the mass of an object decreases its acceleration.*

# 11:7 Moving through the air

When the space shuttle comes in to land, it is travelling very fast. Because it is moving so fast, there is a lot of **air resistance**, which helps to slow it down. The outside of the shuttle gets very hot. It is covered with special heat-resistant tiles to prevent the astronauts inside from being cooked.

**Did you know?**

The space shuttle Challenger exploded shortly after take-off in 1986.

The explosion was caused by burning fuel leaking through a fuel tank seal that did not work properly in cold weather.

## Movement through fluids

The picture shows how you can see the effect of air resistance on a moving object. Drop a ball and a crumpled piece of paper. The ball reaches the ground first. The paper is affected more than the ball by the force of air resistance.

- The Earth pulls the ball and the paper downwards.
- Air resistance acts in the opposite direction to motion.

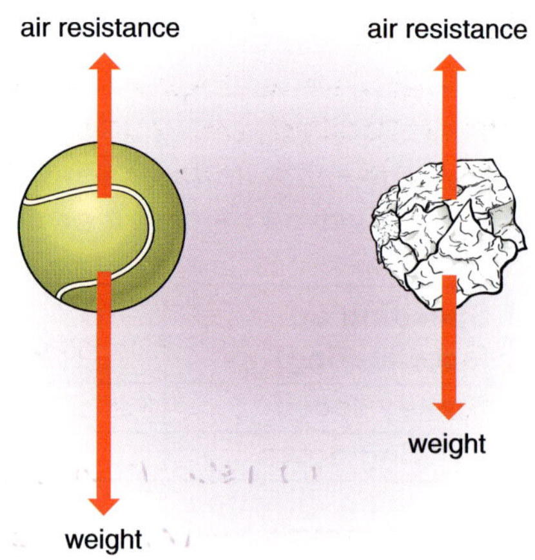


Resistive forces act on any object moving through a gas (such as the air) or a liquid (such as water). Gases and liquids are known as **fluids**, because they can flow. The faster the object moves, the greater the resistive force.

**a Look at the diagram which shows the forces on the ball and the paper as they fall. Explain why the paper falls at a steady speed. Why does the ball accelerate?**

## Falling step by step

How do the forces change as the paper falls?

- At first the only force is the Earth's pull. This makes the paper accelerate.
- Air resistance increases as the paper moves faster.
- When the air resistance is equal in size to the Earth's pull, the forces are balanced.

The paper falls the rest of the way to the floor at a steady speed, known as **terminal velocity**.

**b How can you tell from the picture when the paper reaches its terminal velocity?**

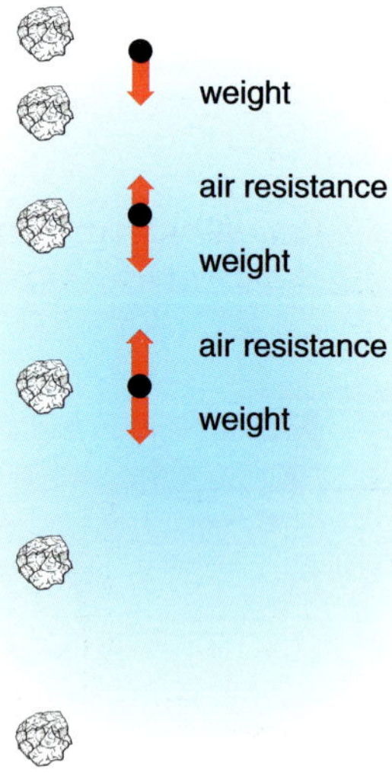

## Skydiving

- After the skydiver jumps out of the aircraft, the forces on her change in the same way as they do on the crumpled paper. She reaches a terminal velocity of about 120 mph.
- It is not a good idea to hit the ground at this speed, so she opens her parachute.
- The increased area causes the air resistance to increase.
- The forces are now unbalanced. The upward force is bigger than the downward force, so she slows down.
- The air resistance decreases as she travels more slowly. A new terminal velocity is reached when the forces on her become balanced.

**This skydiver is moving at terminal velocity. She can feel the air rushing past, making the force of air resistance.**

The graph shows how the speed of the skydiver changes from when she leaves the aircraft.

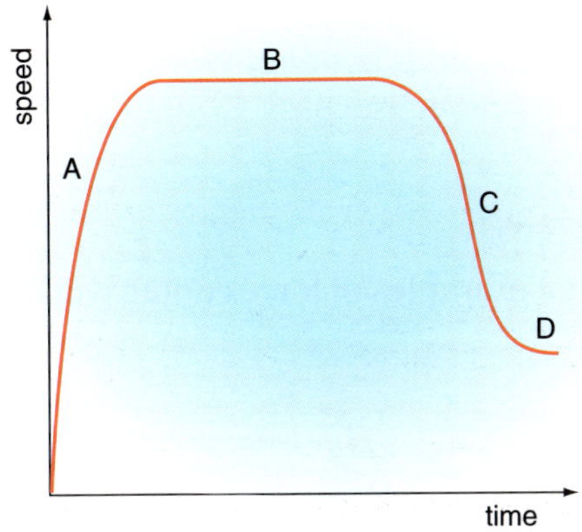


**c Explain what is happening to the speed of the skydiver at each lettered section of the graph.**

## Falling through a vacuum

A parachute is no use on the Moon, where there is no air to provide a resistive force. In 1969 Neil Armstrong carried out a famous experiment that was seen throughout the world on television. He dropped a feather and a hammer onto the surface of the Moon. He released them side-by-side, one from each hand. They fell together and landed together. This confirmed Galileo's prediction that, if there is no air resistance, all objects have the same acceleration when they fall.

**Did you know?**

Galileo dropped a heavy and a light ball from the top of the leaning tower of Pisa.

The heavy ball landed first because air resistance had less effect on it.

## Questions

**1** Copy the sentences below. Use words from the list to fill the gaps.

**accelerate** **balance** **air resistance** **weight**

- If you drop a shuttlecock, its _______ makes it _______ downwards.
- As it moves downwards, the force of _______ increases.
- When the forces _______, the shuttlecock has reached its terminal velocity.

**2 a** Draw a diagram of a car moving at top speed. Show the forces acting on it: the driving force of the engine, and the resistive force.

**b** What can you say about the sizes of these forces?

**c** Suggest two things that could be changed so that the car could go faster.

**3** Look at these graphs. Which graph could show how the force of air resistance changes when a shuttlecock is dropped towards the ground?

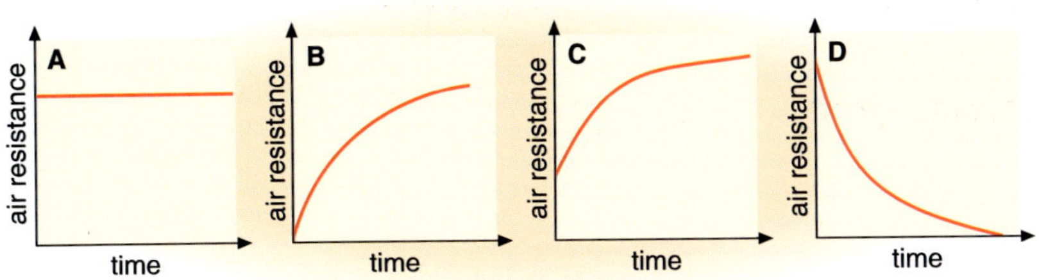


## Key ideas

- *The resistive force increases as an object moves faster through a fluid.*
- *A falling object reaches terminal velocity when its weight and the resistive forces are balanced.*
- *In the absence of air resistance, all falling objects have the same acceleration.*

# 11:8 Forces doing work

Here are some things that you might think of as 'hard work': chopping wood, washing the dishes, writing an essay for your homework, watching a video of a play. But this isn't what scientists mean by **work**.

In science, you do work if you use a force to make something move: pushing or pulling something along, or lifting something up, or changing the shape of something.

**a In the picture, who is doing work (in the scientific sense), the boy or the girl? Explain your answer.**

## Forces moving

Here are some examples of forces doing work:

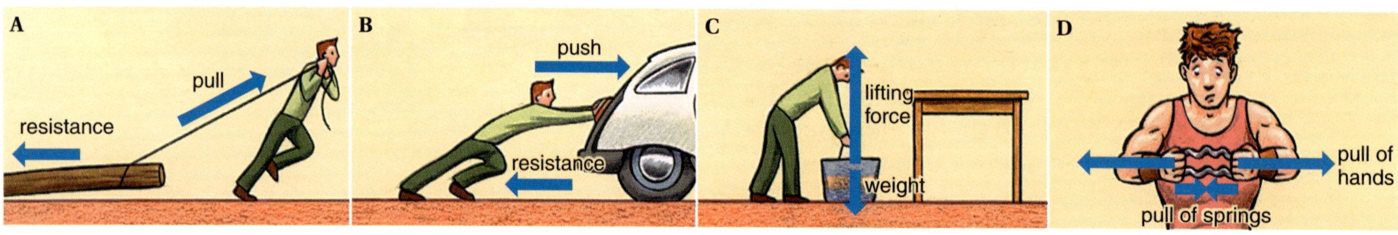


**A** The log will not slide easily along the ground, because of friction. You need to pull it with a force to make it move along.

**B** The car is stationary. You need to push it with a force to start it moving.

**C** The shopping bag is heavy. You need to use a force to lift it onto the table.

**D** The spring is stiff. You need to use a force to stretch it.

## Forces transferring energy

You need **energy** to do work, whether you are pulling, pushing, lifting or stretching. If you carry on doing work, you will eventually run out of energy. The force you use is transferring energy from you to the object you are moving.

Here is where your energy goes in the examples above:

**A** The log and the ground get warm, because of the friction. Your energy has been transferred as **heat**.

**B** The car starts to move. Your energy has been transferred to it as **kinetic energy**.

**C** The shopping bag is higher than before. Your energy is stored as **gravitational potential energy** in the bag.

**D** The spring is ready to snap back when you release it. It stores energy when it is stretched.

**b What happens to the energy when a force does work against friction?**

## How much work?

The amount of energy transferred by a force tells you the amount of work the force has done. The amount of work is measured in joules (J), just like the amount of energy.

Work done = energy transferred

A bigger force transfers more energy, and the further it moves, the more energy it transfers. So the amount of work done is the force multiplied by the distance moved.

Work done = force × distance moved in the direction of the force

The picture shows why we have to say *in the direction of the force.* The lifting force does work when it is raising the bag, because the bag is getting higher and its gravitational potential energy is increasing. The lifting force does no work when the bag is moving sideways, because the bag isn't getting any higher.

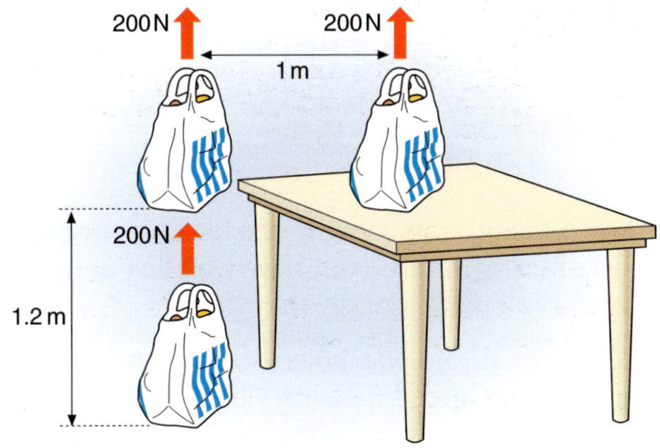


**Example**

The shopping bag is lifted by a 200 N force onto a table, 1.2 m high. How much work is done by the lifting force?

Work done = force × distance moved in the direction of the force

Substitute in the values from the question.

Work done = 200 N × 1.2 m = 240 J

Remember that the answer is in joules (J).

**Did you know?**

You never stop working. Even when you are asleep your heart is pumping blood around your body and your body cells are working as they respire.

So you can reasonably claim to be working 24 hours a day!

**c How much work would be done in lifting the same bag onto a higher table, 1.5 m high?**

## Questions

**1 What are the correct units for the quantities shown in the table? Copy the table and fill in the second column.**

| Quantity | Units |
|---|---|
| energy transferred | |
| work done | |
| force | |
| distance moved | |

**2 Are these people doing work (in the scientific sense)? Explain your answers.**

**a A man pushing a shopping trolley.**

**b A child stretching a rubber band.**

**c A boy sitting watching a science programme on TV.**

**3 How much work is done when someone pushes a car for 50 m with a force of 400 N?**

**4 A crane lifts a car 20 m into the air, using a force of 5000 N. How much work is done by the crane?**

### Key ideas

- *Doing work is a way of transferring energy using a force:*
  *Work done = energy transferred.*
- *To calculate work done:*
  *Work done = force × distance moved in the direction of the force.*
- *Gravitational potential energy is energy that is stored in an object due to its height.*

# 11:9 Kinetic energy and power

Any object that is moving has **kinetic energy**. The car and the lorry in the picture both have kinetic energy. The faster they go, the more kinetic energy they have.

When the photo was taken, the car and the lorry were travelling at the same speed. The lorry has much more kinetic energy than the car, because it has much more mass.

Kinetic energy depends on two quantities: mass and speed.

- Greater mass means more kinetic energy.
- Greater speed means more kinetic energy.

**a A car is accelerating along the road. Is its kinetic energy increasing, decreasing or staying the same?**

## Increasing kinetic energy

**Did you know?**

The kinetic energy of a jumbo jet when it takes off is the same as that of an inter-city train travelling at top speed.

The aircraft needs more powerful engines so that it gains this kinetic energy before it runs out of runway.

This aircraft is increasing its speed as it races down the runway, ready for take-off. Its kinetic energy increases as it goes faster.

To increase its kinetic energy, the aircraft burns fuel. You can see the dirty exhaust fumes coming from its engines. The energy stored in the fuel is being transferred to the aircraft as kinetic energy.

**b Explain why a lorry uses more fuel than a car does to reach its top speed.**

## A fast worker

Which is more **powerful**:

- a fast sports car or a bus?
- a man who can lift bricks or a crane?

The answer to these questions is 'the one that does the same work in the shorter time'. If the work to be done is moving sixty people to the top of a steep hill, the bus is more powerful than the sports car.

**c Explain why the bus is more powerful than the sports car in moving sixty people to the top of the hill.**

If a tonne of bricks needs to be lifted to the top of a skyscraper, the crane is more powerful than the man.

**Power** is a measure of how much work is done each second. It is measured in watts (W), where 1 watt (1 W) is equal to a rate of working or **energy transfer** of 1 joule per second (1 J/s).

Power = **work done** ÷ time taken

**Example**

A crane lifts a 5000 N load of bricks through a vertical height of 15 m.

**a How much work is done by the crane?**

**b It takes the crane 25 s to lift the bricks. Calculate the power output of the crane.**

**Answer**

**a** work = force × distance moved in the direction of the force

= 5000 N × 15 m

= 75 000 J

**b** power = work done ÷ time taken

= 75 000 N ÷ 25 s

= 3000 W

## Questions

1 Copy and complete the sentence.

Kinetic energy is energy due to ________________.

2 Which of the following have kinetic energy?

a A bus that is waiting at a bus stop.

b A spring that has been stretched.

c The Earth in its orbit.

d An aircraft braking as it lands.

3 A car engine has an output power of 76 kW. What does this mean?

4 A weightlifter lifts a 1000 N weight through a vertical height of 1.8 m.

a How much work does the weightlifter do?

b It takes 0.3 s to lift the weight. Calculate the power of the weightlifter.

## Key ideas

- *The greater its mass and the greater its speed, the greater the kinetic energy of a moving object.*
- *Power is the rate of doing work and is calculated as:*

  *Power = work done ÷ time taken*
- *Power is measured in watts (W).*

# 11:10 Inside the Earth

The drawing shows the important features of the structure of the Earth.

- We live on the thin, solid **crust**.
- The **mantle** is made of hot rock. It extends half way to the centre of the Earth.
- The **core** is very dense, because it is made of iron and nickel. The outer core is molten (liquid). The inner core is solid.

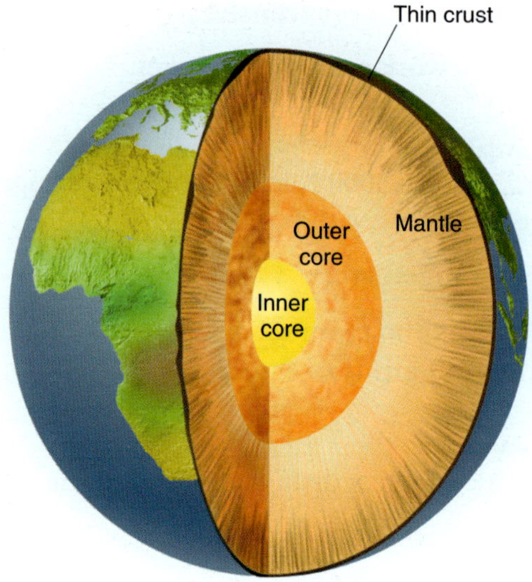


**a Which layer of the Earth is hottest? Which is coolest?**

## A look inside

We can't see inside the Earth, and we can't drill down as far as the mantle. So how do we know about the structure of the Earth?

The answer is that we make use of earthquakes. An earthquake sends strong vibrations right through the Earth. A powerful earthquake can cause great damage; weaker ones may do no damage, but they can still be recorded by scientists using instruments called **seismometers**.

A seismometer produces a trace which is like a graph showing the vibrations which have travelled through the Earth. The stronger the earthquake, and the closer the seismometer is to where it happened, the greater the amplitude of the trace.

**This building was built to be strong enough to withstand an earthquake. Unfortunately, that didn't stop it from falling over when a quake came.**

### Did you know?

Scientists use the shock waves from earthquakes to get an 'X-ray' picture of the Earth. They measure these on machines called seismometers, which are placed all over the globe. The results are analysed by computer.

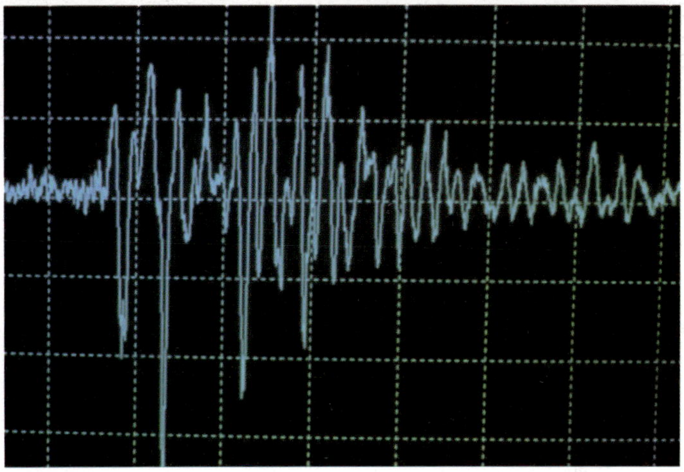

This seismograph shows the trace produced by a major earthquake.

## Reflecting waves

When geologists are looking for oil, they carry out a survey of the rocks in their area of interest. They set off small explosions on the surface, and detect the shock waves which are reflected by layers of rock below. They can then drill down in likely spots to find oil.

**b What instrument do the geologists use to detect the reflected shock waves?**

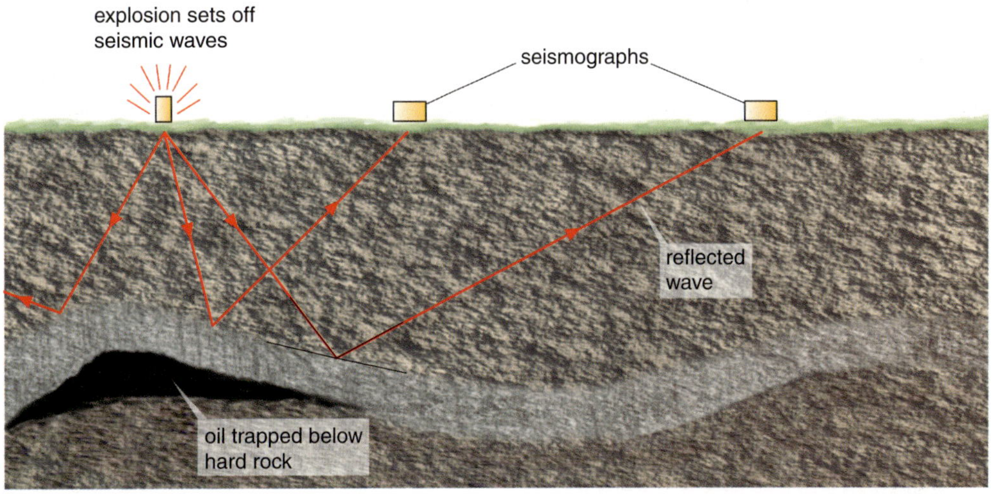


In the same way, geologists can find out about the layers of rock inside the whole Earth. They use the shock waves of an earthquake, which are known as **seismic waves**. These waves travel quickly through the Earth. When they reach the different layers inside the Earth, they are reflected and refracted. They are detected by seismometers at different points on the Earth's surface.

Geologists can use their measurements to build up a picture of the inside of the Earth, in just the same way that an ultrasound scanner builds up an image of an unborn child.

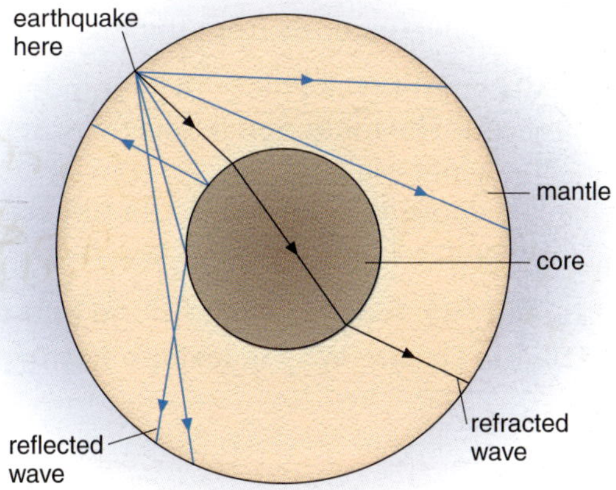


## Key ideas

- *Earthquakes produce seismic waves that can be detected using seismometers.*
- *By studying how seismic waves travel through the Earth, we can find out about its structure.*

## Questions

**1** **Give another name for the shock waves which are produced by an earthquake.**

**2** **When astronauts visited the Moon, they left a seismometer. Later, a disused spacecraft was crashed onto the Moon's surface. Why do you think this was done?**

# Moving plates

Why are there no volcanoes in Britain?

Earthquakes and volcanoes are common enough – but not in Britain. If you plot them on a map they occur in clear belts across the globe.

The reason for this pattern is simple enough. The outer layer of the Earth is broken into jigsaw pieces called **tectonic plates** that are moving about. The **earthquakes** and **volcanoes** occur at the edges of the plates, where they meet.

The plates are quite rigid as they consist of crust that is attached to a slab of upper mantle. This thicker, double layer of crust and upper mantle is called the **lithosphere**.

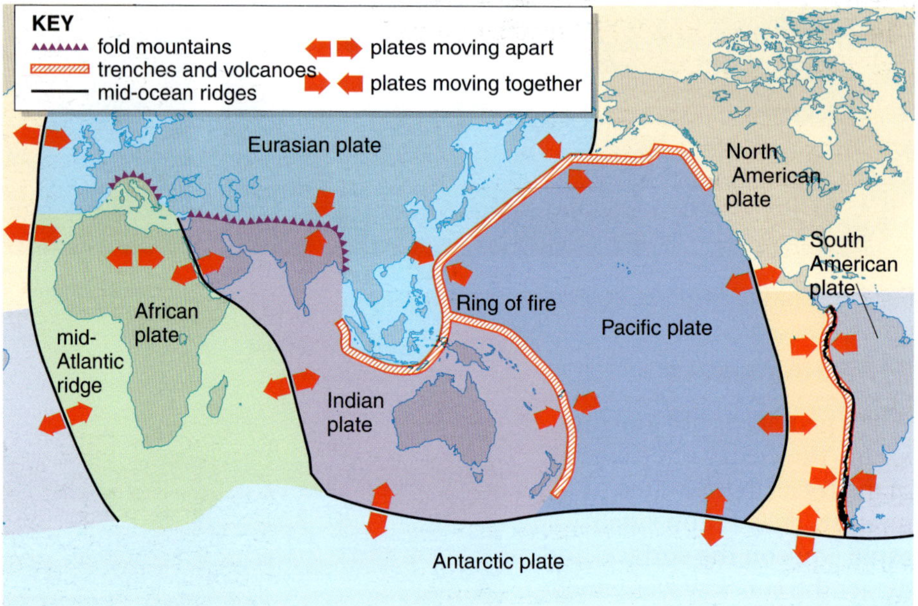


**The map shows the main plates and how they are moving.**

**a From the map, what are the closest places to Britain where powerful earthquakes are common?**

## Moving apart

When plates move apart a crack appears between them. Molten rock called magma flows from the mantle into the crack.

- Most of this volcanic activity is hidden beneath the ocean. The molten rock sets to form new ocean crust made of basalt.
- The deposits of new rock can rise above sea level, forming volcanic islands.

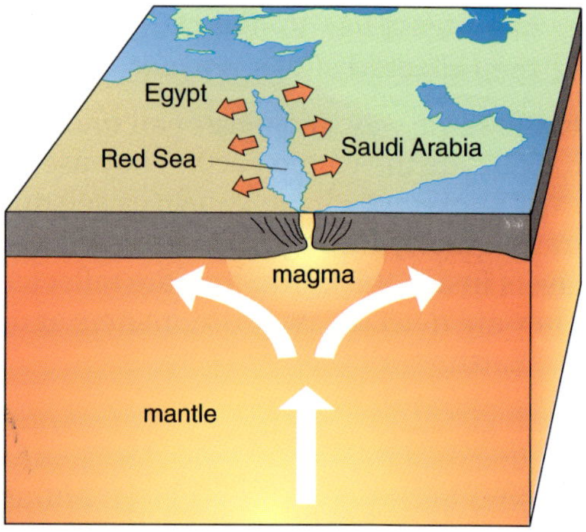


**b Iceland is a volcanic island ridge in the middle of the Atlantic Ocean. Why is Iceland getting wider?**

### Did you know?

Most of the continents now seem to be moving apart, riding on their plates. This means that if you go back in time, they must have been closer together.

Go back 250 million years and the world looked very different. All the continents were stuck together in a supercontinent called Pangaea.

## Come together

Some plates are being pushed together. Along the west coast of South America the thin, oceanic crust of the Pacific is being pushed towards the thicker continental crust. The oceanic crust is made of dense basalt rock. The continental crust is made of less dense rock such as granite.

- The ocean crust is forced down under the continental crust.
- As the rock from the ocean crust goes into the mantle, it melts and becomes magma.

Earthquakes can occur and magma can rise up to form volcanoes.

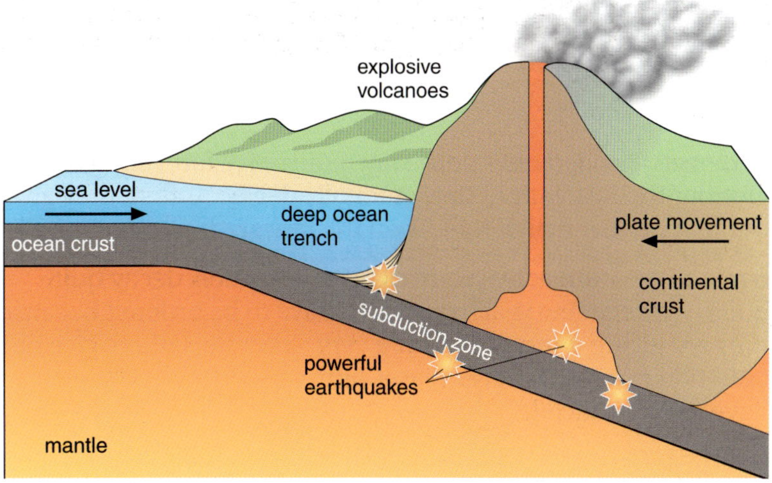


## Slip-sliding away

Along the Californian coast, the two plates are sliding against one another along the San Andreas fault. This causes very powerful earthquakes as the plates jam against one another for several years before jerking forward. San Francisco was destroyed in 1906 and has been struck regularly ever since. Buildings have to be specially designed to withstand earthquakes.

**c The San Andreas fault runs across the Californian orange grove shown here. The rows of trees to the right have been moved 3 m by earthquakes over a 30-year period. How much is this fault moving every year, on average?**

## Questions

**1** Copy the sentences. Use words from the list to complete them.

**edges mantle plates volcanoes**

The crust and the upper ________ form the lithosphere. This is broken up into tectonic ____________. Earthquakes and volcanoes occur along the ___________ of these plates.

**2** The continents seem to be moving apart now, but the Earth is round. What might happen in another 250 million years?

**3** The Atlantic Ocean is getting wider every year. What must be happening to the Pacific? (The world is not getting bigger!)

## Key ideas

- *The lithosphere consists of plates that are moving towards and away from each other.*
- *When plates move towards each other rock goes into the mantle.*
- *When plates move away from each other, new volcanic rock is formed.*
- *When plates slide past each other earthquakes often occur.*

# 11:12 Radioactive decay

Radioactive substances don't stay radioactive forever. As they give out their radiation, they gradually **decay**. At first, they give out radiation at a high rate. Then the rate gradually declines.

Some of the radioactive sources used in schools decay quite quickly. After a few years, new ones have to be ordered because they are giving out radiation at a very slow rate. Others give out radiation at a rate that decreases only very slowly, so they never have to be replaced.

**Did you know?**
All the food that we eat is radioactive, so we take in fresh supplies of radioactivity each day.

This teacher is demonstrating how the amount of radiation coming from a particular radioactive substance decreases quickly.

## Representing radiaoctive decay

The **count rate** tells us the amount of radiation that is detected coming from a radioactive substance. Count rate is measured in **becquerels** (Bq), where 1 Bq = 1 count/s. As a substance decays, its count rate gets less.

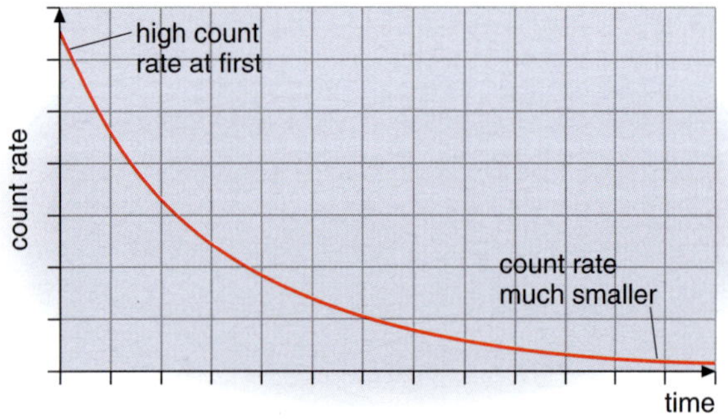


We can show the pattern of radioactive decay as a graph. From the graph you can see:

- at first, the count rate is high;
- after a while, the count rate is less;
- the count rate gradually gets closer and closer to zero as the substance decays away.

**a Look at the graph. Does the count rate decrease steadily to zero?**

## Half-life

When the Earth formed, about four and a half billion years ago, it contained more uranium than it does now. Uranium is radioactive, and about half of it has decayed away.

Other radioactive substances decay much more quickly than uranium. The **half-life** of a radioactive isotope is a measure of how quickly it decays.

- Isotopes with long half-lives decay more slowly than those with short half-lives.

The half-life of a radioactive substance is the time it takes for half of the undecayed nuclei to decay.

The second graph shows that, after twice this length of time, one quarter of the original nuclei still remain. After each half-life, half of the undecayed nuclei that were there at the beginning remain, and half have changed into different nuclei. As the number of undecayed nuclei decreases, so does the count rate.

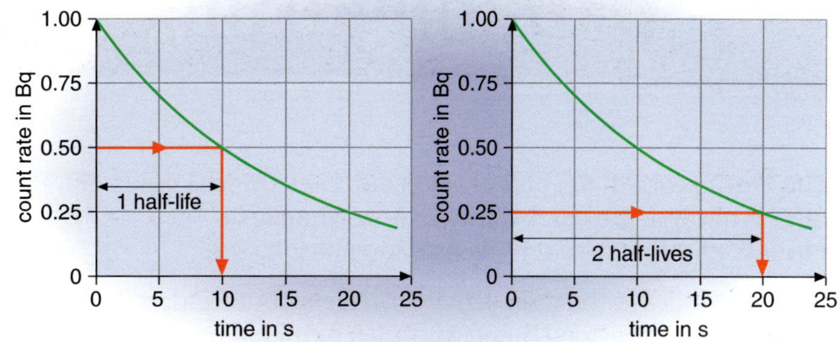


**b A radioactive isotope has a half-life of 2 years. What fraction of the original nuclei are unchanged after:**

**i 2 years?**
**ii 4 years?**
**iii 6 years?**

## Getting rid of waste

Some waste materials from hospitals and nuclear power stations have a short half-life. These decay rapidly. One isotope commonly used in medicine has a half-life of 6 hours. After two days its activity is almost zero and it can be safely disposed of.

Other isotopes have very long half-lives of thousands of years. They need to be stored in places that we are certain will be secure until many half-lives have elapsed.

**c Why is it difficult to find suitable sites for underground storage of some radioactive waste materials?**

## Questions

**1** **Which graph shows the pattern of radioactive decay correctly?**

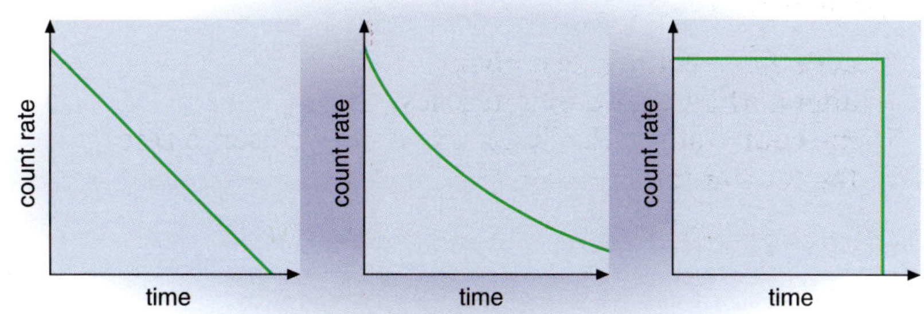


**2** **A sample of a radioactive substance initially contained 100 000 undecayed nuclei. How many of these would remain after two half-lives?**

**3** **The table shows the count rate measured for a radioactive substance.**

| Count rate (Bq) | 300 | 240 | 190 | 150 | 120 |
|---|---|---|---|---|---|
| Time (min) | 0 | 20 | 40 | 60 | 80 |

**a** **What was the initial count rate?**

**b** **How can you tell from the table that the substance was decaying?**

**c** **After how long had the count rate fallen to half its initial value? What is the half-life of the radioactive substance?**

### Key ideas

- *The count rate for a sample of a radioactive substance decreases rapidly at first, then more and more slowly.*
- *The half-life is the time taken for the number of undecayed nuclei to halve.*

# 11:13 Dating using radioactivity

The Earth is about 4.5 billion years old. How do we know that? What was the clock that started as the Earth formed, and that now tells us how long has passed?

The answer lies in the radioactivity of the rocks around us. When the Earth formed there was much more radioactivity around. The rocks of the new Earth contained much more **uranium**, radium and other radioactive isotopes than they do today. The Earth would have been a very dangerous place to live, with high levels of background radiation.

Today, the Earth is much safer because many of the radioisotopes in the rocks around us have decayed away to become stable atoms.

**This geologist is collecting rock samples. By measuring their radioactivity, he can determine their age.**

## The decay of uranium

Uranium is a radioactive substance that is commonly found in rocks. Its atoms are unstable, and they decay until eventually atoms of **lead** are formed. These are stable atoms, and so they do not decay.

This process takes a very long time – billions of years. Even though the Earth is very old, only some of the uranium in its rocks has decayed.

**Did you know?**
Radioactive analysis of Moon rocks shows that the Moon is probably older than the Earth.

**a Which element has unstable atoms, uranium or lead? Which has stable atoms?**

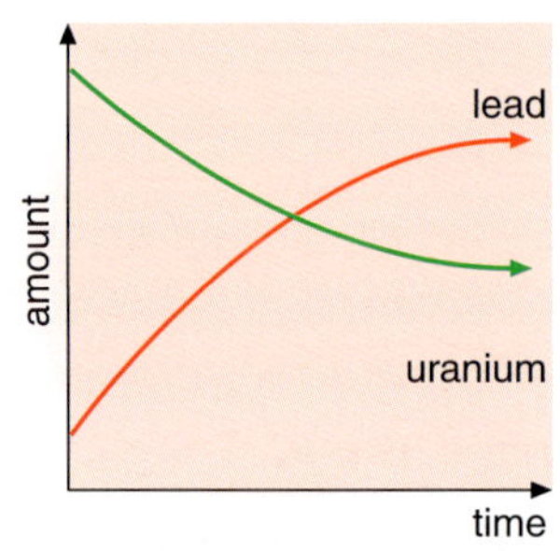


**The amount of uranium in the Earth's rocks has gradually declined; the amount of lead has increased.**

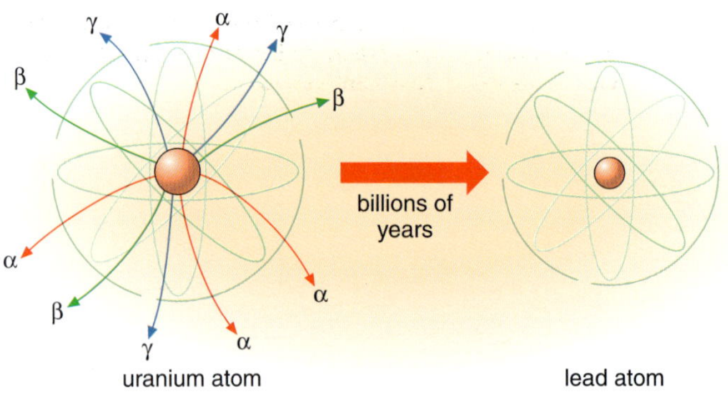


**When uranium atoms decay, they eventually become stable atoms of lead.**

It is interesting to realise that most of the lead in the Earth started off as uranium. Medieval alchemists tried to turn lead into gold; we now know that the reason we find lead in the Earth is that it is a stable element that cannot easily be changed into any other.

Now we can understand the radioactive 'clock' that allows geologists to find the age of the Earth. As time passes – billions of years – the amount of uranium in the Earth's rocks has gradually declined, and the amount of lead has increased. Geologists measure the amounts of uranium and lead in rocks. Then they can work out how old the rocks are.

**b Which is older, a rock with a lot of uranium and a little lead, or one with a little uranium and a lot of lead?**

**This meteorite is a rock from the planet Mars. Geologists have measured the amounts of different isotopes within it to find its age. It is 4.5 billion years old, the same as the age of the Earth.**

## Radiocarbon dating

Living creatures contain carbon. A small amount of this is a radioactive isotope of carbon, called carbon-14. After a living creature dies, the carbon-14 in it gradually decays away.

Archaeologists use this as a way of finding the age of anything that was once alive. They measure the amount of carbon-14 that remains, and this tells them how long ago it died.

This method can be used to find the age of material that died up to 50 000 years ago.

**The Iceman is the body of a bronze age man. It was found frozen, in the Alps. Radiocarbon dating showed that he lived about 5700 years ago.**

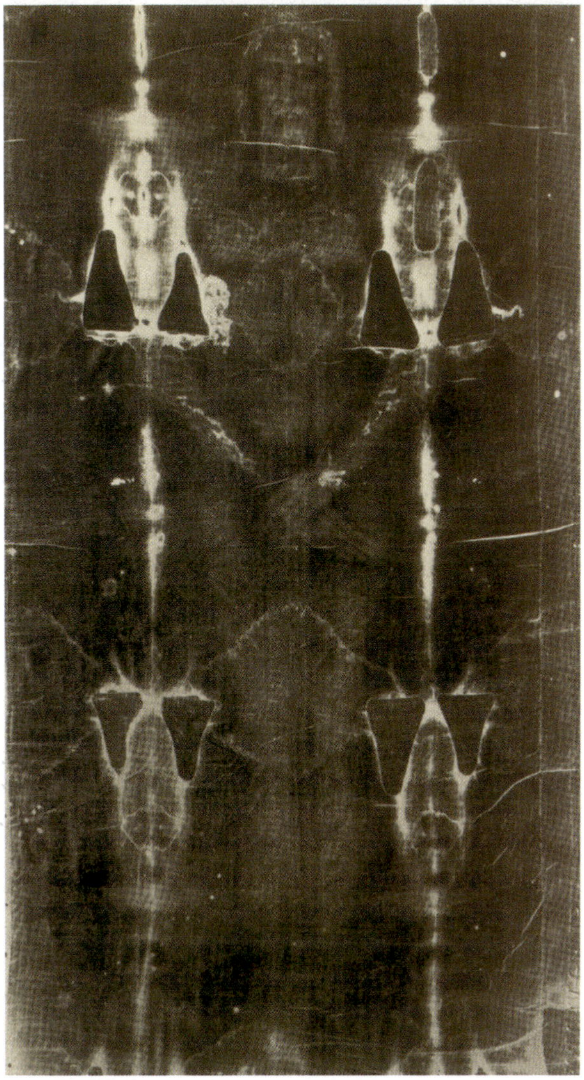

**Some people believed that the Turin shroud is Christ's burial shroud. Radiocarbon dating shows that the cloth was made in the fourteenth century.**

**c Look at the two photos. If you took a gram of carbon from the Turin shroud, and a gram of carbon from the Iceman, which would contain more atoms of radioactive carbon-14? Explain your answer.**

## Questions

**1** Why is there less background radiation today than there was when the Earth formed, 4500 million years ago?

**2** The oldest rocks in the Earth contain less uranium today than when they were formed. They contain more lead.

- **a** Why do they contain less uranium than when they formed?
- **b** Why do they contain more lead?

**3** The photograph shows King Arthur's round table, in Winchester Cathedral. Its age has been found using radiocarbon dating. If you took a gram of carbon from the table, and a gram of carbon from your own body, which would contain more atoms of radioactive carbon-14? Explain your answer.

### Key ideas

- *We can find the age of rocks and materials that were once alive by measuring their radioactivity. The older the material, the less radiation it emits.*

# End of module questions

## Low demand

**Questions 1 and 2**

Here is a distance–time graph for a cyclist.

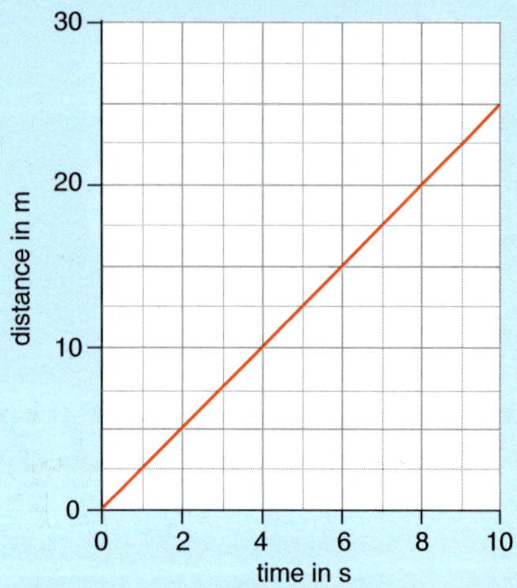


1. How far did the cyclist travel during the first 6 s shown on the graph?

   **A** 10 m

   **B** 15 m

   **C** 20 m

   **D** 25 m

2. What was the speed of the cyclist?

   **A** 0.4 m/s

   **B** 2.0 m/s

   **C** 2.5 m/s

   **D** 250 m/s

3. Stopping distance is made up of

   **A** thinking distance and reaction distance

   **B** thinking distance and acting distance

   **C** acting distance and braking distance

   **D** thinking distance and braking distance

**Questions 4–7**

The diagram shows the forces acting on a car that is moving forwards.

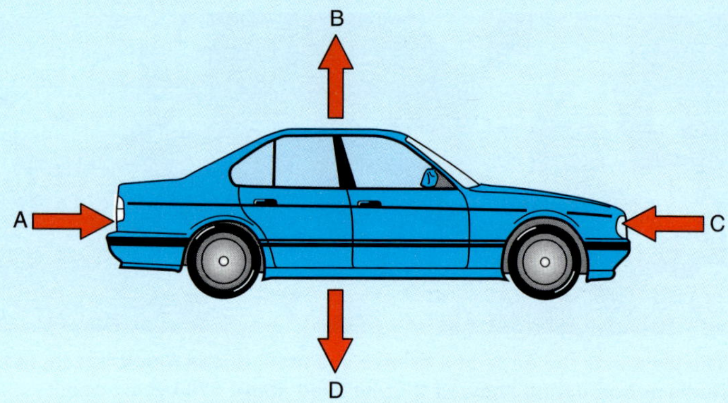


4. Which force is the driving force?

5. Which force is the resistive force?

6. Which pair of forces must be equal in size if the forces on the car are balanced?

   **A** A and B

   **B** B and C

   **C** C and D

   **D** B and D

7. For the car to accelerate forwards

   **A** force A must be bigger than force B

   **B** force B must be bigger than force A

   **C** force A must be bigger than force C

   **D** force C must be bigger than force A

**8** Surplus electricity is used to pump water from a low reservoir to a high one. Water in the high reservoir has more

**A** gravitational potential energy

**B** kinetic energy

**C** movement energy

**D** power

**9** Which two quantities are needed to calculate work?

**A** force and time

**B** force and distance

**C** force and speed

**D** force and power

**10** Tectonic plates are found

**A** in the Earth's core

**B** in the Earth's mantle

**C** on the Earth's mantle

**D** in the Earth's atmosphere

**11** Which graph shows how the activity of a radioactive isotope changes with time?

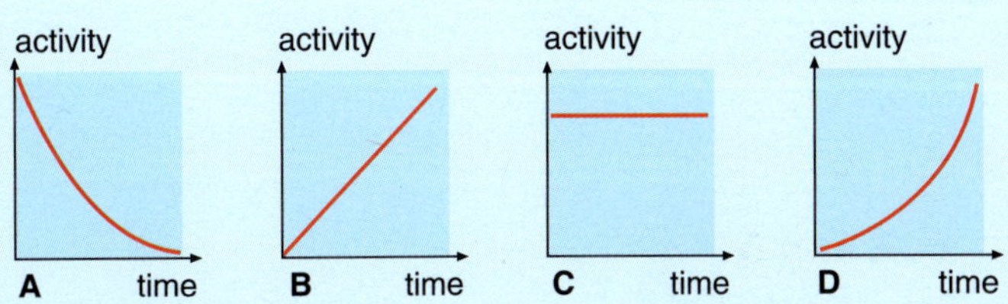


**12** Radioactivity can be used to date

**A** houses

**B** living trees

**C** metals

**D** rocks

## Standard demand

**13** The velocity of a moving object is

**A** its acceleration in a fixed direction

**B** the distance it travels in a certain time

**C** the slope of its speed–time graph

**D** its speed and direction

**14** The gradient of a speed–time graph represents

**A** acceleration

**B** distance

**C** time

**D** velocity

**15** A driver's normal reaction time is 0.4 s.

When travelling at 30 mph, the driver's thinking distance is 5.6 m.

If the driver's reaction time doubles to 0.8 s, the driver's thinking distance is

**A** 2.8 m

**B** 5.6 m

**C** 11.2 m

**D** 22.4 m

**16** The size of the Earth's pull on a person is 750 N.

The person pulls the Earth with a force of

**A** 75 N downwards

**B** 75 N upwards

**C** 750 N downwards

**D** 750 N upwards

**17** Gravitational forces act between objects due to their

**A** electric fields

**B** magnetic fields

**C** charge

**D** mass

**18** When an object falls through the Earth's atmosphere, the upward force that acts on it is due to

**A** air resistance

**B** the Earth's pull

**C** its weight

**D** wind

**19** When a car travels at a constant speed along a level road

**A** it does not need a driving force

**B** there is no resistive force

**C** it needs a driving force that is greater than the resistive force

**D** the driving force and resistive force are equal in size

**20** A person uses a force of 150 N to push a supermarket trolley a distance of 30 m.

The work done in pushing the trolley is

**A** 5 J

**B** 5 W

**C** 4500 J

**D** 4500 W

**21** When a bus accelerates away from a bus stop along a level road it

**A** gains gravitational potential energy

**B** loses gravitational potential energy

**C** gains kinetic energy

**D** loses kinetic energy

**22** The lithosphere is the Earth's

**A** inner core

**B** outer core

**C** mantle

**D** outermost layer

**23** Rock can be taken into the mantle when

**A** tectonic plates slide past each other

**B** tectonic plates move away from each other

**C** tectonic plates move towards each other

**D** a volcano occurs

**24** The activity of a radioactive isotope is measured to be 120 Bq.

6 hours later the activity is 60 Bq.

After a further 6 hours the activity is likely to be

**A** 0 Bq

**B** 30 Bq

**C** 60 Bq

**D** 120 Bq

# Module 12 – Energy, force and communication

The effects of static electricity have been known about for thousands of years. Charge that is not moving is used in modern computer printers and in photocopiers. When large amounts of charge move through the air the effects can be hazardous. By understanding electrostatics, you will learn about how these situations are prevented where possible.

Moving charge is used to transfer energy in circuits. In this module you will learn about the electrical power of different appliances and how transformers are used to transfer energy through the National Grid.

Modern communication systems rely on sending vast quantities of information through the air as radio waves and along optical fibres. You will learn how optical fibres work and why some waves spread out more than others.

The final topic is about the effects of forces on materials and structures and the way in which gases exert pressure.

Before you start this module, try these questions first.

1 Which is the better insulator: plastic or copper?

2 When a current passes in a coil of wire, is the magnetic field similar to that of a bar magnet or that of a horseshoe magnet?

3 Do similar magnetic poles attract or repel each other?

4 Which device uses an electromagnet: a relay or a light switch?

5 Which metal is normally used for the core of an electromagnet: copper or iron?

# 12:1 Static electricity

The Van de Graaff generator in the photograph can be charged up to a very high voltage – hundreds of thousands of volts. If the voltage is high enough, sparks pass through the air.

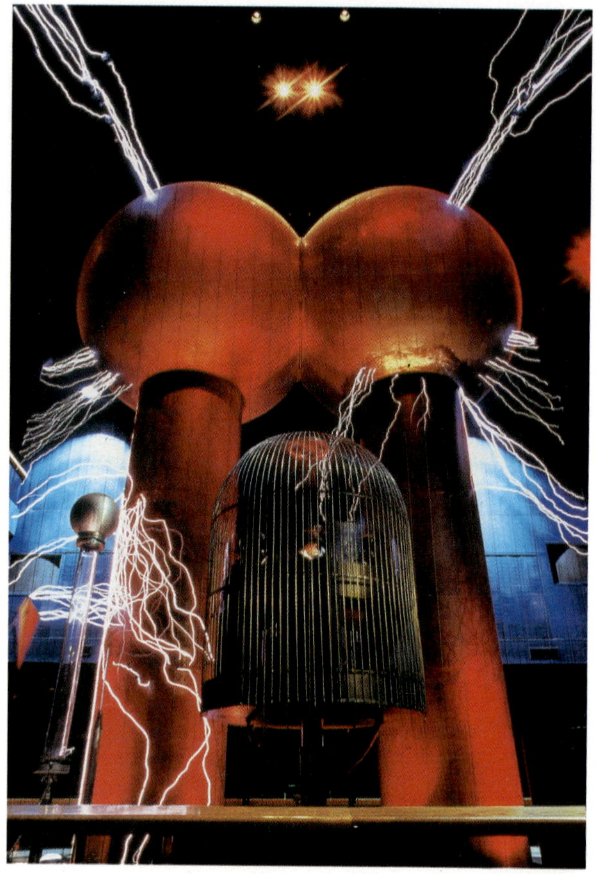

## Charging up

If you rub a rubber balloon on a woollen jumper, they both become **charged**. The charged balloon attracts small pieces of paper and your hair.

Rubber, wool, paper and hair are all examples of electrical **insulators**. Two insulators become charged when they are rubbed together because of the friction between them. A charged material can attract an uncharged insulator.

**Conductors** such as metals are more difficult to charge. They need to be well insulated from the earth, like the dome on the Van de Graaff generator.

**a Which of these materials are insulators?**

**brass iron nylon polythene**

## Two types of charge

There are two types of electric charge, called **positive charge** and **negative charge**.

When the jumper is rubbed, negatively charged electrons pass from it to the balloon. The jumper gains a positive electric charge because it has lost electrons. The balloon gains a negative charge because it has gained electrons. They attract each other because *opposite charges attract*.

Two charged balloons repel each other. Both balloons have a negative charge, and charges that are the same type repel each other (*like charges repel*).

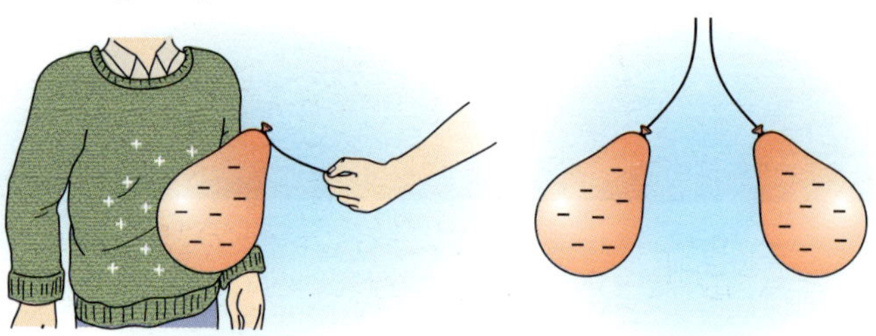

**b Copy and complete the table, to show how these pairs of objects affect each other.**

| First object | Second object | Attract/repel/no effect? |
|---|---|---|
| Negatively charged balloon | Negatively charged balloon | |
| Negatively charged balloon | Positively charged nylon thread | |
| Negatively charged balloon | Uncharged piece of wool | |

**Did you know?**

The name for the electron comes from the Greek word *elektron*. This was the Greek name for amber, a fossil resin. They found that when they rubbed this resin it attracted dust.

## Getting a shock

- If you walk across a nylon carpet, you can become charged: electrons pass from your feet to the carpet because of the friction as you walk.
- Nylon is a very good insulator, so you stay charged until you touch a metal object.
- Some of the charge passes from you to the metal, giving you a shock as the charge moves through you.

A similar thing can happen when you get out of a car. If you are wearing clothing made from a synthetic material such as nylon, you and the car seat become charged as you travel along. When you touch the metal of the car bodywork, you become discharged and you feel a shock.

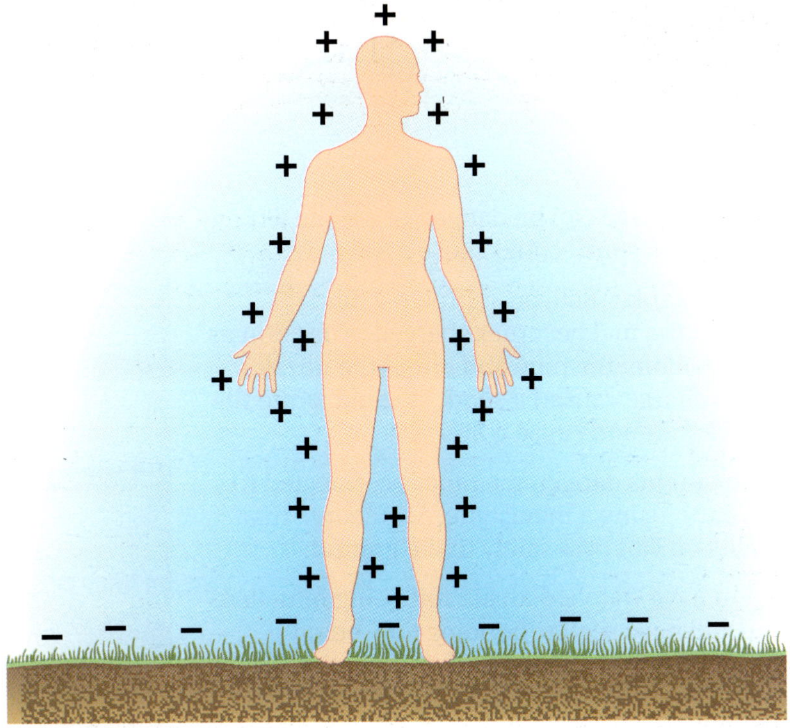

## Questions

1 What force causes two objects to become charged when they are rubbed together?

2 The diagrams show charged balls hanging on strings. Copy the diagrams and complete them to show the charge (+ or –) on each ball.

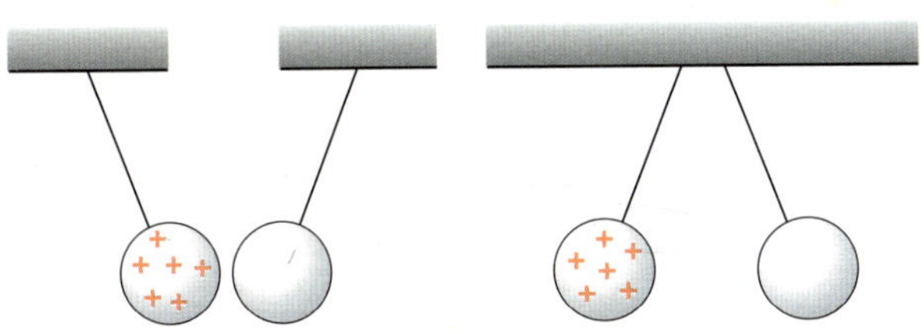

3 Here is something you may have noticed.

- When you comb your hair, your hair is attracted to the comb.
- After combing, your hair is light and fluffy – the hairs are all repelling each other.

What do these observations tell you about the electric charges on the hair and the comb?

4 Explain how you can become discharged after walking across a nylon carpet.

### Key ideas

- *When two different insulating materials are rubbed together they may become electrically charged.*
- *Two objects with the same type of charge repel each other.*
- *Objects with opposite types of charge attract.*
- *Clothing made from synthetic material is easily charged.*

# 12:2 Some dangers and uses of static electricity

Electric charge can be dangerous. In the wrong situation, a **spark** could cause a fire.

When a tanker delivers petrol to a filling station, the fuel becomes charged by friction as it flows along the pipe and out of the nozzle. If this charge caused a spark, it could ignite the fuel vapour and cause a fire.

To avoid this danger, the pipe is connected to the earth using a metal wire. Any charge that builds up can pass safely to the ground.

If you have watched an aircraft being refuelled, you will have seen a 'bonding line' being connected to the metal bodywork of the aircraft first. This prevents a build-up of charge that could cause a spark and a fire.

**a Explain how a bonding line prevents the build-up of static charge.**

## Lightning

Convection currents in clouds can cause charges to move about. Negative charge builds up on the base of a thundercloud.

This creates a large voltage between the cloud and the ground below. When the voltage is big enough, there is a spark between the cloud and the ground as the cloud discharges in a flash of **lightning**.

**Did you know?**

Benjamin Franklin was the first person to use electricity for cooking.

After a picnic he wrote, 'I killed a turkey by the electric spark and roasted it by an electric jack before a fire kindled by the electric bottle'.

## Inkjet printing

Charges can be very useful. If you look at the underneath of a can of baked beans, you will see that it is printed with its 'best before' date and the batch number. The customer knows when it is safe to open the cans, and if there is a problem the whole batch can be recalled.

An **inkjet printer** sprays the ink onto the cans as they move along the production line. The inkjet printer makes use of static electricity to guide the droplets of ink.

The diagram shows how an inkjet printer works. Look for:

- the *gun* that produces the jet of ink droplets;
- the *electrode* that charges them up;
- the *deflecting plates* that move the jet from side to side.

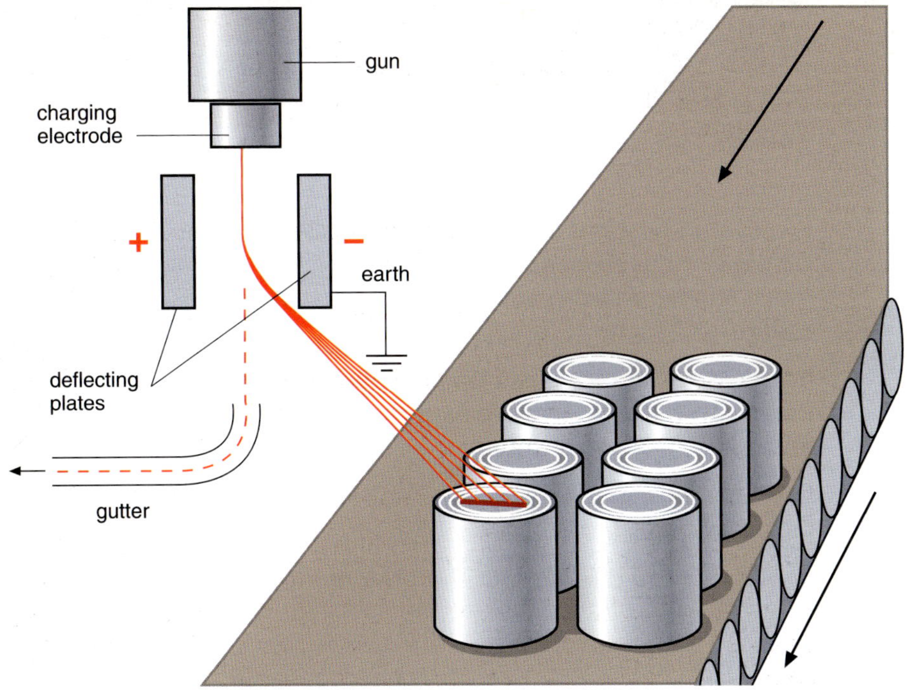


**b Do the ink droplets have positive or negative charge? How can you tell?**

**c How does the jet of ink droplets move if the deflecting plates have no charge?**

## Photocopying

A **photocopier** can make a copy of a black and white page in less than a second. In a photocopier:

- a bright light scans across the page to be copied;
- this forms an image on a special charged drum;
- the bright areas on the drum become discharged;
- the dark areas on the drum remain charged, and these attract the toner (ink);
- the toner is transferred to the paper, which is then heated so that the toner powder melts and sticks to it.

**d What charge does the drum have, positive or negative? What charge does the toner have? What charge does the paper have?**

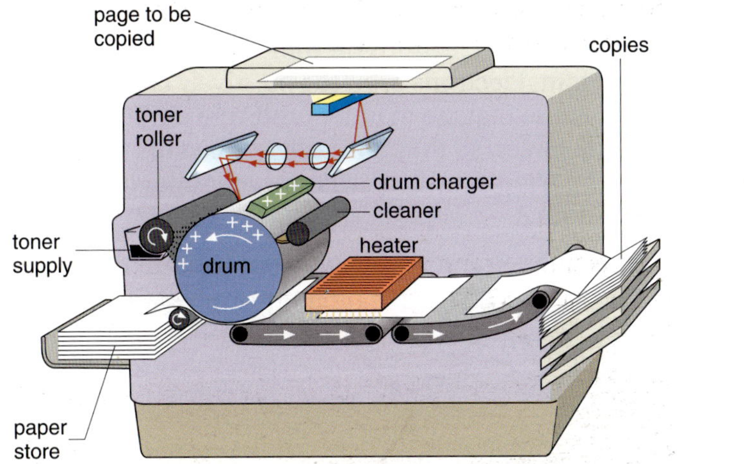


## Key ideas

- *Tankers and aircraft need to be connected to the ground to avoid a spark when fuel is being pumped.*
- *Inkjet printing uses charged droplets of ink. The charged drops are directed to form the shapes of letters by the attraction and repulsion of charged plates.*
- *In a photocopier, light provides the energy for positive charge to escape from the charged drum.*
- *Positive electric charge attracts the black toner powder to the drum, and then to the paper.*

## Questions

**1** Copy and complete the following sentence.

If a drop of ink is given a positive charge, it is attracted by a plate with a _______________ charge.

**2** Look at the diagram of the inkjet printing machine. Explain how the jet moves if the left-hand plate is given more positive charge.

**3** Describe how electrostatic charge is used in a photocopier.

# 12:3 Charge in motion

You can understand the effects of static electricity by thinking about **electrons**. An electron is a tiny particle, much smaller than an atom. It has a negative electric charge.

In an electric circuit, vast numbers of electrons flow from the negative terminal of the battery or power supply towards its positive terminal.

In electronic circuits, a smaller number of charges are on the move.

**a What is the direction of the flow of electrons in a torch lamp?**

## Getting charged

It is easy to rub electrons off some materials. An electron is part of an atom. Electrons orbit the positively charged nucleus of the atom. Those that are in outer orbits are attracted to the nucleus by weak forces, so they are easily rubbed off. Electrostatic charging happens when electrons are rubbed off one material onto another.

**b If a Perspex rod is rubbed with a cloth, the rod becomes positively charged. Explain this in terms of the movement of electrons.**

The result of rubbing a polythene rod with a cloth.

## Electrons and current

In an insulator, the forces on the electrons orbiting a nucleus are large enough to keep them in their orbits. They stay in orbit unless a bigger force acts to pull them away.

In a conductor, electrons are free to move about. It only takes a small force, such as that from a battery or low voltage supply, to make them drift towards the positive terminal.

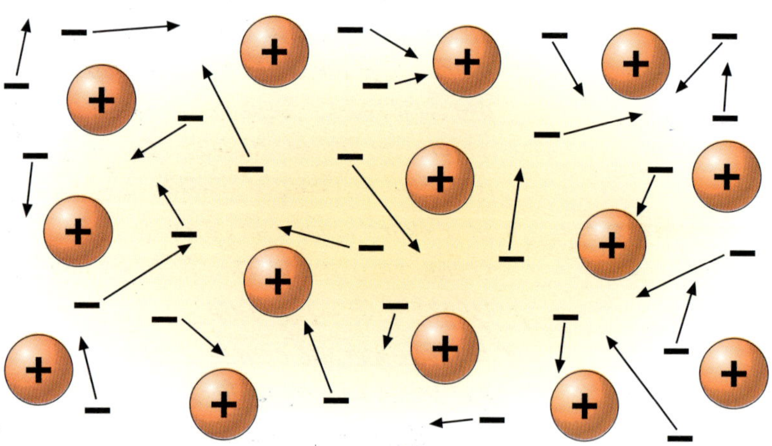

Electrons are free to move about in a conductor. Their movement is random in speed and direction.

When there is an overall movement of electrons from negative towards positive there is an **electric current**.

## How much charge?

You get an electric current when **electric charges** flow. The more charge that flows past a point each second, the greater the current. Electric current is *the rate of flow of charge* or the *charge flow per second.*

The relationship between charge flow and current is:

charge flow = current × time or $Q = I \times t$

where charge ($Q$) is measured in coulombs (C), current ($I$) is measured in amps (A), and time ($t$) is measured in seconds (s).

**Example**

The current in a lamp filament is 2.0 A. How much charge flows through the lamp in 1 minute?

charge flow = current × time

= 2.0 A × 60 s

= 120 C

**c How much charge flows in a heater when a current of 4 A passes for 5 s?**

**Did you know?**

It used to be thought that there were two different types of electricity, static electricity and current electricity.

Now we know that both are due to electric charge. Static electricity describes charge that is not moving. Current electricity is charge on the move.

## Questions

**1** A piece of fur is used to rub a plastic rod. Electrons are rubbed off the fur onto the rod. Which of the following statements are true?

- The fur gains positively charged electrons.
- The rod gains a negative charge.
- The charged fur repels the charged rod.
- The charged rod attracts the charged fur.

**2** Copy and complete the table.

| Quantity | Unit |
|---|---|
| | amp (A) |
| charge | |
| time | |

**3** Conductors and insulators both contain electrons.

**a** What type of charge does an electron have?

**b** Describe how electrons behave differently in conductors and insulators.

**4** The current in a car battery is 5.5 A. How much charge flows through the battery in 5 minutes?

## Key ideas

- *Objects become charged because of the movement of electrons. Electrons have a negative charge.*
- *An electric current in a metal is a flow of electrons. Metals are good conductors because some of their electrons are free to move throughout the metal.*
- *Charge, current and time are related by:*

*charge = current × time*

$Q = I \times t$

# Electrical power

Electricity is a very convenient way of transferring **energy** from place to place. Wherever you are at home, there is probably a socket near you that you can plug an electrical appliance into.

Energy from electricity is easily transferred to:

- *heat* in a resistor such as the heating element of a hairdryer;
- *movement* by a motor such as the fan of a hairdryer;
- *light* by the lamps used at home.

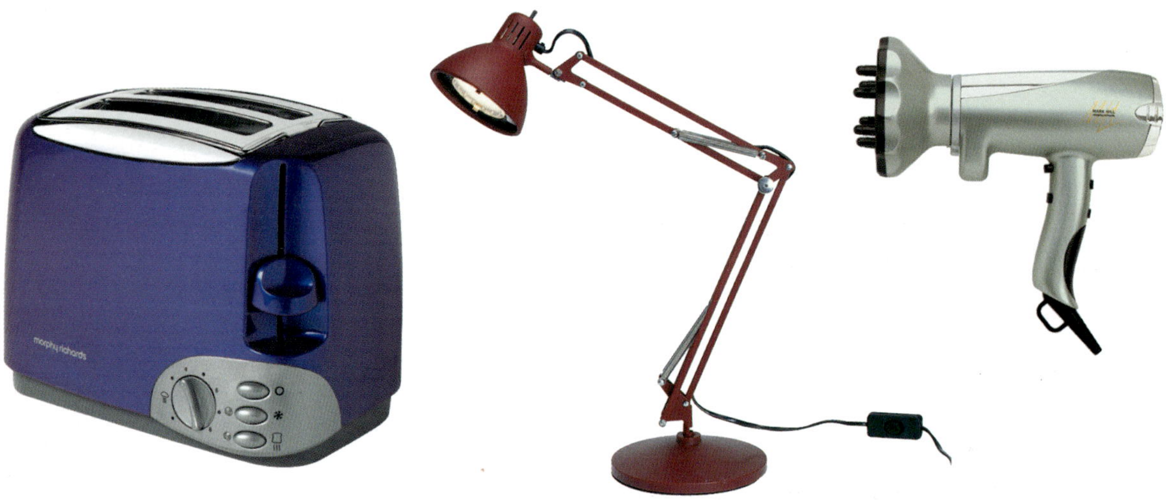

These devices transfer energy from the mains electricity supply to heat, light and movement.

**a What is the main energy output of an electric toaster? What other type of energy does it give out?**

## Power

If you buy a new light bulb or a new hairdryer, you have a choice. Ordinary filament lamps are available in different **powers**, the common ones being 40 W, 60 W and 100 W. Remember, W stands for watt. 1 watt is a rate of energy transfer of 1 joule per second.

Hair dryers are available with powers ranging from 100 W (for a baby) to 2000 W (2 kW).

The more powerful the hair dryer, the faster it should dry your hair. You might expect that the more powerful the lamp, the brighter it is. This is not always the case. Some types of lamp are better than others when it comes to transferring energy from the electricity supply to light.

The electrical power of an appliance is the rate of energy input, how many joules of energy are supplied to it each second.

**b How much energy is supplied to a 60 W lamp in 1 minute when it is operating normally?**

**Did you know?**

Devices used for electrical heating are much more powerful than those used for lighting. They are also more expensive to operate.

## Working out the power

The electric motors that are used to start an engine in a motor vehicle are very powerful. They operate from a low **voltage**, usually 12 V or 24 V. Very large currents are needed to supply the energy at the rate required. The same power can be supplied from the higher voltage mains supply using a much smaller **electric current**. The electrical power supplied to a device depends on both the current and the voltage:

power = current × voltage or $P = I \times V$

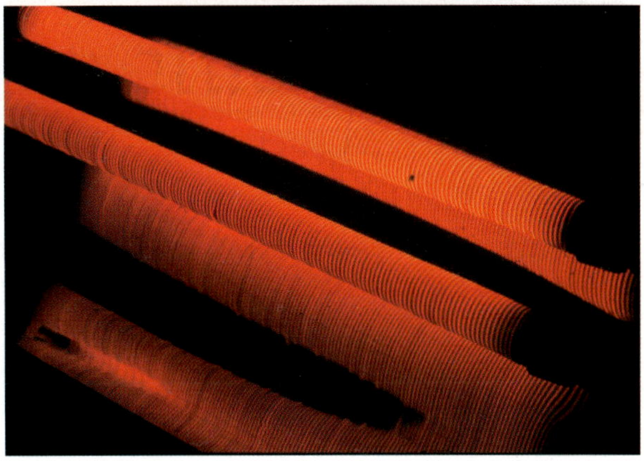

Each bar of this electric fire transfers energy at a rate of 1000 watts.

**Example 1**

The current in the rear windscreen heater of a car is 15 A when the voltage across it is 12 V. Calculate the power of the heater.

power = current × voltage

= 15 A × 12 V

= 180 W.

**Example 2**

The current in a mains soldering iron is 0.75 A. The mains voltage is 240 V. Calculate the power of the soldering iron.

power = current × voltage

= 0.75 A × 240 V

= 180 W.

You can see from these examples that the higher the voltage, the smaller the current required to deliver the same power.

**c Explain why the heater in Example 1 needs thicker cable than the soldering iron in Example 2 to connect it to the electricity supply.**

## Questions

**1 Calculate the power of each device in the table.**

| | Device | Current (A) | Voltage (V) |
|---|---|---|---|
| a | car headlamp | 5 | 12 |
| b | torch lamp | 0.15 | 3 |
| c | iron | 5.6 | 240 |
| d | kettle | 9.5 | 240 |

**2 A kettle can be operated from a mains supply of 120 V or 240 V. Explain why it takes four times as long to boil some water when it is connected to a 120 V supply as it does when connected to a 240 V supply.**

**3 Explain why a 1000 W car starter motor needs a much greater current than a 1000 W mains heater.**

### Key ideas

- *The electrical power of a device is the rate at which energy is transferred to it from the voltage supply.*
- *Power = current × voltage,* $P = I \times V$.

# 12:5 Electric motors

Some cars are powered by electricity. Each wheel has an electric motor to turn it. Electric motors use electromagnets.

Petrol-driven cars also have electric motors in them. They have a starter motor to get them going, and motors for the windscreen wipers. There are motors to work the fuel pump and the screen washers, and there may be electrically operated windows and locks.

## A moving wire

When a wire is placed at right angles to a **magnetic field**, it moves when a current passes in it. The picture shows that the direction of the **force** is at right angles to both the magnetic field and the *current*.

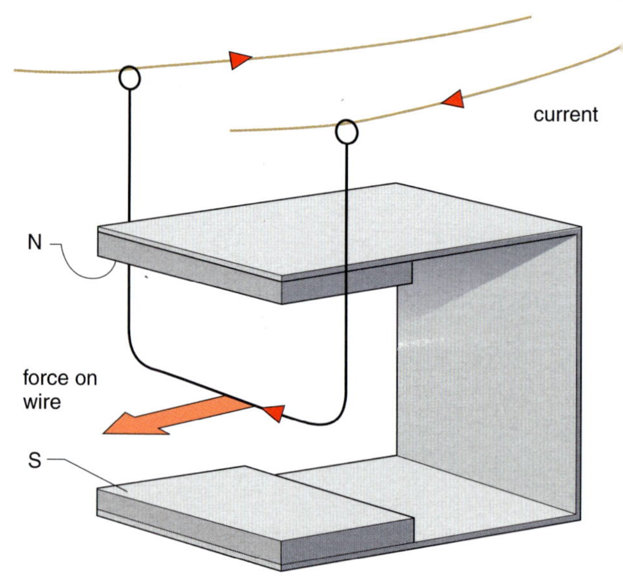


In the picture a 'swing' has been made of copper wire. It hangs in a magnetic field.

When a current passes in the wire, it is pushed sideways. You can make the force bigger in two ways:

- increase the current;
- use stronger magnets.

If the current passes the other way, or if the magnets are reversed, the swing is pushed in the opposite direction.

**a How does the force change if the current is decreased?**

## Parts of a motor

The diagram shows a simple direct current **motor**. These are its important parts:

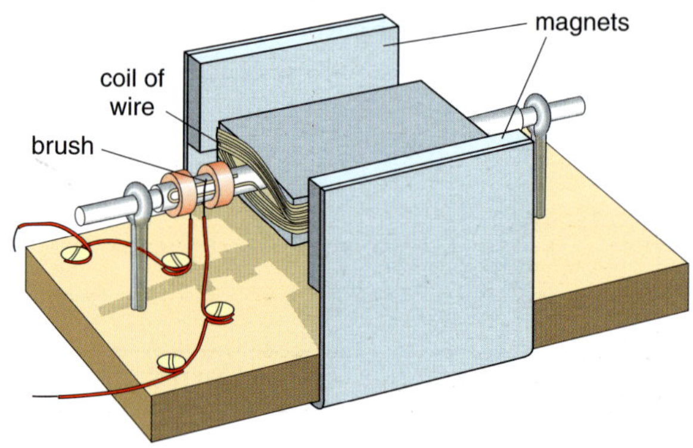


- a *coil of wire*, which becomes an electromagnet when current passes in it;
- two *permanent magnets* with opposite poles facing, to make a strong magnetic field;
- two *brushes* that touch onto the wire of the coil.

Electric current passes into the coil through one of the brushes, around the coil and back out through the other brush.

**b If you make a motor like the one shown, how can you check that the magnets have opposite poles facing?**

**Did you know?**
Electric motors were first used for domestic tasks in the vacuum cleaner, invented by Cecil Booth in 1901.

## How it works

This is how the forces on the sides of the **coil** make the motor turn.

- On one side of the coil, the current is passing from front to back. The force on this side is upwards.
- On the other side of the coil, the current is passing the other way, from back to front. The force on this side is downwards.

This pair of forces makes the motor spin round.

The brush connections are a clever way of making sure that the coil keeps turning in the same direction.

**c If the connections to the motor's power supply are reversed, what happens to the direction of the current? Explain how this affects the rotation of the coil.**

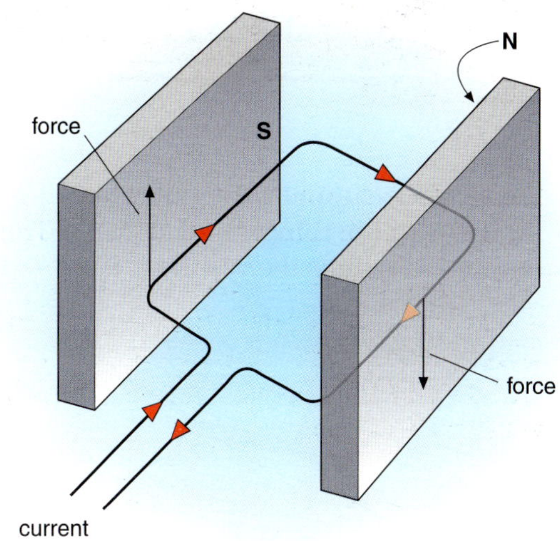


## Questions

**1** **Look at the picture of the wire swing. The force on the wire can be changed in several ways. Copy the table, and tick the correct boxes to show how the force will change.**

| Change made | Force increases | Force reverses |
|---|---|---|
| increasing the current | | |
| reversing the magnets | | |
| using stronger magnets | | |
| reversing the current | | |

**2** **Copy and complete the sentences using the words provided.**

**brushes  coil  field  magnets**

**When a current passes in the __________ of a motor it becomes an electromagnet. Current passes into and out of the coil through connections called __________. Two permanent __________ are needed to provide the magnetic __________.**

**3** **Explain why brushes are used to connect the coil of an electric motor to the power supply, rather than fixed connections.**

### Key ideas

- *A force acts on a wire that is carrying a current when it is at right angles to the direction of a magnetic field.*
- *The direction of the force is at right angles to both the direction of the magnetic field and the current.*
- *This force is used to make a motor turn.*

# 12:6 Transformers

Electricity is supplied to houses at 240 V. This voltage is too high for many of the things used at home. They have **transformers** in them to reduce the voltage.

**Radio plugged into mains. The radio has a transformer built into it.**

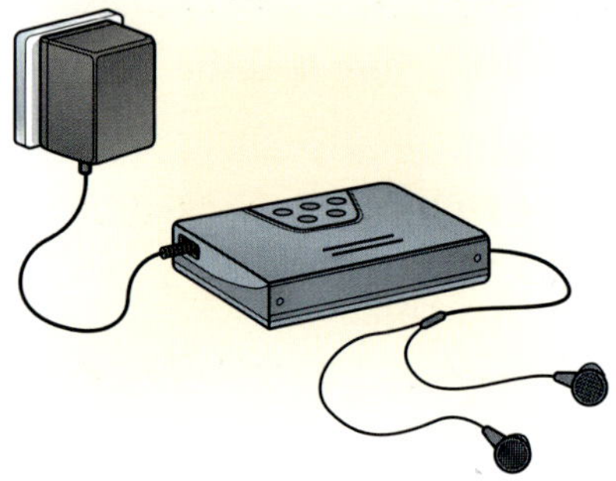

**Walkman plugged into mains via a transformer.**

Mains electricity is alternating current (a.c.). This means that the current passes back and forth in the wires. Transformers only work with a.c. electricity.

**a Why does the personal stereo in the picture need a transformer if it is to be plugged into the mains electricity supply?**

## Coils and cores

Transformers can be used to make an alternating voltage bigger or smaller.

- A **step-up transformer** increases the size of an alternating voltage.
- A **step-down transformer** decreases the size of an alternating voltage.

A transformer is made of two coils of wire, wound on an iron core. The two coils are not wired together, they are linked by the core. The input voltage is applied to the **primary coil** and the output voltage is taken from the **secondary coil**.

The diagram shows the different structures of step-up and step-down transformers.

**b A radio is fitted with a transformer so that it can run from the 240 V mains instead of a 9 V battery. Is this a step-up or a step-down transformer?**

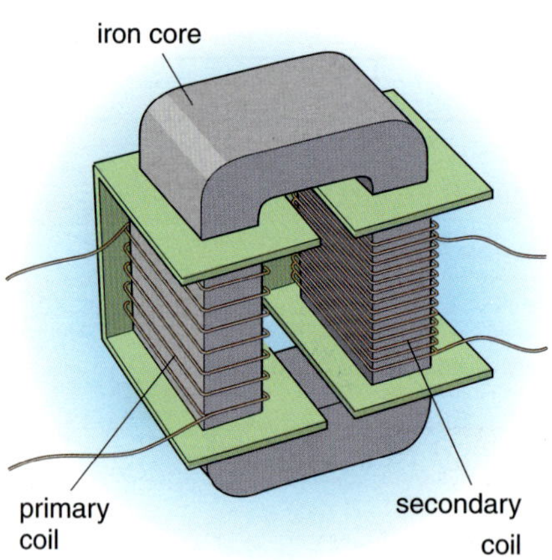


**A step-up transformer has more turns on the secondary coil.**

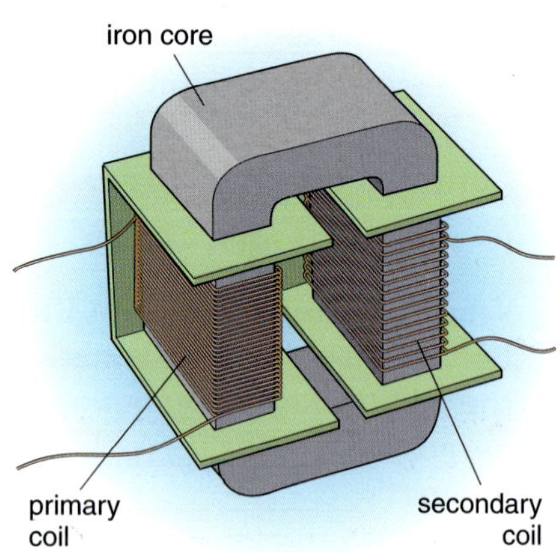


**A step-down transformer has fewer turns on the secondary coil.**

## Supplying power

You know that the higher the voltage, the smaller the current that is required to deliver a given power. A typical power station generates electricity at the rate of 2000 MW, two thousand million watts. This is enough to supply a city the size of Birmingham.

To transmit the power at mains voltage, 240 V, would require a huge current. Very thick cables would be required that would be very expensive to manufacture and too heavy to be supported on pylons.

To keep the size of transmission cable down, and to minimise the energy wasted as heat in these cables, electrical power is transmitted at a very high voltage.

- Electricity is generated at 25 000 V.
- The voltage is increased by a step-up transformer to 400 000 V.
- Electricity at this voltage passes into the national grid network.
- Transformers are used to step down the voltage in stages before the electricity reaches consumers.

**Did you know?**

The cables that you see suspended from pylons are all live wires. They are at a high voltage and carry the energy from power stations to consumers. The ground is used to complete the circuit between power stations and substations.

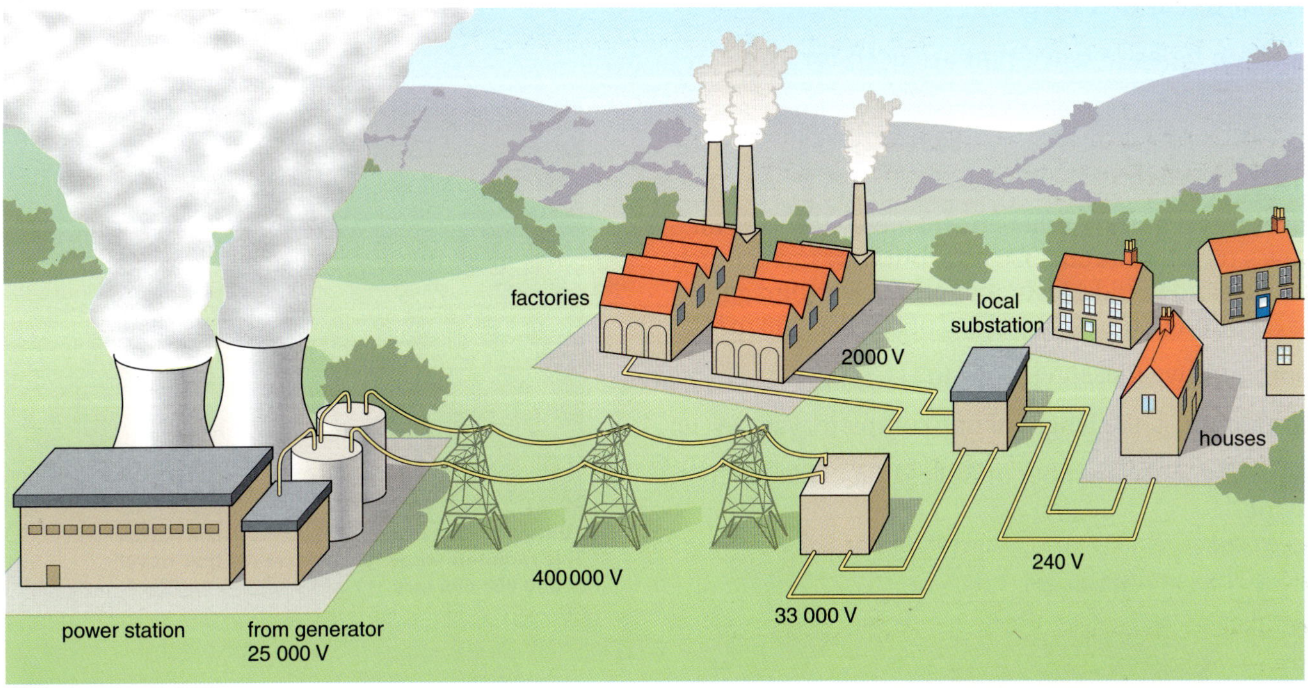


**c What type of transformer is used:**

**i at a power station?**

**ii at a substation?**

## Key ideas

- *A transformer can change the size of an alternating voltage.*
- *A step-up transformer is used to increase the voltage of electricity generated at a power station.*
- *A step-down transformer is used to decrease the voltage of the mains supply before it reaches consumers.*

## Questions

**1** When the voltage of the electricity generated at a power station is increased, what happens to the current?

**2** Not all the power generated at a power station reaches the consumers. What happens to the power that is wasted?

**3** Explain why electrical power is transmitted at high voltage.

# 12:7 The wave equation

Waves are used to transfer *energy* from one place to another. They have many uses.

- Communications by sound, telephone, radio and television all use waves.
- Grills and microwave ovens use waves to cook food.
- X-rays and gamma rays are waves that are used to treat cancers.
- Vision uses light, another example of a wave.

When you speak to a friend, the sound is carried by vibrations of the air particles. These particles vibrate to transmit the energy of the sound wave. There is no movement of any material from you to your friend.

**a Name three types of wave that are used for communicating.**

**This oven uses the energy in microwaves to cook food.**

**This radiotelescope receives waves that travel at 300 000 000 m/s.**

## The speed of waves

Some waves travel quickly, others travel more slowly. In air, sound waves travel at around 320 m/s, but they travel much faster in solids and liquids. Light and other electromagnetic waves travel through the air at a *speed* of 300 000 000 m/s.

Two important wave measurements are:

- **wavelength**, $\lambda$, the length of one complete wave cycle;
- **frequency**, $f$, the number of waves that occur each second.

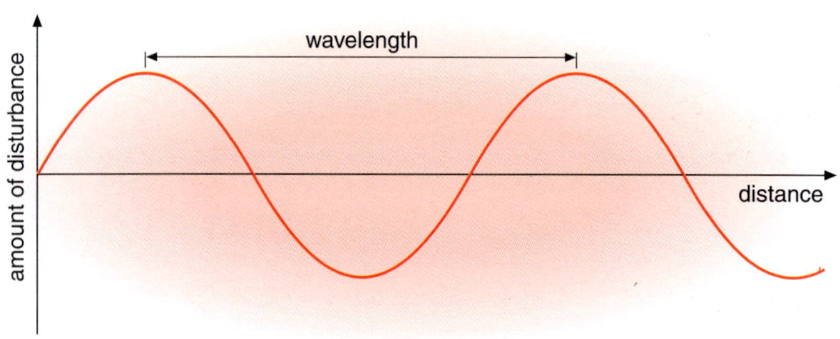


The speed of a wave depends on the type of wave and the material that it travels in.

**b What is the speed of radio waves in air?**

Waves on the sea move at a few metres per second; the water in a ripple tank is much shallower, and the waves travel more slowly.

The diagram shows a line of waves. After 1 s, the red wave has moved 6 m to the right. The speed of the waves is 6 m/s.

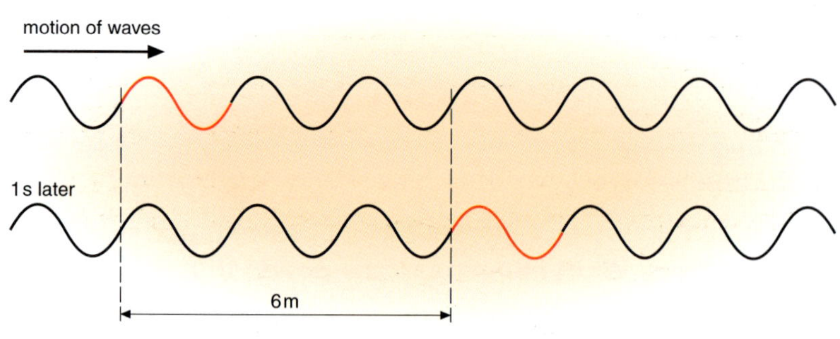

The speed of a wave can be calculated from its frequency and wavelength:

wave speed = frequency × wavelength or
$v = f \times \lambda$

**Example**
Some waves on the sea have a wavelength of 20 m and a frequency of 0.2 Hz. What is their speed?

wave speed = frequency × wavelength
= 0.2 Hz × 20 m
= 4 m/s

**c Some waves are travelling along a spring. Their wavelength is 1.5 m and their frequency is 2 Hz. Calculate the speed of the waves.**

A surfer can ride along on the top of a breaking wave. It can be quite a fast ride!

**Did you know?**
Ships use *sonar* (***so***und ***n***avigation ***a***nd ***r***anging) to find the position of shoals of fish, shipwrecks and submarines.

## Questions

1 Copy and complete the sentences using the words provided.

**speed** **material** **energy**

All waves transfer ______________. When a wave transfers energy from one place to another, there is no transfer of any ______________. The ______________ of a wave depends on its type and the material it is travelling in.

2 Calculate the speed of each wave in the table.

| | Wave | Frequency (Hz) | Wavelength (m) |
|---|---|---|---|
| a | sound in water | 300 | 5.0 |
| b | surface water wave | 2.5 | 2.0 |
| c | sound in air | 80 | 4.0 |
| d | sound in a metal | 1250 | 0.8 |

3 A loudspeaker cone completes 3000 vibrations each minute. It produces waves that have a wavelength of 6.0 m in air.

**a** Calculate the frequency of the waves.

**b** Calculate the speed of the waves in air.

## Key ideas

- *For all waves*

*wave speed = frequency × wavelength*
*or* $v = f \times \lambda$

# 12:8 Total internal reflection

A doctor may use an instrument called an endoscope to look inside a patient. To see inside the patient's stomach, a long, flexible device is passed down their throat. This contains a bundle of **optical fibres**. Light that enters one end of a fibre travels along inside it until it emerges at the other end. The fibre carries the light round bends and curves.

Some of the fibres in an endoscope carry light into the patient, to provide illumination; others carry the light rays back to a camera that shows an image of the stomach.

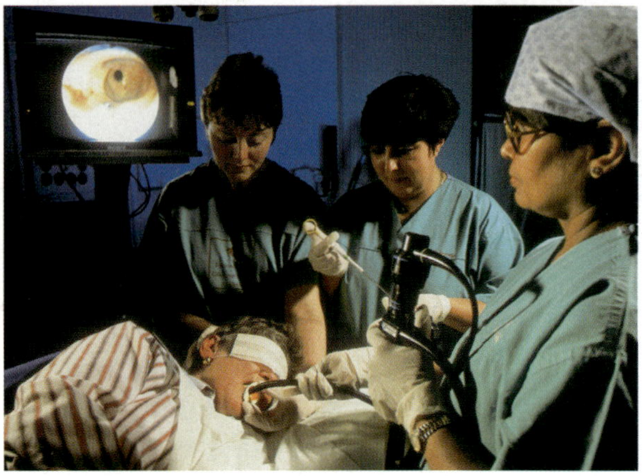

The image of the patient's insides appears on a monitor screen, so that the whole medical team can see it.

**a What is unusual about the way that light travels in an optical fibre?**

## Inside glass

Optical fibres are made of very pure glass. They are quite flexible, so that they can be bent into a curved shape. The diagram shows how light is reflected when it strikes the inside surface of the fibre. This reflection is total, all of the light is reflected. The inside surface of the fibre behaves like a perfect mirror.

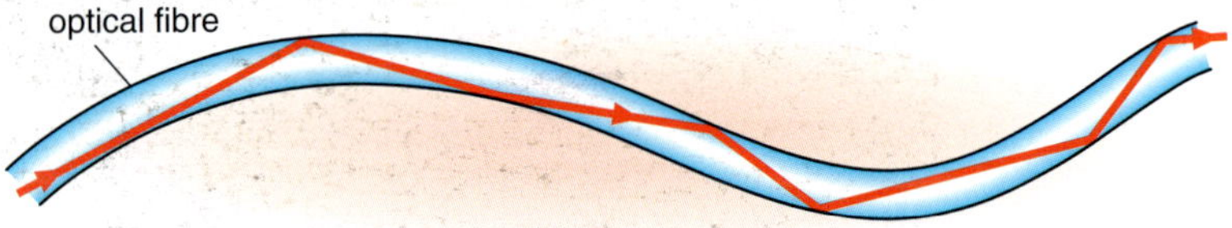


This type of reflection is known as **total internal reflection** (TIR). It is called *internal* because it happens *inside* the glass.

**b Why is it called *total*?**

The diagrams show what happens when light travels from glass (or Perspex or water) into air.

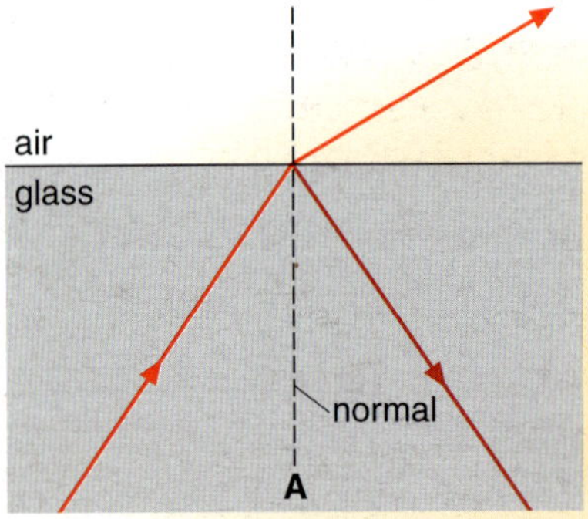


The ray of light strikes the surface of the glass at a narrow angle. Some of the light is refracted as it passes through; some is reflected.

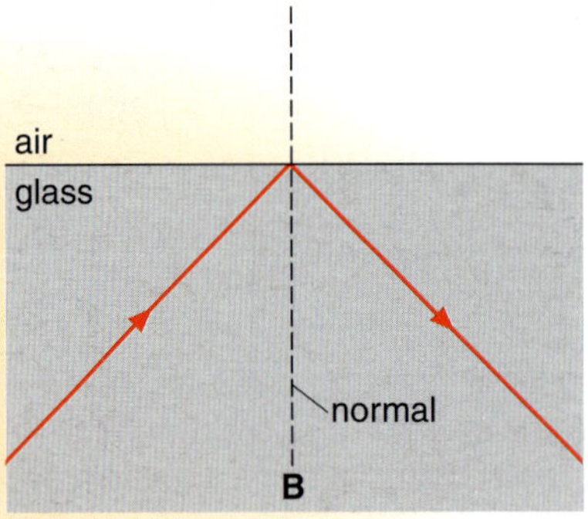


Here the ray strikes the surface at a greater angle. There is no refracted ray; all of the light is reflected.

**Did you know?**

Optical fibres are used in eye surgery. Light from a laser travels through an optical fibre. It can be used to 'spot-weld' a detached retina onto the back of the eye.

TIR occurs when the angle between the direction of the light and the normal line is greater than a certain angle called the **critical angle**.

**c Look at the first of the two diagrams. What happens when the angle between the direction of the light and the normal is less than the critical angle?**

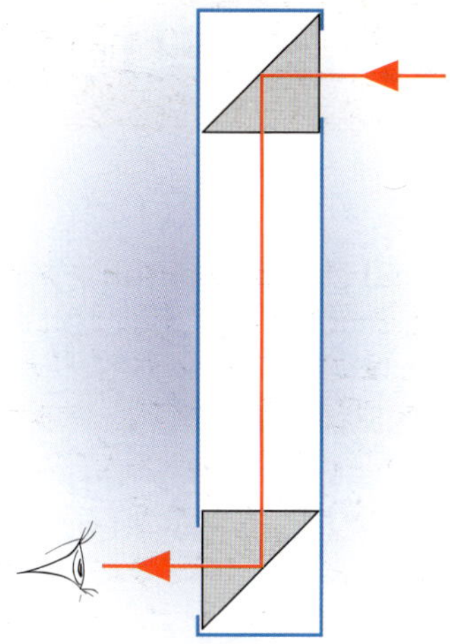

A periscope

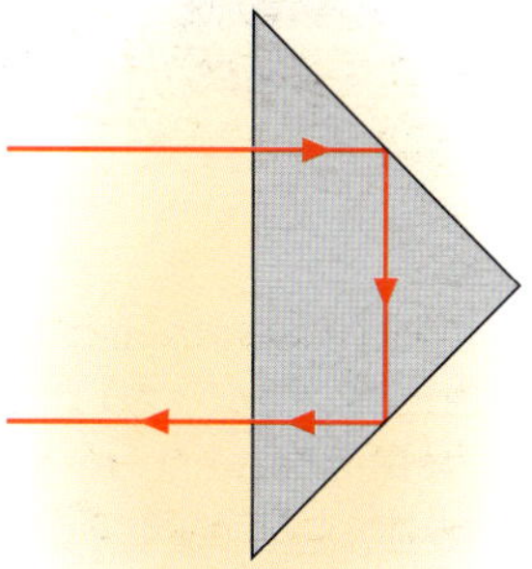

The action of a prism in a cycle reflector. Each reflector consists of hundreds of prisms.

## Up and over

A periscope allows the user to see over an obstacle. Some periscopes are made with two mirrors; others use two glass prisms to reflect the light. The light is totally internally reflected inside each prism.

Cycle reflectors also use **reflecting prisms** to reflect light from the headlights of a car.

## Getting the picture

Today, many houses are connected to a cable TV network that also provides a telephone system. Optical fibres are used to transmit television, radio and telephone signals to the user. The signals are carried by light. This is better than using electrical signals in cables (wires).

- Light in a thin fibre can carry much more information than electrical signals in a cable of the same thickness.
- The light signals can travel much further than electrical signals before they become too weak to detect.

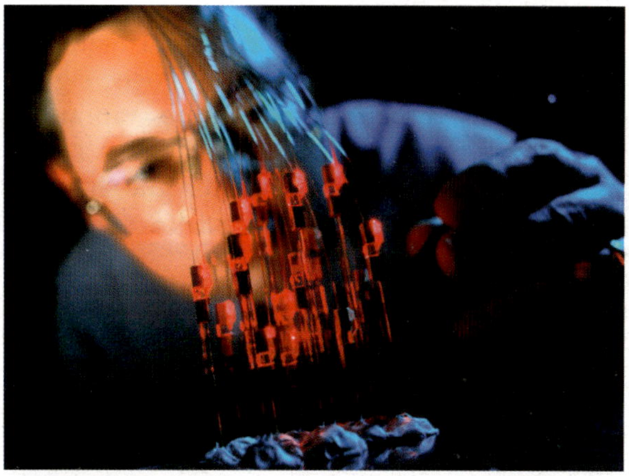

Optical fibres use light to carry television, radio and telephone signals.

## Questions

**1 Copy and complete the two diagrams to show what happens when light strikes the inside of a Perspex block.**

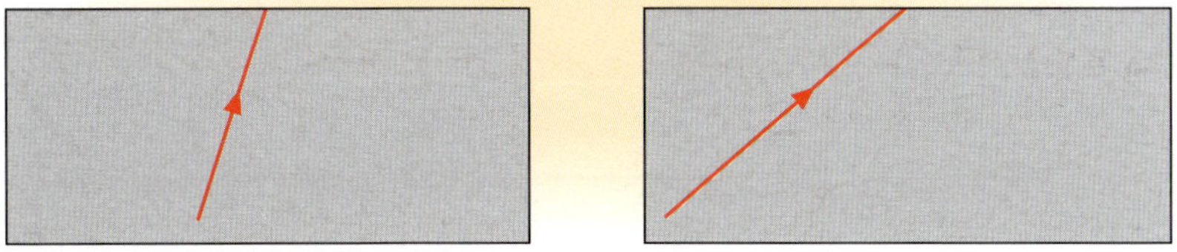

**2 List three uses of total internal reflection.**

**3 Why would you expect to see a brighter image using a periscope that contains two prisms, rather than one with two mirrors?**

**4 Copy and complete the sentences below, which explain why cable TV systems use optical fibres instead of electrical cables. Use the words *more* or *less*.**

An electrical cable can carry ______________ information than an optical fibre of the same thickness.

There is ______________ weakening of the signal in an electrical cable than in an optical fibre.

## Key ideas

- *When light strikes the inside surface of glass (or another transparent material), some is reflected and some passes through, provided the angle between the ray and the normal is small.*
- *If the angle is greater than the critical angle, it is totally internally reflected.*
- *Total internal reflection occurs in optical fibres, which are used in endoscopes and for transmitting information over long distances.*

# 12:9 Analogue and digital

Today, we are surrounded by information – pictures, speech, music, text, and data. It reaches our eyes and ears in the form of light and sound.

Information travels around in many forms – it may be carried by radio waves or microwaves through the air, as electrical signals along wires and cables, or as light or infrared signals along optical fibres.

**a What type of wave is used to transmit television signals through the air?**

A computer with Internet access can connect you to many sources of information including text, data, images and music.

## Waves of information

Information is transferred as a signal. Signals can have two forms: **analogue** or **digital**. An analogue signal varies like a wave, to carry the information. The amplitude or the frequency of the wave changes continuously, like a sound wave. The diagrams show two forms of analogue signal.

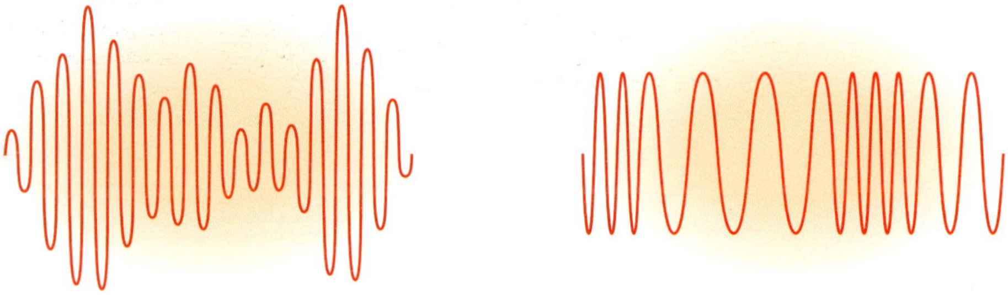

The analogue signal on the left has a varying amplitude. The one on the right has a varying frequency.

A loudspeaker makes use of analogue signals. An electric current in the wires varies in amplitude and frequency. It passes in the loudspeaker coil and makes the cone move backwards and forwards. This pushes the air to and fro to make a sound wave.

## Dot dash dot

A digital signal is similar to Morse code. The information is coded as a series of pulses (on and off). A source of light or infrared radiation, such as a laser, flashes on and off to send the signal down an optical fibre. When it is received the signal is translated back into sounds and pictures that can be understood.

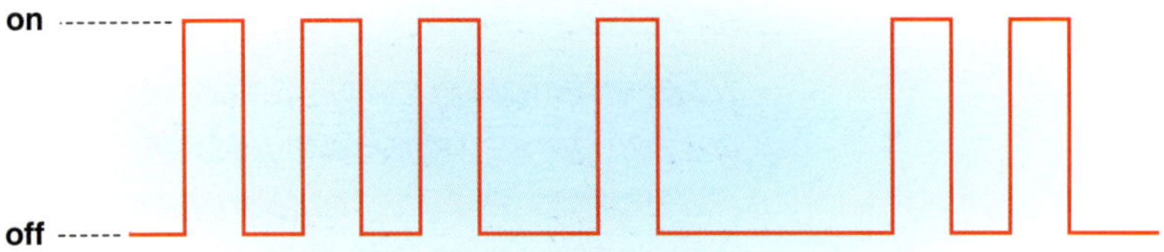


A digital signal is a series of on–off pulses.

**Did you know?**

Samuel Morse invented the Morse code in 1835, when the only means of long distance communication was by telegraph wire. His code used dots and dashes to represent each letter of the alphabet.

The use of Morse code has now been discontinued.

**b** Look at the diagram of the digital signal. How many 'on's are there? How many 'off's?

## Digital quality

In many ways, digital signals are a better way of transmitting information than analogue signals.

- Digital signals give higher quality sound and pictures because noise and distortion is easily removed. Once received, the original quality of the signal can be restored.
- A digital signal can travel long distances along an optical fibre before it needs amplifying.

**c** A digital signal can be carried along an optical fibre by light waves. What other form of electromagnetic radiation can be used?

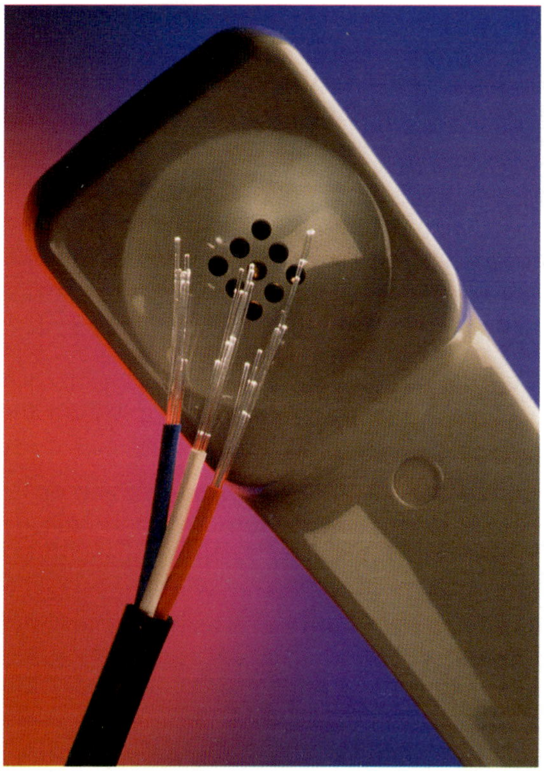

A conventional telephone wire can only carry a signal for a few kilometres before it needs amplifying. If it is replaced with an optical fibre, the signal has a much greater range.

## Questions

**1** Copy the table. Write *analogue* or *digital* in the first column.

| Type of signal | Description |
|---|---|
| | a series of on–off pulses |
| | a wave with varying frequency or amplitude |

**2** Computers can send information to each other along cables. Which type of signal transfers information more rapidly, analogue or digital?

**3** Look at the diagrams.

**a** Which shows an analogue signal?

**b** Which shows a digital signal?

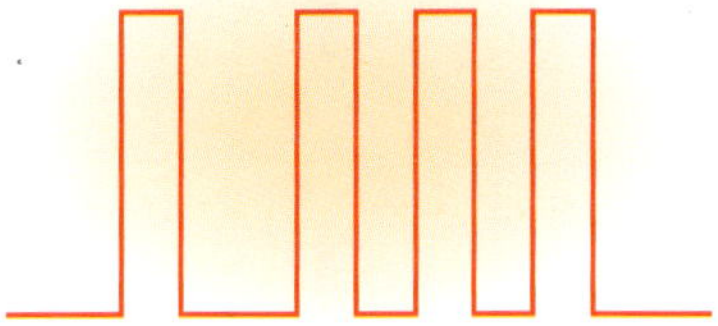

A

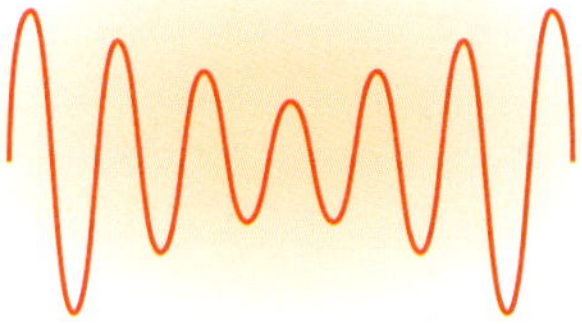

B

**4** State one advantage of transferring information in digital form.

### Key ideas

- *Information is transferred in the form of a signal. Signals can be carried by varying electric currents, by electromagnetic waves, or by light or infrared waves along optical fibres.*
- *Signals can be digital (on-off pulses) or analogue (varying amplitude or frequency).*
- *Digital signals give clearer reception than analogue signals.*

# 12:10 Wave diffraction

A harbour can provide protection from big waves on the open sea. The photograph shows what happens when waves enter a harbour. They spread out as they enter the harbour mouth into the space beyond, so that boats in the furthest corners are rocked up and down.

You can study this effect using a ripple tank. Straight ripples approach a **gap** in a barrier, just like the mouth of the harbour. As they pass through the gap, they spread out into the space beyond.

In a similar way, ripples spread around the corner as they pass an obstacle to fill the space behind it.

This spreading out of waves as they pass through a gap or around an obstacle is known as **diffraction**. Diffraction is an effect that is only observed with waves. Particles move in straight lines, and their paths do not bend when they pass through a gap. Sound and light both travel as waves, so they can also be diffracted.

**Did you know?**
Loudspeakers are designed so that sound spreads out through diffraction as it leaves the loudspeaker cone.

## Longer wavelengths

The diagrams show how waves of different *wavelengths* are diffracted as they pass through a gap. Waves with a long wavelength spread out more than those with a short wavelength.

**a** **Look at the first diagram of ripples being diffracted. What would happen if the gap was made narrower? Would the ripples spread out more, or less?**

**b** **Look at the diagrams of waves being diffracted. Does their wavelength change when they are diffracted? How can you tell?**

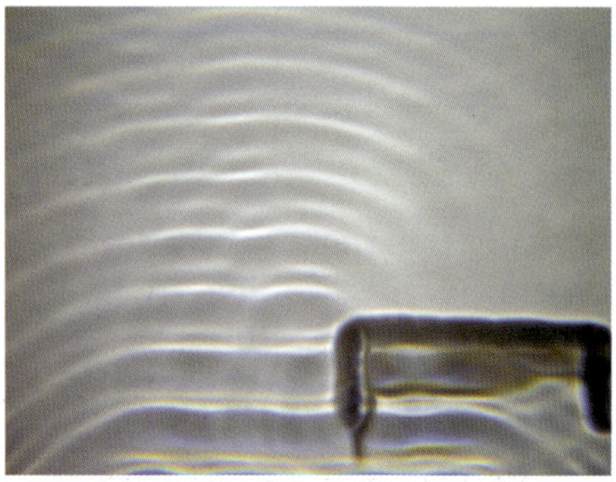

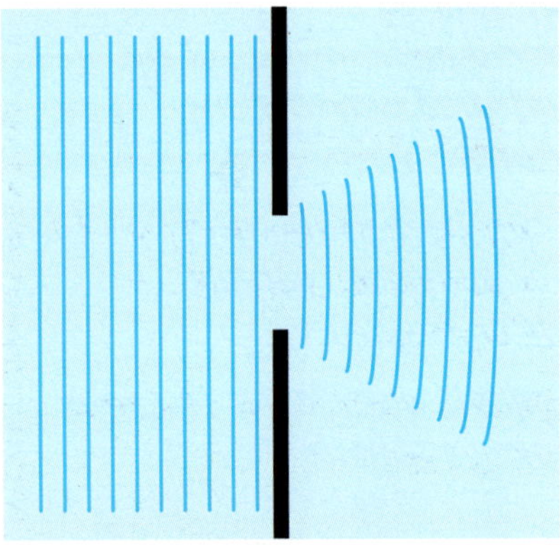

short wavelength (ripples close together): very little diffraction

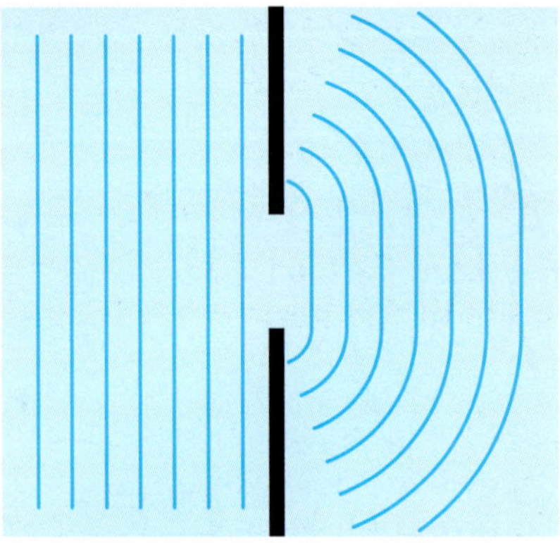

longer wavelength: more diffraction

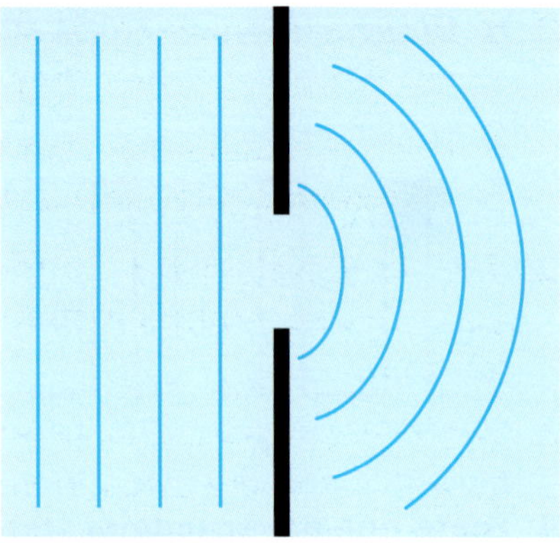

longest wavelength: strongest diffraction

## Diffracting sound and radio waves

If you are in the next room to some people who are speaking to you, you may be able to hear them even though you cannot see them. The sound waves of their voices are diffracted as they pass through the doorway and spread out around the room that you are in.

Sounds are easily diffracted at a doorway because the wavelength of sound is about the same as the width of the doorway.

Radio waves are a form of electromagnetic radiation (like light). They have long wavelengths, usually over 1 m and sometimes as much as 1 km. There may be a hill between you and the transmitter, but the longer wavelengh waves are diffracted round the hill so that you can still pick up the signal.

Radio waves can also be reflected from a large flat surface such as a nearby building. Your television or radio aerial than detects two signals, one a short time after the other. This can cause a 'ghost' image on your television screen, or make your radio sound fuzzy.

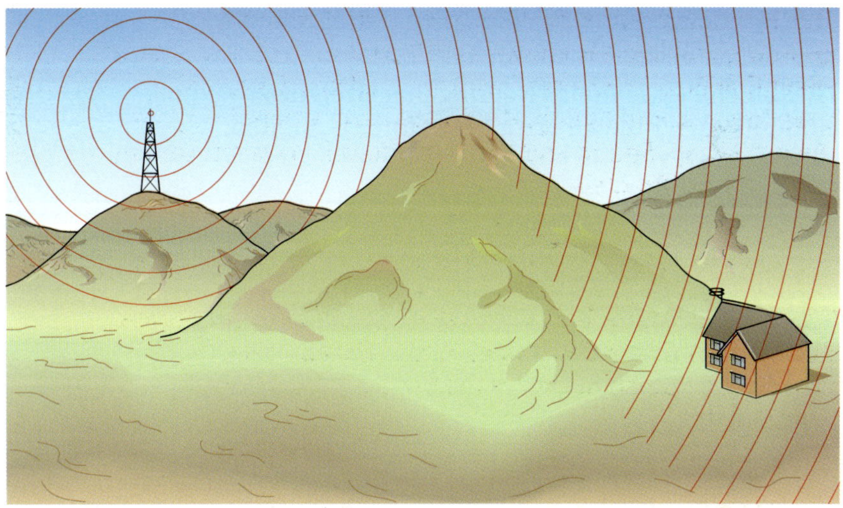

Light waves have a very short wavelength, less than a millionth of a metre. They can also be diffracted, but they need to pass through a very tiny gap for the effects to be seen.

**c Which radio waves are more likely to reach the radio aerial, those for FM (wavelength 3 m) or those for AM (wavelength over 200 m)? Explain your answer.**

## Questions

**1** Copy this table and complete the definitions in the second column.

| | |
|---|---|
| **Reflection** | Waves change direction when ... |
| **Refraction** | Waves change direction when ... |
| **Diffraction** | Waves spread out when ... |

**2 a** Draw a diagram to show how straight, parallel ripples are diffracted when they pass through a narrow gap.

**b** Draw a second diagram to show how the situation would be altered if the ripples had a longer wavelength.

**3** You are standing at your friend's front door. Explain how you can hear someone mowing the lawn in the back garden.

**4** You receive radio signals from a transmitter a few kilometres away. Explain how your radio set can pick up these signals even though there may be a block of flats in the way.

### Key ideas

- *Waves spread out when they go through a gap or past an object. This is diffraction.*
- *The longer the wavelength, the more the waves spread out.*

# 12:11 Changing shape

As you walk across a solid concrete floor, you are not aware that the floor changes shape as you walk. You are more aware of the change in shape of a chair or a bed when you sit or lie on it. The floor, the chair and the bed all become **compressed**. This enables them to exert an upward force so that the vertical forces acting on you are balanced.

**When you sit in a chair, the squashed springs exert an upward force on you.**

## Patterns of change

Some objects follow a simple pattern of behaviour when they are stretched or compressed, others do not. If you look at the scale on a forcemeter you will see that it is linear, the pointer moves the same distance between 1 N and 2 N as it does between 3 N and 4 N.

The forcemeter contains a spring that **stretches** by equal amounts each time an extra 1 N of force is applied.

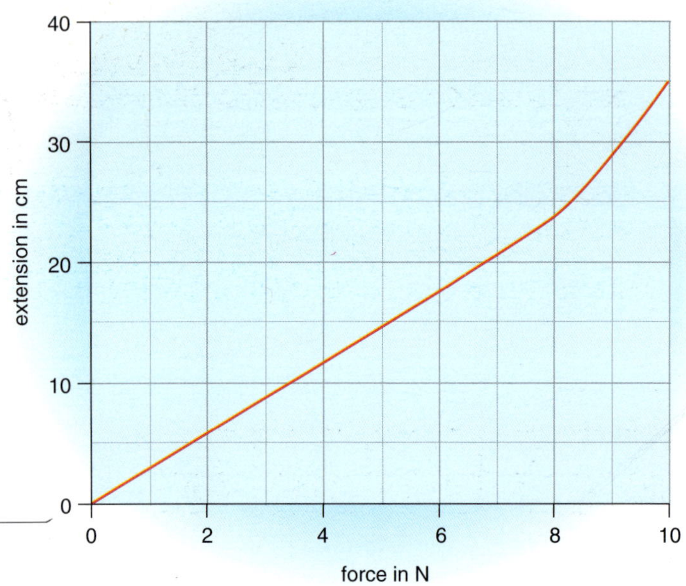


The graph shows the pattern of stretching when the force on a **spring** is steadily increased.

- Initially the spring follows a simple pattern, *doubling* the force *doubles* the **extension**.
- After a certain force, the spring becomes easier to stretch.
- Beyond this force, the spring may not return to its original size when the force is removed.

**a i For the spring shown on the graph, at what force does the simple pattern stop?**

**ii What *extension* does this force cause?**

**Did you know?**

Most scales that are used for weighing people use springs. When a person stands on the scales, a spring is compressed. The heavier the person, the greater the amount of compression.

## A rubber band

**Rubber bands** do not show the same pattern of stretch that a spring shows. If you pull on a rubber band you find that it is easy to stretch at first and then it becomes stiffer. If you continue to stretch it, eventually the band will break.

**b i How much does the band stretch when the force is increased from 0 to 1 N?**

**ii How much does the band stretch when the force is increased from 4 to 5 N?**

**iii How can you tell that the band has become stiffer?**

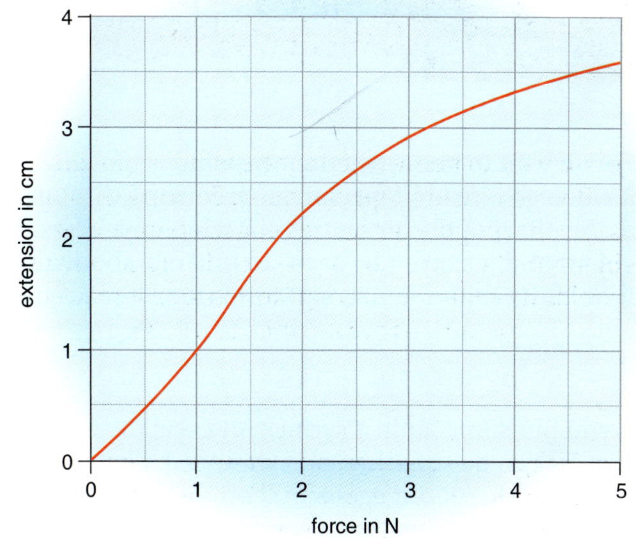


## Bridge supports

A simple bridge consists of a beam resting on two concrete pillars. The pillars are compressed so that they provide an upward force to balance the weight of the beam.

When traffic is on the bridge the forces change.

- The downward force on the pillars increases.
- The pillars become compressed to provide a greater upward force.
- The upward and downward forces remain in balance.

The diagram shows the extra forces from the pillars due to the weight of a lorry on the bridge. As the lorry crosses from right to left, the force from the right hand pillar decreases and that from the left hand pillar increases.

**c What is the position of the lorry when the forces from the pillars are equal?**

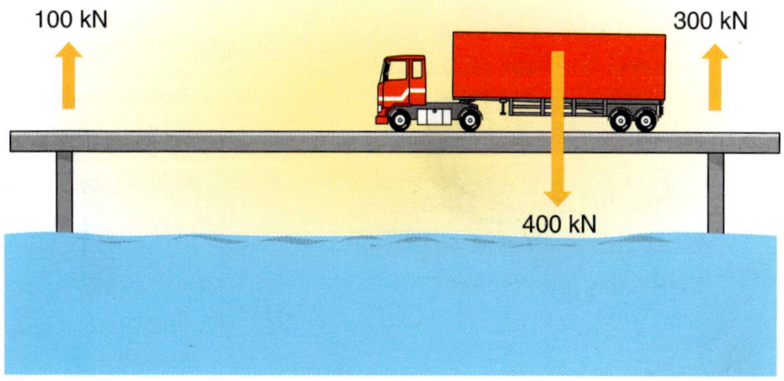


## Questions

**1 The data in the table show how the length of a spring changes as the force on it is increased.**

| Force (N) | 2 | 4 | 6 | 8 | 10 |
|---|---|---|---|---|---|
| Length (cm) | 10.0 | 12.5 | 15.0 | 18.5 | 23.0 |

**a Plot a graph of length of spring against force. Use scales similar to those in the graph above.**

**b i What is the length of the spring when there is no force on it?**

**ii For what range of forces does the spring follow a simple pattern of stretching?**

**iii Describe this pattern.**

**iv Describe how the spring stretches when the force is increased further.**

**2 a Explain why the upward forces from the pillars of a bridge change when a heavy lorry drives onto the bridge.**

**b How do the forces change as the lorry crosses the bridge?**

### Key ideas

- *For a limited range of forces, springs stretch in a regular and predictable way.*
- *Rubber bands do not show a simple pattern of stretching.*
- *The sizes of the upward forces on a horizontal beam change with the position of the load.*

# 12:12 Gas pressure

If you want to know whether the wind is blowing, you do not have to go outside. You can tell by looking through the window at the effect of the air on trees or telephone wires. Air has no colour and it cannot be seen. To find out about air scientists have done experiments on it to see how it reacts.

You can tell whether the wind is blowing by the effects it has.

## Squashing up

If you put some air in a syringe and seal the end, you notice that air can be squashed and stretched. Push in the plunger and the air pushes it out again. Pull on the plunger and the air pulls back. It behaves just like a spring.

One of the first people to try to explain this springy property of air was Robert Boyle, a seventeenth century scientist. He suggested that air is made of **particles** that are hard in the middle and springy on the outside.

Had Boyle been putting forward his model today, he would probably have suggested that air is made of bits of material like foam rubber.

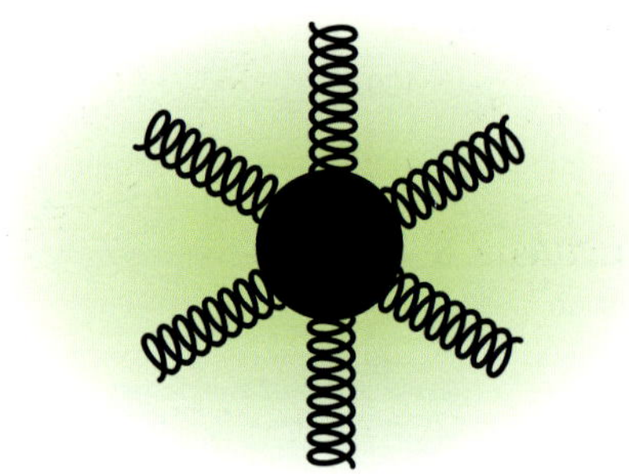

**a Why did Boyle think that air is made up of squashy particles?**

## Moving pollen

The next significant discovery was made by Robert Brown, a botanist. He was studying different types of pollen under a microscope. The pollen grains were suspended in water. He noticed that they were moving in a dithery, jerky motion. This motion of pollen grains is called '**Brownian motion**'.

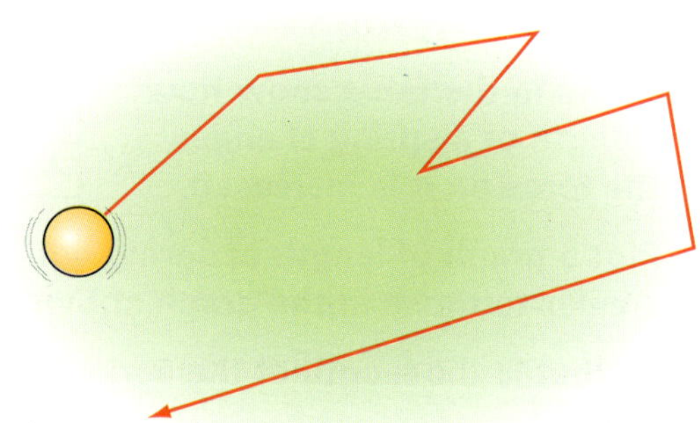

Particles of smoke suspended in air show a similar type of motion.

Although he observed it, Brown was not able to explain the motion of the pollen grains.

**b Explain why Brown was able to see pollen grains, but he could not see the particles that make up water.**

## A stroke of genius

The explanation for Brownian motion came from Albert Einstein at the beginning of the twentieth century. This explanation led to the current model of the structure of liquids and gases. Einstein's explanation goes like this.

- Something must be hitting the pollen grains to make them move.

- The particles hitting the pollen grains must be very tiny, because they cannot be seen under the microscope.
- The particles must be very fast-moving to be able to have this effect on the larger pollen grains.
- The motion of the particles is disordered.

**c Explain why Einstein thought that particles of water must be moving very fast.**

**Did you know?**
When Einstein put forward his explanation of Brownian motion, he was working as an obscure clerk in the Swiss patent office.

## The particles in a gas

The picture shows a model of the particles in a gas.

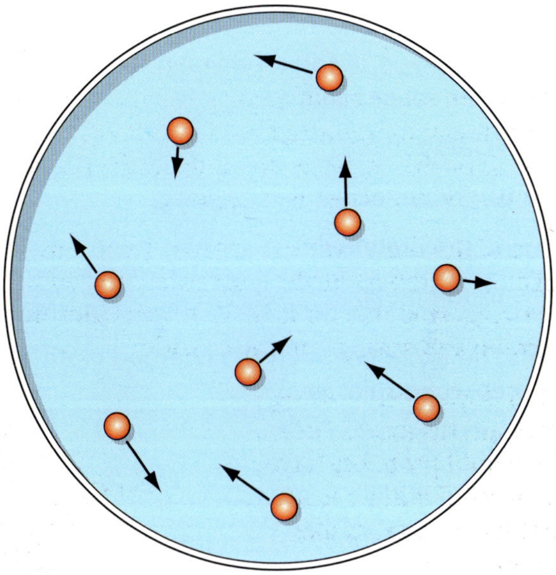

- The motion of an individual particle is constantly changing in speed and direction, it is **random** and cannot be predicted.
- On average, the particles are very fast-moving, typically 300 m/s in air at room temperature.

The particles in a gas collide with each other and with the container walls. These collisions result in a change of speed and direction.

**Gas pressure** is caused by the forces exerted in collisions with the container walls. The pressure of a gas can be increased by:

- squashing it, so that collisions with the container walls are more frequent;
- heating it, so that the particles move faster, on average, and exert a greater force at each collision.

**d Which type of collision causes gas pressure?**

## Questions

**1** Copy and complete the sentences using the words provided.

**container walls** **direction** **particles** **pressure**

Gases are made up of lots of ____________. These are moving all the time, constantly changing speed and ____________. When they collide with the ____________ they exert a force, which results in gas ____________.

**2** How did Boyle explain the springiness of air?

**3** Describe Einstein's explanation of the movement of pollen grains in water.

**4** Some air is sealed in a syringe. The piston is pushed in. Explain why the gas pressure increases.

## Key ideas

- *The particles in a gas have a random motion.*
- *Gas pressure is a result of the forces exerted when gas particles collide with the walls of their container.*

# End of module questions

## Low demand

**Questions 1–2**

When a Perspex ruler is rubbed with a cloth, the ruler becomes positively charged.

1 What type of force between the cloth and the ruler causes this?

**A** attractive

**B** frictional

**C** gravitational

**D** magnetic

2 The force between the charged cloth and the charged ruler is

**A** attractive

**B** frictional

**C** gravitational

**D** magnetic

3 Lightning is caused by a build up of charge

**A** in the air

**B** on power lines

**C** on telephone wires

**D** at the base of a cloud

4 A shock from a car door is caused by the movement of

**A** electrons

**B** neutrons

**C** nucleons

**D** protons

5 The diagram shows a transformer.

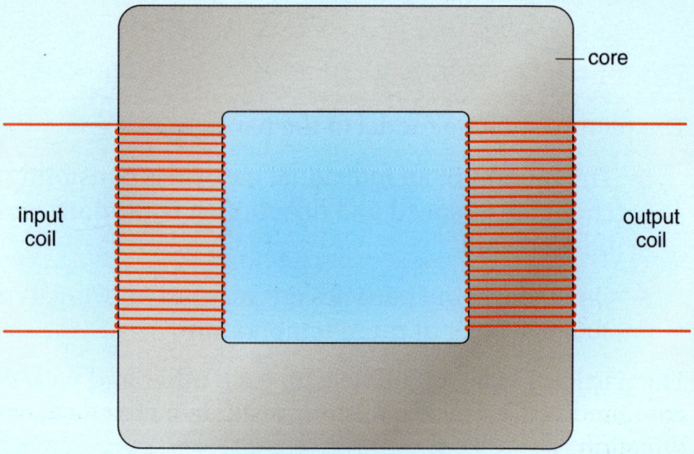


The best material for the core is

**A** copper

**B** iron

**C** plastic

**D** steel

6 In a simple d.c. motor the coil

**A** moves in and out

**B** moves from side to side

**C** moves up and down

**D** turns round

7 Waves can transfer

**A** energy

**B** gases

**C** liquids

**D** solids

**Questions 10–11**

The diagram shows light passing through a prism.

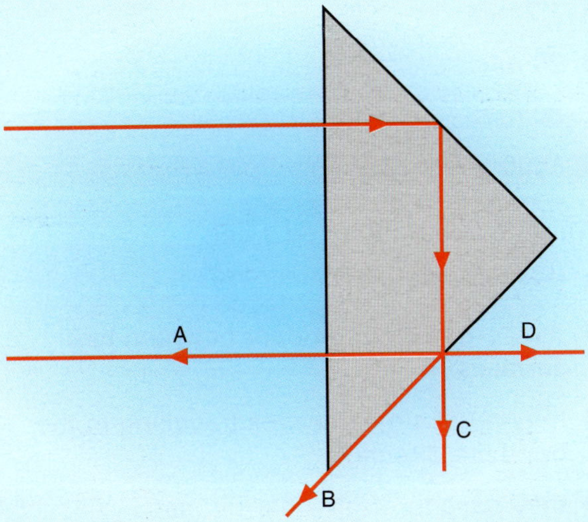


8 Which lettered arrow shows the direction of the light as it leaves the prism?

9 Prisms are used like this in

**A** cameras

**B** cycle reflectors

**C** optical fibres

**D** periscopes

10 A spring stretches by 6 cm when a 10 N weight is hung on it.

If the 10 N weight is replaced by a 5 N weight the spring could stretch by

**A** 3 cm

**B** 4 cm

**C** 5 cm

**D** 6 cm

11 The particles in a gas

**A** do not move

**B** move up and down

**C** move from side to side

**D** move randomly

12 A lorry crosses a simple road bridge.

The sizes of the forces P and Q change when the lorry changes

**A** acceleration

**B** gear

**C** position

**D** speed

## Standard demand

**Questions 13–14**

When a person walks across a nylon carpet, the carpet becomes negatively charged.

13 What type of charge does the person gain?

**A** earthed

**B** negative

**C** neutral

**D** positive

14 What charge transfer takes place?

**A** electrons move from the person to the carpet

**B** electrons move from the carpet to the person

**C** protons move from the person to the carpet

**D** protons move from the carpet to the person

15 Electrostatic charge is a hazard when

**A** photocopying

**B** refuelling an aircraft

**C** using an inkjet printer

**D** using a laser printer

16 A current of 2.0 A passes in a lamp filament for 60 s.

The charge flow through the filament is

**A** 15 C

**B** 30 C

**C** 120 C

**D** 240 C

17 A current of 2.5 A passes in a lamp when the voltage across it is 12 V.

The power of the lamp is

**A** 4.8 J

**B** 4.8 W

**C** 30 J

**D** 30 W

18 When a current-carrying wire is placed at right angles to a magnetic field, the wire experiences a

**A** force parallel to the magnetic field

**B** force at right angles to the magnetic field

**C** force in the direction of the current

**D** force in the opposite direction to the current

19 A transformer

**A** changes the power of an alternating voltage

**B** changes the power of a direct voltage

**C** changes the size of an alternating voltage

**D** changes the size of a direct voltage

20 Which line in the table shows the action of a step-down transformer?

| | Input voltage | Output voltage |
|---|---|---|
| **A** | 240 V a.c. | 12 V a.c. |
| **B** | 240 V a.c. | 12 V d.c. |
| **C** | 12 V a.c. | 240 V a.c. |
| **D** | 12 V a.c. | 240 V d.c. |

21 A sound wave has a wavelength of 50 m and a frequency of 30 Hz.

The speed of the wave is

**A** 1.7 m/s

**B** 20 m/s

**C** 80 m/s

**D** 1500 m/s

22 Waves can be diffracted when

**A** they strike a mirror

**B** they cross the boundary between two surfaces

**C** they meet similar waves travelling in the opposite direction

**D** they pass through a narrow gap

23 The extension of a spring

**A** always doubles when the force is doubled

**B** always halves when the force is doubled

**C** is proportional to the force for small extensions

**D** is inversely proportional to the force for small extensions

24 The particles in a gas exert a pressure by

**A** becoming squashed

**B** expanding

**C** colliding with other particles

**D** colliding with the container walls

## The periodic table of elements

**KEY**

| | |
|---|---|
| Mass number A | 1 |
| Symbol | **H** |
| Name | Hydrogen |
| Atomic number (Proton number) Z | 1 |

| 1 | 2 | | | | | | | | | | | 3 | 4 | 5 | 6 | 7 | 0 |
|---|---|---|---|---|---|---|---|---|---|---|---|---|---|---|---|---|---|
| | | | | | | | | | | | | | | | | | 4<br>**He**<br>Helium<br>2 |
| 7<br>**Li**<br>Lithium<br>3 | 9<br>**Be**<br>Beryllium<br>4 | | | | | | | | | | | 11<br>**B**<br>Boron<br>5 | 12<br>**C**<br>Carbon<br>6 | 14<br>**N**<br>Nitrogen<br>7 | 16<br>**O**<br>Oxygen<br>8 | 19<br>**F**<br>Fluorine<br>9 | 20<br>**Ne**<br>Neon<br>10 |
| 23<br>**Na**<br>Sodium<br>11 | 24<br>**Mg**<br>Magnesium<br>12 | | | | | | | | | | | 27<br>**Al**<br>Aluminium<br>13 | 28<br>**Si**<br>Silicon<br>14 | 31<br>**P**<br>Phosphorus<br>15 | 32<br>**S**<br>Sulphur<br>16 | 35<br>**Cl**<br>Chlorine<br>17 | 40<br>**Ar**<br>Argon<br>18 |
| 39<br>**K**<br>Potassium<br>19 | 40<br>**Ca**<br>Calcium<br>20 | 45<br>**Sc**<br>Scandium<br>21 | 48<br>**Ti**<br>Titanium<br>22 | 51<br>**V**<br>Vanadium<br>23 | 52<br>**Cr**<br>Chromium<br>24 | 55<br>**Mn**<br>Manganese<br>25 | 56<br>**Fe**<br>Iron<br>26 | 59<br>**Co**<br>Cobalt<br>27 | 59<br>**Ni**<br>Nickel<br>28 | 63<br>**Cu**<br>Copper<br>29 | 64<br>**Zn**<br>Zinc<br>30 | 70<br>**Ga**<br>Gallium<br>31 | 73<br>**Ge**<br>Germanium<br>32 | 75<br>**As**<br>Arsenic<br>33 | 79<br>**Se**<br>Selenium<br>34 | 80<br>**Br**<br>Bromine<br>35 | 84<br>**Kr**<br>Krypton<br>36 |
| 85<br>**Rb**<br>Rubidium<br>37 | 88<br>**Sr**<br>Strontium<br>38 | 89<br>**Y**<br>Yttrium<br>39 | 91<br>**Zr**<br>Zirconium<br>40 | 93<br>**Nb**<br>Niobium<br>41 | 96<br>**Mo**<br>Molybdenum<br>42 | 99<br>**Tc**<br>Technetium<br>43 | 101<br>**Ru**<br>Ruthenium<br>44 | 103<br>**Rh**<br>Rhodium<br>45 | 106<br>**Pd**<br>Palladium<br>46 | 108<br>**Ag**<br>Silver<br>47 | 112<br>**Cd**<br>Cadmium<br>48 | 115<br>**In**<br>Indium<br>49 | 119<br>**Sn**<br>Tin<br>50 | 122<br>**Sb**<br>Antimony<br>51 | 128<br>**Te**<br>Tellurium<br>52 | 127<br>**I**<br>Iodine<br>53 | 131<br>**Xe**<br>Xenon<br>54 |
| 133<br>**Cs**<br>Caesium<br>55 | 137<br>**Ba**<br>Barium<br>56 | 139<br>**La**<br>Lanthanum<br>57 | 178<br>**Hf**<br>Hafnium<br>72 | 181<br>**Ta**<br>Tantalum<br>73 | 184<br>**W**<br>Tungsten<br>74 | 186<br>**Re**<br>Rhenium<br>75 | 190<br>**Os**<br>Osmium<br>76 | 192<br>**Ir**<br>Iridium<br>77 | 195<br>**Pt**<br>Platinum<br>78 | 197<br>**Au**<br>Gold<br>79 | 202<br>**Hg**<br>Mercury<br>80 | 204<br>**Tl**<br>Thallium<br>81 | 207<br>**Pb**<br>Lead<br>82 | 209<br>**Bi**<br>Bismuth<br>83 | 210<br>**Po**<br>Polonium<br>84 | 210<br>**At**<br>Astatine<br>85 | 222<br>**Rn**<br>Radon<br>86 |
| 223<br>**Fr**<br>Francium<br>87 | 226<br>**Ra**<br>Radium<br>88 | 227<br>**Ac**<br>Actinium<br>89 | | | | | | | | | | | | | | | |

Elements 58–71 and 90–103 have been omitted.

The value for mass number is normally that of the commonest isotope, e.g. $^{35}Cl$ not $^{37}Cl$.

Bromine is approximately equal proportions of $^{79}Br$ and $^{81}Br$.

# Key words

The key words listed below are terms that you need to understand for your exams. It might prove helpful to copy them out and provide definitions from the relevant spread whilst revising for exams.

## Module 7 – Food and the environment

**Spread 7:1**
nucleus
cell membrane
cell wall
chlorophyll
chloroplast
cyctoplasm
vacuole

**Spread 7:2**
carbon dioxide
glucose
oxygen
photosynthesis

**Spread 7:3**
cellulose
protein
respiration
starch

**Spread 7:4**
carbon dioxide
light
limiting factor
temperature

**Spread 7:5**
cuticle
diffusion
osmosis
selectively permeable membrane
turgid

**Spread 7:6**
fertiliser
mineral
root hair

**Spread 7:7**
diffusion
guard cells
phloem
stomata
transpiration
xylem
xylem vessel

**Spread 7:8**
auxin
cutting
plant hormone
rooting powder
selective weed killer
tissue culture

**Spread 7:9**
biomass
ecosystem
food chain
food web
producer
pyramid of biomass
pyramid of numbers

**Spread 7:10**
carbon compounds
carbon cycle
carbon dioxide
decay
microorganisms
oxygen
photosynthesis
respiration

**Spread 7:11**
carbon dioxide
deforestation
sustainable forestry

**Spread 7:12**
nitrogen
rainforest

**Spread 7:13**
biological pest control
fungicide
herbicide
insecticide
pesticide
predator
sterile male

**Spread 7:14**
food chain
DDT
insecticide
malaria

**Spread 7:15**
biodiversity
ecosystem
endangered species
habitat
species

## Module 8 – Health and exercise

**Spread 8:1**
air passage
alveolus (plural alveoli)
bronchiole
bronchus (plural bronchi)
diaphragm
intercostal muscle
rib
thorax
trachea
ventilation

**Spread 8:2**
addictive
bronchitis
cilia
diffusion
emphysema
mucus
tumour

**Spread 8:3**
artery
atrium (plural atria)
circulatory system
double circulatory system
pulse
vein
ventricle

**Spread 8:4**
artery
capillary
vein

**Spread 8:5**
diabetes
glucagon
glycogen
insulin
pancreas

**Spread 8:6**
aerobic respiration
anaerobic respiration
cramp
lactic acid
oxygen debt

**Spread 8:8**
hormones
steroids

**Spread 8:9**
carrier
cystic fibrosis
inherited disorder

**Spread 8:10**
anaemia
carrier
malaria
sickle cell anaemia
sickle cell disease

**Spread 8:11**
genetic counselling
gene therapy
rejection

## Module 9 – Chemicals and the Earth

**Spread 9:1**
alloy
conductor
ductile
malleable

**Spread 9:2**
mineral
ore
oxidation
reactivity series
reduction
stable

**Spread 9:3**
displacement reaction
thermit reaction

**Spread 9:4**
blast furnace
carbon reduction

**Spread 9:5**
electrodes
electrolysis

**Spread 9:6**
bauxite
cryolite
re-cycled

**Spread 9:7**
catalyst
transition metals

**Spread 9:8**
alkali
alkali metals
brine
halite

**Spread 9:9**
fossil
metamorphic rock
sedimentary rock
succession

**Spread 9:10**
basalt
granite
igneous rock
magma
minerals
volcano

**Spread 9:11**
atmosphere
photosynthesis

**Spread 9:12**
global warming
greenhouse effect
respiration

**Spread 9:13**
dynamic equilibrium
fertilisers
Haber process
yield

**Spread 9:14**
blue baby syndrome
eutrophication

**Spread 9:15**
monatomic gases
noble gases

## Module 10 – Understanding chemical reactions

**Spread 10:1**
atomic number
isotope
mass number
nucleons

**Spread 10:2**
chemical bond
electrostatic forces
ion
ionic bonding

**Spread 10:3**
crystal
giant structure
lattice
molten

**Spread 10:4**
covalent bond
diatomic

**Spread 10:5**
molecule

**Spread 10:6**
exothermic

**Spread 10:7**
endothermic

**Spread 10:8**
formula
symbol

**Spread 10:9**
balance
product
reactant
state symbols
symbol equation
word equation

**Spread 10:10**
relative formula mass

## Module 11 – Movement and change

**Spread 11:01**
speed
velocity
distance--time graph
slope
gradient

**Spread 11:02**
acceleration
speed–time graph

**Spread 11:03**
accelerating

**Spread 11:04**
reaction time
thinking distance
braking distance
stopping distance

**Spread 11:05**
balanced forces
unbalanced forces

**Spread 11:06**
direction
mass

**Spread 11:07**
air resistance
fluid
terminal velocity

**Spread 11:08**
work
energy
gravitational potential energy
heat
kinetic energy

**Spread 11:09**
powerful
power
work done
energy transfer

**Spread 11:10**
crust
mantle
core
seismograph
seismic wave

**Spread 11:11**
tectonic plates
lithosphere
earthquake
volcano

**Spread 11:12**
decay
count rate
becquerel
half-life

**Spread 11:13**
uranium
lead
radiocarbon dating

## Module 12 – Energy, force and communication

**Spread 12:01**
charged
insulator
conductor
positive charge
negative charge

**Spread 12:02**
spark
lightning
inkjet printer
photocopier

**Spread 12:03**
electron
electric charge
electric current

**Spread 12:04**
energy
power
voltage

**Spread 12:05**
coil
magnetic field
force
motor

**Spread 12:06**
transformer
step-up transformer
step-down transformer
primary coil
secondary coil

**Spread 12:07**
wavelength
frequency

**Spread 12:08**
optical fibre
total internal reflection
critical angle
reflecting prism

**Spread 12:09**
analogue
digital

**Spread 12:10**
diffraction gap
diffraction

**Spread 12:11**
compress
stretch
extension
spring
rubber band

**Spread 12:12**
particles
Brownian motion
random
gas pressure

# Index


acceleration 122–125, 131, 132–133
  measurement 124–125
acid reactions 67, 106, 113, 114
addictive smoking 39
aerobic respiration 46
Africa, sickle cell disease 55
air
  breathing 38
  gas concentrations 38
  plant water loss 15
air passages 36–37, 52, 56
air pressure 37, 172
air resistance 128, 132–133
airships 90
alchemists 144
algal bloom 89
alkali metals 76–77
alkaline solutions 62, 76
alleles 53, 54–55
alloys 63
alternating current (a.c.) 160
aluminium
  extraction 64, 66, 68, 70, 72–73, 108
  ion 110
  in magma 80
  reactivity 64, 66, 70
  uses 62
aluminium alloy 63
aluminium oxide 66, 72, 108
aluminium sulphate 110
alveoli 36, 38–39, 43
Amazonian rainforest 20, 24
ammonia
  in the atmosphere 82
  covalent bonding 104
  fertilisers 86, 88
  Haber process 75, 86–87, 88, 115
ammonites 79
ammonium hydroxide 88
ammonium ions 110
ammonium nitrate 88
amplitude 166
amps (A) 155
anaemia 54–55
anaerobic respiration 46–47
analogue signals 166
anhydrous copper sulphate 86, 109
animals 2–3, 18–19
anodes 70–73
anti-lock braking system (ABS) 126
antibiotics 52, 54
aquatic plants 2, 5
aqueous solutions 113
archaeological dating 97, 144–145
argon 90, 91, 98
Armstrong, Neil 133
arteries 41, 42, 43
artificial fertilisers 12–13
asexual reproduction 17
athletes, performance 50–51
atmosphere
  balance 84–85
  carbon dioxide 21, 23, 25, 84–85
  composition 82–83, 91
atomic number 96
atoms 96, 98–99, 102–103
atria 40–41
auxins 16, 17

bacteria
  chlorine action 77
  diseases 52
  genetically engineered 45
  in respiration 38, 39
baking soda 108
balanced equations 112, 113
balanced forces 128–129, 132
Bannister, Roger 120
basalt 80, 81, 140–141
bauxite 64, 72
beams 171
becquerels (Bq) 142
biodiversity 30–31
biological pest control 27
biomass 18–19, 23
birds, and pesticides 26, 28
bivalves 79
blast furnace 68–69
blood
  breathing system 38
  circulatory system 40–43
  glucose 44, 46
  nitrite effects 89
blood cells 38, 43, 54–55
blood pressure 42, 43
blood vessels 38–39, 40, 42–43, 54
blue baby syndrome 89
body temperature 46
boiling points 76, 87, 90, 104
bond breaking 107, 108
bonding
  covalent 102–105
  ionic 98–101
bones 50
Booth, Cecil 158
Boyle, Robert 172
brachiopods 79
braking distance 126
braking force 126, 127
breathing
  during exercise 37, 46–47
  exchange of gases 38–39
  inhalation/exhalation 36–37, 48
bridge supports 171
brine 77
bromide 110
bromine 114
bronchioles 36, 38
bronchitis 39
bronchus 36
Brown, Robert 172
Brownian motion 172, 173
brushes (motors) 158–159
burning
  alkali metals 76
  carbon 68
  fuel 8, 21, 23, 85, 106
  wood 20–21, 22, 23, 86

cable TV 165
calcium 64, 110
calcium carbonate 68–69, 78, 84, 114, 115
calcium chloride 114
calcium hydrogencarbonate 85
calcium hydroxide 114, 115
calcium oxide 69, 114, 115
calcium silicate 69, 115
cancer 39, 51
capillaries 38, 40, 41, 42–43, 54
carbohydrates 4, 19, 44
carbon
  anodes 72
  fullerene 105
  isotopes 97, 145
  oxidation 114
  recycling 20–21
carbon cycle 20–21, 23, 84–85
carbon dating 97, 145
carbon dioxide
  in the atmosphere 21, 23, 25, 82, 83, 84–85, 91
  carbon cycle 20–21, 23, 84–85
  catalytic converters 75
  covalent bonding 104
  detection of 7
  fizzy drinks 108
  formation 114, 115
  formula 111
  fossil fuel burning 85
  metal extraction 68–69, 72
  in photosynthesis 4, 5, 8–9, 12, 14, 23
  in respiration 7, 23, 36, 38, 84
carbon monoxide 69, 83, 114
carbon reduction 68–69, 70, 71, 72
carbonate ion 110
carcinogens 39
carriers of diseases 53, 54–55
cars 122, 126–127, 128–129
cartilage rings 36
catalysts 75, 87
catalytic converters 75
cathodes 70–73
cell membranes 2–3, 10–11, 12

cell sap 2–3
cell walls 2–3, 7, 11
cells
  animal 2–3
  blood 38, 43, 54–55
  growth and repair 46
  plants 2–3, 7
cellulose 7
cementation 78
Cenozoic era 79
cereal crops 17, 19
charge (chemical) 110, 114
charge (electrical) 150–151, 152, 153
chemical energy 106–109
chemical equations 112–113
chemical properties 62, 97
chickens 19
chlorine
  atom 98, 102, 103
  formula 111
  gas 70, 77, 102, 114
  ion 110
  molecules 102
chlorophyll 3, 5, 12
chloroplasts 2–3, 9
cigarettes 39
cilia 38, 39
circulatory system 40–43
citric acid 108
cloning 56
coils 158–159, 160
coke 67, 68–69
colour 74–75, 76, 86
combustion reactions 106
common salt 70, 76, 77, 100–101
communication 162, 166–167, 169
compaction 78
compost 20, 88
compression
  gases 87
  solids 170–171
computers
  greenhouse controls 9
  Internet access 166
  measurement of acceleration 124
concrete 78
conductors
  electrical 62, 74, 76, 101, 104, 150, 154
  thermal 74, 76
conglomerate 78
conservation 25
copper 74
  extraction 64, 65, 66, 67, 71, 114
  ion 110
  purification 73
  reactivity 64, 66, 67, 68
  uses 62
  wire 158
copper alloys 63
copper carbonate 74
copper hydroxide 74
copper nitrate 74
copper oxide 65, 67, 74, 114
copper sulphate 66, 71, 73, 74, 114
  anhydrous 86, 109
corals 79, 84
core of the Earth 138
coronary blood vessels 41
coronary heart disease 43
coulombs (C) 155
count rate 142
covalent bonding 102–105
cramp 47
critical angle 165
crop growing 8–9, 12–13, 19, 22, 88–89
crystallisation 80–81, 100–101
current 154–155, 157–159, 161, 166
  alternating 160
cuticle 11
cuttings 17
cystic fibrosis 52–53, 56
cytoplasm 2–3

Dalton, John 111
dangerous driving 127
dating 79, 97, 144–145
DDT insecticide 26–29
  world-wide ban 27, 29
decay
  plants 20, 24
  radioactive substances 142–143
decomposers 31
deflecting plates 153
deforestation 22–23, 25
density 74, 76, 90
deuterium 96–97
deuterium oxide 97
diabetes 44–45
diaphragm muscle 36–37, 48
diatomic molecules 102
diet 43, 44
diffraction 168–169
diffusion 10
  circulatory system 38–39, 43
  water in plants 14–15
digestive system 20, 52
digital signals 166–167
direct current motors 158–159
direction 121, 131, 135
disorder 173
displacement reactions 66–67, 68
dissolving
  alkali metal compounds 76
  gases in water 5
  sodium chloride 101
distance moved 120–121, 135
distance–time graphs 120–121
diversity 30–31
DNA molecules 57
double circulatory system 40
drinking water 89
drug tests 50
ductile metals 62
dust particles 38
dynamic equilibrium 86, 115
Earth
  age 79, 82–83, 142, 144
  crust 138–141
  metal occurrence 64, 72
  molten rock 80, 81, 140–141
  structure 138–141
  temperature 84
earthing 152
earthquakes 138, 140–141
Earth's pull effects 16, 128, 129, 132
ecosystems 1, 18–19, 30
Einstein, Albert 172, 173
ejector seat 128
elastic fibres 42
electric current 154–155, 157–159, 161, 166
electric motors 157–159
electric shocks 151
electrical appliances 156–157
electrical conductors 62, 74, 76, 101, 104, 150, 154
electrical discharge 90, 151, 153
electrical power 156–157, 160–161
electricity 156–157, 160–161
electrodes 70–73, 153
electrolysis 65, 70–73, 77, 108
electromagnetic waves 162, 169
electromagnets 158
electron arrangements 98–99, 102–103
electron energy levels 91
electron shells 98–99, 102–103
electron transfer 98–99
electronic circuits 154
electrons
  atomic structure 96, 98–99, 102–103, 154
  and electricity 150–151, 154
electroplated nickel silver (EPNS) 71
electrostatic forces 98
emphysema 39
endangered species 30
endoscope 164
endothermic reactions 108–109
energy
  chemical reactions 106–109
  from electricity 156
  food chains 18–19
  loss 19
  from respiration 7, 37, 46–47, 48
  transfer 134–135, 136, 137
environment
  balance 83, 84, 85
  effects of DDT 28–29
enzymes 20, 45
epidermis 14
equations 112–113
equilibrium sign 86, 115
eutrophication 89
evaporation 11, 14–15, 25
evolution of life 83
excretion 10, 19

exercise
benefits 48–49
changes in breathing 37, 46–47
circulatory system 43
exhalation 37, 38
exothermic reactions 106–107
extension 170

falling 132–133
farming 26–27
fats 7, 75
ferns 79
fertilisers 12–13, 20, 69, 86, 88–89
fire 20, 152
fish 89
fitness 48–49
flacid plant cells 11
flames 76
fluids 132
food
energy 19
exothermic heating 107
small intestine 43
food chain 18–19
DDT effects 27, 28
forcemeter 170
forces
changing shape 170–171
electric motors 158–159
movement 120, 128–129, 134–135
forest fires 20
forests 22–23
formulae 98, 110–113
fossil fuels 8, 23, 84, 85
fossils 78–79
Franklin, Benjamin 152
free-fall acceleration 124
French Revolution 82
frequency 162, 166
friction 126, 128, 134, 150, 151, 152
fruit 17, 46
fuel
burning 8, 21, 23, 85, 106
energy transfer 136
fullerene 105
fungicides 26

galena 64, 65
Galileo 128, 133
gaps for wave diffraction 168–169
gases
covalent bonding 104
particle collisions 173
pressure 172–173
resistive forces 132
state symbol 113
gene therapy 56–57
genes 53, 55, 56
genetic counselling 56
genetic engineering 3, 45, 56–57
geology 78–81
giant structures 100, 105
glass optical fibres 164–165
global warming 84
glucagon 44
glucose
blood sugar control 44–45
circulatory system 41, 43
energy release 46
from photosynthesis 4, 84, 109
in respiration 6–7, 37, 48, 109
glycogen 45
gold 64, 144
gradient of graphs 121–123, 125
granite 80–81, 141
graph plotting 120–123, 133, 142–143
gravitational attractive forces 129
gravitational potential energy 134, 135
green colour of plants 5
greenhouse effect 84
greenhouses 8–9, 28
groups in the periodic table 62, 74, 76, 90, 98
guard cells 14–15

Haber, Fritz 86
Haber process 75, 86–87, 88
habitats 30–31
haematite 64, 68
haemoglobin 54, 89
hair dryers 156
half-life 142–143
halite 64, 77
hardening of the arteries 43
Harvey, William 41, 42
heart
beats 40, 41, 43, 48
mechanical 57
muscles 41, 43, 48
pumping action 40–41, 43, 48, 135
valves 40–41
heart attacks 51
heart disease 43, 48
heart transplants 57
heat conductors 74, 76
heat energy 134
heating 156, 157
heavy water 97
helium 82, 90, 91, 98
herbicides 26
high blood pressure 43, 48
high energy drinks 46
Highway Code 127
hormones 16–17, 44, 50–51
humans
DDT effects 29
effects on habitats 30
waste recycling 2
humidity 15
Huntington's disease 53
hydrated copper sulphate 86, 109
hydrochloric acid 106, 111, 113, 114, 115

hydrogen
acid reactions 67, 106, 113, 114
in airships 90
in the atmosphere 83
atom 102, 103
electrolysis of water 108
formula 111
Haber process 75, 115
isotopes 96–97
margarine production 75
metal extraction 65, 67
molecules 102
water reactions 76
hydrogen chloride 103, 104, 111
hydrogen peroxide 75, 114
hydrogencarbonate ion 110
hydroxide ions 110

ice cap melting 84
impurities 69, 73
industrial electrolysis 72–73
information transfer 166–167
infrared beams 124
inhalation 37, 38
inherited disorders 52–56
inkjet printing 152–153
insecticides 26–29
insulators 150, 151, 154
insulin 44–45, 57
iodide 110
iodine starch test 4–5
ionic bonding 98–101
ionic compounds 70, 72, 98–101
ions 110
displacement reactions 66
electrolysis 70–73
electron arrangements 98–99
lattice structure 100
iron 74
alloys 63
in blood 89
catalyst 87
cores in transformers 160
Earth core 138
exothermic reactions 107
extraction 64, 65, 66, 67, 68–69, 114
Haber process 75
ions 110
in magma 80
reactivity 64, 66, 67, 114
symbol 110
iron oxide 66, 68–69, 114
iron sulphate 114
isotopes 96–97, 142–145

joules (J) 135, 137, 156

kinetic energy 134, 136–137
krypton 90, 91

lactic acid 46–47
lady's slipper orchid 30
land use 22
lasers 90, 164
lattice structure 100–101
lava 80, 81

Lavoisier 82
lead 64, 65, 67, 68, 110, 144
leaves 3, 5, 14–15
lifting force 134–135, 137
light
  effect on plant growth 3, 4–5, 9, 12, 16, 89
  optical fibres 164–165
  waves 162, 168, 169
lightbulbs 90, 156
lighting 156
lightning 152
limestone 68–69, 78, 79, 84
limiting factors 8–9
lipids 56
liquefaction of ammonia 87
liquids 113, 132, 172
lithium 76, 77, 115
lithium chloride 76
lithium oxide 115
lithosphere 140
liver 45, 51
loudspeakers 166, 168
lubricants 105
lungs
  cancer 39
  circulatory system 40
  gene therapy 56
  respiration 26–27, 38–39, 52

magma 80–81, 140–141
magnesium
  acid reactions 106, 113, 114
  atom 99, 115
  ion 99, 110
  ore 64
  for plant growth 12
magnesium chloride 113
magnesium hydrogencarbonate 85
magnesium oxide 99, 115
magnesium sulphate 106, 114
magnetic fields 158
magnets 129, 158–159
malachite 64, 65
malaria 26, 28, 29, 55
malleable metals 62
Malpighi 42
manganese oxide 75
manned spacecraft 2
mantle 138, 140
manure 13, 88
marble 78
margarine 75, 77
Mars 83, 144
mass
  and acceleration 131
  and kinetic energy 136
mass number 96–97, 115
medicines 25
melting points 72, 74, 76, 77, 90, 100, 104
membranes
  lungs 56
  osmosis 10–11
meningitis 52
Mesozoic era 79
metal hydroxides 76
metal oxides 66–67, 76
metals
  discovery 64
  extraction 65–71
  ores 64, 65
  properties 62
  reactivity 64–67, 70, 76–77
  uses 62–63
metamorphic rocks 78, 79
meteorites 144
methane
  in the atmosphere 82
  covalent bonding 104
  reaction with oxygen 114
microorganisms 20, 38, 52
microwave ovens 162
minerals
  metal compounds 22, 64
  for plant growth 12–14
  rock formation 78, 80
moisture 20
molecules 91, 102–105
molten aluminium oxide 72
molten sodium chloride 70, 77, 101
monatomic gases 91
Moon 133, 144
moorland food chain 18
Morse, Samuel 166
Morse code 166
mosquitoes 28
mountain air 36, 54
movement 120–135
moving wire 158
mucus 38, 39, 52
mudstone 78
muscles
  arteries 42
  diaphragm 36–37, 48
  glucose use 46, 48
  heart 41, 43, 48
  ribs 36, 48
  steroid misuse 50
  tissue 43
mutations 39, 56

Napoleon III 64
National Grid network 161
negative charge 150–151, 152, 154–155
negative ions 98–99, 110
neon 90, 91, 98
nervous system 53
neutral solutions 62
neutralisation reactions 88, 106, 112–113, 115
neutrons 96
Newton 128, 129
newtons (N) 128
nickel 75, 138
nicotine 39
nitrates 7, 20, 24, 89, 110
nitric acid 75, 88
nitrites 89
nitrogen
  in the atmosphere 82, 83, 91
  the bends 90
  formula 111
  Haber process 75, 86–87, 115
  molecules 91
  for plant growth 12, 24, 86, 88
  in respiration 38
nitrogen gases 75
nitrogen oxide 75
noble gases 82, 90–91, 98
noise 167
non-metals 62, 67, 76, 90
  covalent bonding 102, 104–105
nose 39
nucleons 96
nucleus of cell 2–3
nutrients 20, 31
nylon 151

obesity 48
oestrogen 29
oil surveys 139
oils 75
oilseed rape 3
optical fibres 164–167
ores 64, 65, 68–69, 70, 72
organic farming 13, 20, 88
organic solvents 100, 104
osmosis 10–12
ospreys 30
oxidation 65, 68
oxides 62, 66–67, 99, 110
oxygen
  in the atmosphere 82, 83, 91
  atom 99, 103
  blood transport 30, 54, 89
  carbon cycle 20–21, 83, 84
  combustion reactions 106
  decay 20
  electrolysis of water 108
  formula 111
  in magma 80
  metal extraction 68–69, 72
  molecules 91, 103
  from photosynthesis 4, 5
  pollutant in early atmosphere 83
  reduction/oxidation reactions 65
  in respiration 7, 36, 38, 46–47, 84
oxygen debt 47

Palaeozoic era 79
pancreas 44–45
Pangaea 140
parachutes 133
parasites 27
particle motion 172–173
periodic table of elements 96, 110, 115
  groups 62, 74, 76, 90, 98
periscope 165
permanent magnets 158–159
pesticides 26–27, 28, 39
pH values 62

phloem 14
phosphorus fertilisers 12
photocopying 153
photosynthesis
 carbon cycle 20–21, 23, 83, 84
 equation 4–5, 8, 109
 limiting factors 8–9
 rate increase 8–9
physical properties 62, 74, 97
pillars 171
plants
 cell structure 2–3
 growth 3–9
 hormones 16–17
 respiration 6–7, 12, 14, 19, 84, 85
plasma 43
plating 66, 71
platinum catalyst 75
playing field habitat 30
pollen grains 172–173
pollutants 83
positive charge 150–151, 154
positive ions 98–99, 110
potassium 12, 64, 76, 77, 110
potassium nitrate 76
potatoes 6, 11
power (mechanical) 136–137
power stations 143, 161
predators 27, 28
pressure
 gases 172–173
 Haber process 87
primary coil 160
products of reactions 112
propane 8, 9
proteins 7, 12, 19, 24, 50, 56, 88
protons 96
puberty, DDT effects 29
pulse 41, 48, 49
purification of copper 73
pylons 62, 161
pyramid of biomass 18
pyramid of numbers 18
pyrites 64, 65

radar 162
radio waves 169
radioactivity
 dating 97, 144–145
 decay 142–143
 waste disposal 143
radium 144
rain
 carbon dioxide effects 21
 effect on rocks 78
 and pesticides 26
rainforests
 carbon cycle 20
 deforestation 22, 25
 rainfall 24, 25
 species 24, 25
random motion 173
raw materials 68, 72
reactants 112
reaction time 126, 127
reactivity series 64–67, 70, 76–77, 90, 91
recycling
 aluminium 73
 carbon 20–21, 85
 Haber process 87
 human waste 2
red blood cells 38, 43, 54–55
reduction 65
reflecting prisms 165
reflection 139, 164–165
refraction 139, 164–165
rejection of transplants 57
relative atomic mass 115
relative formula masses 115
resistive forces 130, 132, 133
respiration
 of animals 7, 19
 breathing system 36–37, 48
 carbon cycle 20–21, 23, 84
 energy use 46–47, 109, 135
 microorganisms 20
 of plants 6–7, 12, 14, 19, 84, 85
reversible reactions 86, 109, 115
rhodium catalyst 75
rib muscles 36, 48
ribcage 36
ribs 36–37
ripple tanks 168
road chippings 69
rocks
 dating 79, 144
 formation 78–81, 82, 140–141
 metal occurrence 64
 oil surveys 139
 salt deposits 77
root hairs 7, 12
roots
 growth 16–17
 osmosis 11, 12
 section 14
rubber bands 171
rusting 107

salt deposits 77
salt solutions 10–11
San Andreas fault 141
San Francisco 141
sandstone 78
scuba diving 54, 90
seas
 environmental balance 83, 84, 85
 rising levels 84
 rock formation 78, 79
 waves 162–163, 168
secondary coil 160
sedimentary rocks 78, 79
seedless grapes 17
seismic waves 139
seismometers 138–139
selective weed killers 17
selectively permeable
  membranes 10–11
shale 78, 79
shape changes 170–171
shellfish 78, 79, 84, 85
shock waves 138–139
shoots 6–7, 16–17
sickle cell disease 54–55
signals 162, 166–167, 169
silicon 80
silicon dioxide 69, 115
silver 110
skidding 126, 127
skin 50
skydiving 133
slag 69
slope of graphs 121–123, 125
smoke 172
smoking 39, 43
snails 79
soda lime 4, 107
sodium 76–77, 114, 115
 atom 96, 98
 ion 70, 98, 110
 ore 64
sodium bromide 114
sodium chloride
 bonding 98, 100–101
 electrolysis 70, 77
 formation 76, 106, 114, 115
 formula 110
sodium citrate 108
sodium hydrogencarbonate 108
sodium hydroxide 76, 77, 106, 112, 113, 115
sodium sulphate 76, 110, 112, 113
sodium thiosulphate 114
soil
 erosion 25
 microorganisms 20
 nitrates 24, 88
 water movement 12
solidification of rock 80–81, 140–141
solids, state symbol 113
sonar 163
sound 162, 167, 168–169
spacecraft 2, 132
sparks 152
species 24, 25, 30–31
speed
 moving objects 120–127, 130–133, 136
 waves 162–163
speed–time graphs 122–123, 125, 133
sport 48, 50
springs 170–171, 172
stable compounds 64–65
starch
 storage in potatoes 6
 test for 4–5
state symbols 113, 114–115
static electricity 150–154
steam 82, 83
steel 63
stems 14
step-up transformers 160–161
step-down transformers 160–161
sterile insect pest control 27

steroid misuse 50–51
stomata 14–15
stopping distance 126–127, 130
stretching 170–171
succession 78
sugar
in blood 44–45
osmosis 11
in plants 6–7, 14
sulphate ion 110
sulphur 12, 114
sulphur dioxide 114
sulphuric acid 106, 111, 112, 113, 114, 115
Sun's energy 19, 84
sustainable forestry 22
symbol equations 112, 113, 114–115
symbols 110, 112, 113

tachograph 123
tectonic plates 140–141
temperature
body temperature 46
chemical reactions 106–109
decay 20
Haber process 87
photosynthesis 9
water loss 15
terminal velocity 132–133
testosterone 50–51
tests
for starch 4–5
for water 86
thermit reaction 66
thinking distance 126, 127
thorax 37
throat 38
time taken 120–123, 125–127, 133, 137
tin 64, 68
tissue culture 16
total internal reflection 164–165
tourism 25
tower of Pisa 133
trachea 36–39
transformers 160–161
transition metals 74–75
transmitters 169
transpiration 14–15
trees 22–23
trilobites 79
tritium 96
tubers, potatoes 6–7
tumours 39
turgid plant cells 11

unbalanced forces 128, 130–131, 133
unstable compounds 64
uranium 142, 144
urine test 50

vacuoles 2–3
vacuum 133
vacuum cleaner 158
valves
heart 40–41
veins 42
Van de Graaff generator 150
variegated leaves 5
veins 41, 42
velocity 121
ventilation 36
ventricles 40–41
Venus atmosphere 83
vibrations 162
viruses 52, 56
visibility 126
volcanoes 80, 82, 140–141
voltage 150, 152, 157, 160–161
volts (V) 150

waste products
blood transport 43
recycling in space 2
respiration 46–47
water
aqueous solutions 113
electrolysis 108
formula 111
heavy 97
loss 14–15
movement through plants 14
osmosis 10–12
in photosynthesis 4
reaction with alkali metals 76–77
in respiration 7
test for 86
watts (W) 137, 156
wave diffraction 168–169
wave equation 162–163
wavelengths 162, 168–169
weed killers 17
welding 66, 90
wild flowers 30–31
wilting 11
wind
carbon dioxide effects 21
effects 172
rate of water loss 15
rock weathering 78
wood
burning 20, 22, 23, 86
structure 14, 23
uses 22–23
woodland habitat 31
word equations 112, 113, 114–115
work done 134–135, 136–137

xenon 91
xylem 14
xylem vessels 14

yield
crops 12–13, 88–89
Haber process 86–87

zinc 64, 67, 68, 110
zinc blende 64